John G. Stoessinger

WHY NATIONS GO TO WAR

Second Edition

New York   St. Martin's Press

For My Son
Richard
and
His Generation

Cover design: Mies Hora

Library of Congress Catalog Card Number: 77-86304
Copyright © 1978 by St. Martin's Press, Inc.
All Rights Reserved.
Manufactured in the United States of America.
098
fedcba
For information, write: St. Martin's Press, Inc.,
175 Fifth Avenue, New York, N. Y. 10010

cloth ISBN: 0–312–87851–6
paper ISBN: 0–312–87852–4

ACKNOWLEDGMENTS

Excerpts from *Nations in Darkness: China, Russia and America*
by John G. Stoessinger. Copyright © 1971 by Random House, Inc.
Reprinted by permission of the publisher.

WHY NATIONS GO TO WAR

Second Edition

Even in our sleep
Pain that we cannot forget
Falls drop by drop upon the heart
Until in our own despair
Against our will
Comes wisdom
Through the awful grace of God.

Aeschylus

Preface to the Second Edition

No new wars have broken out since the first edition of this book appeared. Instead, the Vietnam war came to an end and President Anwar el Sadat of Egypt embarked on his dramatic peace mission to Israel. For the first time in a generation, the guns on the world stage are silent.

It is a good time to take stock. How do wars begin? Are they inevitable? How is the threshold crossed from peace to war? What are the roles of personalities? Why did no nation that began a war in this century come out a winner? What might be the face of future wars?

I first wrote this book in order to transmit an understanding of twentieth-century warfare to my students. Over the past three years, I have had a multitude of letters from students and teachers all over the world. Many of these contained suggestions for improvement that have found their way into the present work. Thus, this book is more than an updated version of the earlier edition. It now represents a common quest for more fundamental answers.

Wars seem to occur in generational cycles. The war between Catholics and Protestants more than three centuries ago was fought for thirty years. The recent conflict involving French,

Americans, and Vietnamese in Indochina, the struggle between Hindus and Moslems on the Indian subcontinent, and the modern thirty years' war fought between Arabs and Israelis in the Middle East: all these seem to have run their course within a single generation.

As I write these lines, these wars have yielded to diplomacy. No new ones have erupted. Perhaps the pause is a mere accident of history. But perhaps the present generation is also more determined to say No.

JOHN G. STOESSINGER

Introduction

This book makes an attempt to take a new look at the age-old scourge of war. Ever since I was a student, I have found most explanations somehow wanting. I read that wars were caused by nationalism, militarism, alliance systems, economic factors, or by some other bloodless abstraction that I could not understand. Often I was told that war was an ineradicable part of human nature. I wondered if this could be true. Having lived through most of the major wars of this century, I yearned to understand more deeply. I had the hope that insight might bring healing. The conventional wisdom left me totally dissatisfied, both intellectually and emotionally. It somehow always missed the human essence of the problem. After all, wars were begun by men. Yet this personality dimension was seldom given its due weight in traditional books on war. Instead, forces over which men had no control often were enthroned as "fundamental" causes. Out of my need to know the human truth behind the mechanistic forces grew the outline for this book.

I decided to embark on six case studies of the major international wars fought in this century: the two world wars, Korea, Vietnam, India and Pakistan, and the Arab states and

Israel. What interested me most in each case was the "moment of truth" when leaders crossed the threshold into war. I decided to "blow up" that fateful moment, to capture it in flight, as it were, in all its awesome tragic meaning. In the process, I sought answers to the questions that have always haunted me: At what moment did the decision to go to war become irreversible? Who bore the responsibility and why? Could the disaster have been averted? Did the six cases, different though they were, reveal some common truths about war in our time?

My first unforgettable exposure to World War I was Erich Maria Remarque's classic *All Quiet on the Western Front*. The author dedicated the book to the memory of a generation that "had been destroyed by war even though it may have escaped its guns." Yet many old people to whom I spoke about the war remembered its outbreak as a time of glory and rejoicing. Distance had romanticized their memories, muted the anguish, and subdued the horror. I have attempted to recapture the atmosphere of those few weeks in July 1914 that changed the world forever, and I have tried to portray the leading personalities who contributed to the disaster.

I remember well the charismatic nature of Hitler's grip upon the German nation. Most of my boyhood years were spent in fleeing from the Nazi terror. I have always been haunted by the personality of Hitler and driven by a need to understand his demon. That is why I chose to examine the attack upon the Soviet Union which witnessed Hitler at the zenith of his power, but also bore within it the seeds of his ultimate destruction. Why did he launch this suicidal assault? Why did Stalin, who trusted no one, place his trust in Hitler? And what explains the fact that so many German soldiers followed Hitler to their doom in Russia like obedient boys in school?

When the Korean War broke out, I remember that I applauded President Harry Truman for repelling the armed aggression from the north. But when General Douglas Mac-Arthur's forces crossed the parallel into North Korea, I began to wonder. And when the general drove on toward the Chinese border, I shuddered with anxiety that China might intervene. My fear was justified. I have attempted in this case study to recapture each decision separately and to place responsibility where it belongs.

In no war did personalities play a greater role than in Vietnam. I believe that, in the course of a single generation, five American presidents based their policies in Indochina not on Asian realities but on their own fears and, later, on their hopes. Each president made a concrete policy decision that escalated the war and left it in worse shape than before. It is for this reason that this case, like a Greek tragedy, has five "acts," each a virtually new step in a gradually escalating conflict that became the "Thirty Years' War" of our century.

Three of the most dreadful wars of our time were fought on the Indian subcontinent. The human suffering that accompanied them took place on a scale so vast that it defies the imagination. I have attempted to study the personalities of the Hindu and the Moslem leaders for whom religious war was just as real in our secular era as it was at the time of the Crusades a thousand years ago.

Yet another Thirty Years' War has been fought in this century between Arab and Jew. Four times in a single generation these two peoples have turned upon each other with a terrible ferocity. Both Arab and Jewish leaders have seen their cause as just and firmly based upon the will of God, morality, and reason. And in the name of two appeals to justice, they have done things to one another that neither side will easily forget. I have attempted to capture the human truth of this great tragedy in which right does not clash with wrong, but with another right.

Upon completing my six cases and surveying the entire spectacle of war in our time, a number of new themes emerged that I had never seen before. I have presented these in the concluding chapter of this book. A pattern *did* emerge that, I hope, will point to new directions and start a dialogue about man's most terrible self-imposed affliction.

Perhaps chaos is a name we give an order that, as yet, we do not understand. I hope that this book may bring some order to the chaos by presenting some original perspectives. And such insight, I dare hope, may be a first step to liberation.

Contents

WHY NATIONS GO TO WAR

Second Edition

1.

The Iron Dice:
World War I

If the iron dice must roll, may God help us.

Theobold von Bethmann-Hollweg
German Chancellor, August 1, 1914

Most men do not believe that everything is possible. The
emperors and generals who sent their men to war in August
1914 thought in terms of weeks, not months, let alone years.
"You will be home before the leaves have fallen from the
trees," the German Kaiser told his troops in early August
while, at the same time, members of the czar's Imperial Guard
wondered whether they should take their dress uniforms with
them for their victorious entry into Berlin or whether they
should have them brought to the front by the next courier.
Few foresaw the world catastrophe that would snuff out the
lives of an entire generation and consign the next to disillusion
and despair. When it was all over, no one was the man he
used to be and, as D. H. Lawrence put it, "all the great words
were cancelled out." In one of history's most consummate
touches of irony, one of the few who did see the shadow of
war lengthening into years was the chief of the German

General Staff, Helmuth von Moltke, who predicted "a long
and wearisome struggle," but who also believed that war was
sooner or later inevitable and saw fit to pronounce on June 1
that Germany was "ready, and the sooner the better for us."

This theme of inevitability is a haunting and pervasive one.
Most of the statesmen who made the crucial decisions behaved
like actors in a Greek tragedy. The terrible dénouement was
foreseen, but somehow it could not be prevented. Time and
again, men shifted responsibility from themselves to an im-
personal God or Providence that was deemed to be beyond
their control. In the words of the German Chancellor Theobold von Bethmann-Hollweg, on August 1, "if the iron dice
must roll, may God help us," or in those of Emperor Francis
Joseph of Austria-Hungary: "We cannot go back now." Historians, too, have been affected by this fatalistic attitude. As
one leading scholar has summed up his analysis of the outbreak of the war: "All the evidence goes to show that the beginning of the crisis . . . was one of those moments in history
when events passed beyond men's control." [1]

The thesis of this chapter is that such a view is wrong:
mortal men made these decisions. They made them in fear
and in trembling, but they made them nonetheless. In most
cases, they were not evil men bent upon destruction but
frightened men entrapped in self-delusion. They based their
policies on fears, not facts, and were singularly devoid of empathy. Misperception, rather than conscious evil design, seems
to have been the leading villain in the drama.

In this analysis, I shall not dwell upon the underlying
causes of the world war. Not only have these been discussed
exhaustively by leading historians,[2] but I seriously question
whether they can be related directly and demonstrably to the
fateful decisions that actually *precipitated* the war. Historians
are virtually unanimous, for example, in their belief that the
system of competitive alliances that divided Europe into two

camps in 1914 was a principal factor that caused the war to spread. This strikes me as a mechanistic view that does not leave enough room for psychological and personality considerations. On July 5, Germany gave her ally Austria-Hungary full support to punish Serbia for the assassination of the Austrian crown prince. By late July, however, when Austrian policy threatened to produce a general mobilization in Russia on Serbia's behalf, Germany attempted to restrain her ally. In this attempt she failed and the result was world conflagration. Supposing, however, that the German Kaiser or his chancellor had *succeeded* in restraining the Austrians, historians would have had to credit the alliance system with the *prevention* of a war. In other words, a study of the leading personalities of the time and of the manner in which they perceived one another may be a more fruitful undertaking than to formulate such abstractions as alliance systems, militarism, or nationalism.

The crucial events to be examined on the threshold of war are the German pledge of support to Austria in her policy toward Serbia; Austria's ultimatum to Serbia and the rejection of the Serbian response; Germany's efforts to mediate and to restrain Austria; and the actual outbreak of general war on August 1, precipitated by Germany's declaration of war on Russia and the invasion of Luxembourg and Belgium.

The Kaiser's Fateful Pledge

The news of the assassination of the Austrian Crown Prince Franz Ferdinand on June 28, 1914 reached the German Kaiser on his yacht near Kiel. According to an eyewitness, Wilhelm II turned deathly pale as he heard the fatal news from Sarajevo.[3] He had been drawn to the Austrian archduke and his wife and had just returned from visiting the couple at their castle. Franz Ferdinand's marriage to a lady-in-waiting had aroused the sullen opposition of the aged emperor, Francis Joseph, who had only relented on the condition that the marriage would be a "morganatic" one, that is, the couple's children would be deprived of the right of succession to the throne. This act of renunciation had embittered Franz Ferdinand, a condition further aggravated by the condescension of the Austrian court toward his wife Sophie.

Kaiser Wilhelm was a moody man with a mercurial temper. The romantic predicament of his Austrian friend had appealed to him and he had formed a deep and, apparently, quite genuine personal attachment. He was deeply shaken when he heard about the archduke's last words to his wife, "Sophie, Sophie, do not die, live for our children," [4] before death claimed them both. His fury and indignation against the Serbians were thoroughly aroused. In his marginal comments, he described them as "bandits" and "murderers." In addition to his personal grief, he believed that the assassination represented a profound threat to the monarchical principle. Hence, it is not surprising that Admiral von Tirpitz reports in his *Memoirs* the Kaiser's conviction that the Russian czar would not support "the assassins of royalty." [5] The crowned heads of Europe would have to make a common stand against the threat of regicide. With the impetuosity that marked his nature, the Kaiser wanted Austria to punish Serbia as quickly as possible. He was convinced that the entire civilized world, including Russia, would be sympathetic. As he put it in no uncertain terms: "Matters must be cleared up with the Serbians and that soon. That is self-evident and the plain truth." [6] On July 5, he took the fateful step of assuring Austria that she could count on Germany's "faithful support" even if the punitive action that she was planning to take against Serbia would bring her into conflict with Russia. In other words, the Kaiser issued Austria-Hungary a blank check. Before he went off on a vacation cruise the next morning, he exclaimed confidently: "I cannot imagine that the old gentleman in Schönbrunn will go to war, and most certainly not if it is a war over the Archduke Franz Ferdinand."[7]

The incredible fact is that the German Kaiser had not the slightest idea of what the Austrians would do. Propelled by a generous impulse of loyalty to his dead friend, he offered what he thought would be moral support to the aggrieved party. That this guarantee would entail military support never seriously occurred either to him or to the German military and governmental apparatus that fully supported his move. Even more important, the Kaiser believed that a common loyalty to monarchy would be a stronger bond than the links of ethnic kinship; that is, the czar would support the Kaiser against his fellow Slavs in Serbia. On both these counts, Wilhelm II proved to be terribly mistaken.

The Kaiser used a special term for his pledge to Austria: *Nibelungentreue*. There is no adequate English translation for this term. The *Nibelungen* are mystical German sagas peopled with heroes whose highest virtues are honor, courage, and loyalty. The pledge of a *Nibelung* is a blood bond that is sacred and irrevocable. Once given, it can never be retracted. Wilhelm's cousin, Ferdinand I of Bulgaria, understood its significance when he observed:

> I certainly do not like my cousin Kaiser Wilhelm, but I feel sorry for him all the same. Now he will be dragged into the whirlpool, be entangled, and he will have to fight, whether he wants to or not. That is all he gets out of his Nibelungentreue.[8]

The Kaiser's decision to support Austria-Hungary under any circumstances demonstrated an extraordinary confusion of personal ethics and political judgment. His friendship with the archduke prompted him to place the fate of his nation in the

hands of another power. His view of the Russian czar as a
kindred-spirited fellow monarch made him assume that such
a relinquishment of control carried no risk whatever. And his
romanticism robbed him of all flexibility in the emerging crisis.

It is not true, as many historians have stated, that the Kaiser
wanted war. Nor is it true, however, as his definitive biog-
rapher has said, that he "succumbed to a power he had not
reckoned with: the power of Fate; had it not been for that,
the war would never have started." [9] Such thinking is guilty
of a blind determinism. The Kaiser was indeed to blame. His
flaw was both moral and political, for his form of loyalty demanded sacrifice beyond himself. It offered up the German
nation, and it emboldened the senile monarchy of Austria-
Hungary to take a desperate gamble. The cliché of the saber-
rattling Kaiser is misleading. What is closer to the truth is that
he permitted others to rattle and, ultimately, use the saber
for him.

The Austrian Ultimatum to Serbia

During the fateful days of July 1914, the fate of Austria-
Hungary was in the hands of three men: the Emperor Francis
Joseph, his foreign minister, Count Leopold von Berchtold,
and the chief of staff, Conrad von Hötzendorff.

At the time of the Sarajevo assassination, Francis Joseph
was an exhausted old man. The wars he had waged in the
past had resulted in defeat or in loss of territory. Personal dis-
asters had embittered his declining years: the murder of his
wife, the tragic death of his son, and now the murder of his
nephew. "Everyone is dying around me," he said mournfully.
There is little doubt that above all he wished to end his days
in peace. Shortly after the assassination of Franz Ferdinand,
he spoke of plans for a summer respite in order to regain his

strength. Evidently, he had no expectation of even a local war with Serbia. When Conrad von Hötzendorff urged mobilization measures, after receiving Kaiser Wilhelm's promise of support on July 5, the emperor refused to approve them. He pointed out the danger of an attack from Russia and the doubtfulness of German support. During the next three weeks, however, Francis Joseph's strength began to fail and his signature affixed to the crucial documents laid before him by his foreign minster betrayed a trembling and uncertain hand. More important, the marginal annotations no longer showed the probing mind of earlier years. One distinguished historian even maintains that the foreign minister dispatched the crucial ultimatum to Serbia "without the knowledge or approval of Francis Joseph."[10] While this is difficult to prove, it is likely that the aged sovereign no longer fully grasped the consequences of the policies that Count Berchtold and his chief of staff were now pursuing.

Conrad von Hötzendorff, Austria-Hungary's chief of staff and head of the militarist party in Vienna, believed passionately in the need to preserve his nation's status as a great power. Even before Sarajevo, he feared the disintegration of the Habsburg empire, from either internal decay or violent overthrow by its enemies. If Austria-Hungary accepted this final insult, then, indeed, the dual monarchy would become a "worm-eaten museum piece." Thus, Serbia had to be dealt a punishing blow quickly before the situation deteriorated even further. Von Hötzendorff's own words are illuminating:

For this reason, and not as vengeance for the assassination, Austria-Hungary must draw the sword against Serbia. . . . It (is) not a question of knightly duel with "poor little" Serbia, as she like(s) to call herself, nor of punishment for the assassination. It (is) much more the highly practical importance of the prestige of a Great Power. . . . The Monarchy ha(s) been seized by the throat, and ha(s) to choose between allowing itself to be strangled and making a last effort to prevent its destruction."[11]

In the view of Austria-Hungary's chief of staff, then, the monarchy's status as a great power was in desperate peril. Both pride and prestige motivated his policy.

Count Leopold von Berchtold, the foreign minister, has been described by Sidney B. Fay as "as helpless and incompetent a person as was ever called to fill a responsible position in time of danger."[12] The record of his behavior during the critical weeks of July 1914 reveals a striking difference between his attitude toward Serbia before July 5, the date of the Kaiser's blank check to Austria, and his approach to the problem after that date. When informed of the tragedy of Sarajevo, Berchtold vacillated. He hesitated to take military action against Serbia for fear that the Kaiser would not support him, but he shared von Hötzendorff's conviction that something had to be done to preserve Austria's great power status. The Kaiser's pledge resolved Berchtold's indecision, and the promise of German support enabled him to use the Sarajevo assassination as the final justification for clearing up, once and for all, Austria's Serbian problem. He drafted an ultimatum that he was certain Serbia would reject. Protected by Germany, he could then deal a mortal blow without fear of Russian intervention.

Count Berchtold's outstanding character trait seems to have been his duplicity. Though outraged by Sarajevo, he took no action until presented with the German guarantee, but then he went a great deal further than the Kaiser would have wanted him to go. Austria-Hungary's failing prestige could now be buttressed by a German guarantee. The German *Nibelungentreue* could be translated into an ironclad commitment with no exit. Germany could thus be made to pay

the price of Austria-Hungary's last and fateful effort to remain
a world power.

Berchtold seems to have been the main, possibly even the
sole, author of the Serbian ultimatum. He communicated its
general tenor to Berlin, and the Kaiser, incredibly enough, did
not demand to see the precise text. Thus, when Berchtold
transmitted the note to Serbia, Wilhelm was faced with a *fait
accompli*. The terms of the ultimatum were stern and unyield-
ing: they included demands for the dissolution of Serbian nationalist groups, the dismissal of key military officers, the arrest
of leading political figures, and the right for Austria-Hungary
to implement these measures to her complete satisfaction.
Serbia was given forty-eight hours to respond or else to face
the consequences.

The Serbian Prince Regent Peter and his ministers were
deeply shaken by the harshness of the ultimatum. They suspected that it was a pretext to eliminate Serbia as a sovereign
state. After all, even though the assassins were Slav nationalists with Serbian ties, they were subjects of the empire and
the assassination itself had taken place on Austro-Hungarian
soil. In desperation, the prince regent cabled the following
plea to the Russian czar:

> We are unable to defend ourselves and beg your Majesty to
> come to our aid as soon as possible. The much-appreciated
> goodwill which your Majesty has so often shown toward us
> inspires us with the firm belief that once again our appeal to
> your noble Slav heart will not pass unheeded.[13]

The Serbian ministers then began to work around the clock
on their reply. They argued bitterly over the intent of the
ultimatum. A minority felt that the demands were honestly
calculated to exact punishment for the assassination and to
guarantee Austria's future security, but the majority was con-

vinced that the document had been framed deliberately to elicit a rejection. The final reply was actually conciliatory and accepted most of the Austrian demands. Only those that would virtually have abrogated Serbia's sovereignty were treated somewhat evasively. The consensus was reached within minutes of the deadline. To add to the tension, the only remaining typewriter broke down and the final text was copied out in a trembling hand by a secretary. Just before the deadline which was at 6 P.M., July 25, Nikola Pashich, the Serbian minister of interior, arrived at the Austrian legation in Belgrade with the reply. Baron W. Giesl, the Austrian ambassador, was under strict instructions from Berchtold to break off diplomatic relations unless Serbia yielded on every point. He hurriedly glanced at the document, noted the Serbian qualifications on some of the demands and immediately dispatched a note to Pashich informing him that Austria-Hungary had ruptured diplomatic relations with Serbia. The note overtook Pashich during his return to the ministry and he found it there upon his arrival. So great was Giesl's eagerness that he and the entire staff of the Austrian legation managed to catch the 6:30 P.M. train from Belgrade.

The news reached Emperor Francis Joseph two hours later at his summer villa in Ischl. According to an eyewitness, the old man looked at the message, sank into a chair, and muttered in a choked voice: "Also doch!" (so it has come about after all).[14] Berchtold now convinced the broken man of the need to order partial mobilization. On July 28, Austria-Hungary officially declared war on Serbia. One day later Belgrade was under bombardment.

During these fateful days the Kaiser was cruising on his yacht in the North Sea. He showed so little interest in the matter that he did not even ask to see the text of the Serbian reply until the morning of July 28, a few hours before Austria declared war. After reading it, he jotted down the following words in the margin:

> A brilliant performance for a time-limit of only 48 hours. This is more than one could have expected! A great moral success for Vienna; but with it every reason for war drops away, and Giesl ought to have remained quietly in Belgrade! After such a thing I should never have ordered mobilization.[15]

To his secretary of state, Gottlieb von Jagow, Wilhelm issued the following instruction:

> I propose that we say to Austria: Serbia has been forced to retreat in a very humiliating manner and we offer our congratulations; naturally, as a result, every cause for war has vanished.[16]

A few hours later, however, when Austrian bombs fell on Belgrade, Kaiser Wilhelm was compelled to face the dreadful consequences of the heedless pledge to Austria that he had made less than a month before.

The Closing Trap

The war that broke out on July 28 was a localized conflict between Serbia and Austria-Hungary. The Austrians gambled that it would remain so. Count Berchtold was convinced that there was nothing to fear from Russia; after all, the czar, who lived in fear of assassination himself, was sure to sympathize with a determined Austrian move against Serbia for the cause of monarchy. And even if this assumption was incorrect, then a swift and decisive military victory over Serbia would confront the czar with a *fait accompli*. But most important, Berch-

told was sure that the Kaiser's guarantee to Austria would prevent Russian intervention. Thus, the war would remain
localized and could safely be brought to a quick and successful
conclusion.

It now becomes essential to this analysis to consider the
actual situation in Russia at the time of Sarajevo. Russia's
foreign policy rested on the shoulders of three men: Czar
Nicholas II, Foreign Minister Sergei Sazonov, and the minister of war, Vladimir Sukhomlinov.

The czar, though kind and considerate in his personal relations, was a study in apathy and indifference in matters of
public policy. Barbara Tuchman, in a devastating vignette,
describes the czar's reaction to the news of Austrian and German plans for mobilization. "Nicholas listened," she writes,
"and then, as if waking from a reverie, said gravely, 'God's
will be done.'" [17] His main concept of government was to preserve intact the absolute monarchy that had been bequeathed
to him by his father. The czarina had fallen under the spell
of the magnetic personality of Rasputin and life at the imperial court was totally out of touch with the people whom the
monarchy was supposed to govern.

Sazonov, the czar's foreign minister, was a highly emotional man who had originally wanted to become a monk but
had abandoned the idea because of his frail health and instead
had entered the diplomatic service. The German ambassador
at St. Petersburg described him as "filled with glowing patrio-
tism bordering on chauvinism. When he talk[ed] of past
events in which he thought Russia suffered injustice, his face
assumed an almost fanatical expression." [18] According to
another eyewitness, his lips trembled with emotion as he once
remarked that he could not survive another defeat such as
Russia had suffered in her war with Japan. [19]

The man responsible for Russia's preparations for war was
Sukhomlinov. The minister of war was a pleasure-loving man

in his sixties. Sazonov, who disliked him intensely, said that "it was very difficult to make him work but to get him to tell the truth was well-nigh impossible." [20] He held office at the whim of the czar and through the artful cultivation of Rasputin. Naturally lazy, he left his work largely to subordinates and, in the words of the French ambassador, Maurice Paléologue, kept "all his strength for conjugal pleasures with a wife 32 years younger than himself," whom he had married after a sensational divorce scandal. The evidence for the divorce was supplied by an Austrian named Altschiller, who then became a close friend of the minister. In January 1914, Altschiller was exposed as Austria's chief espionage agent in Russia. Totally unreceptive to new ideas, Sukhomlinov prided himself for not having read a military manual for twenty-five years. The phrase "modern war" irritated him. "As war was," he said, "so it has remained." As a result, he clung stubbornly to obsolete theories and ancient glories and believed without question in the supremacy of the bayonet over the bullet.

This, then, was the trio of men to whom the prince regent of Serbia appealed for help against Austria-Hungary. The popular response in Russia to the Austro-Serbian rupture was extremely heated. On July 26, crowds marched through the streets of St. Petersburg chanting "Down with Austria," and "Long live Serbia." Hostile demonstrations were held in front of the Austrian embassy and the police had to protect the members of the legation from being attacked by the incensed crowd. The czar, when informed of the ultimatum, displayed mild irritation and requested Foreign Minister Sazonov to keep him informed. Sazonov's own reaction, however, was explosive: "C'est la guerre Européenne." He was convinced that the ultimatum was a pretext for Austrian aggression against Serbia. When Count S. Szápáry, the Austro-Hungarian ambassador at St. Petersburg, made an effort to defend his country's action by emphasizing the need for a common stand against revolutionary agitation and regicide, Sazonov shouted heatedly: "The fact is, you want war and you have burned your bridges. You are setting Europe on fire." [21] Sazonov was particularly infuriated by Berchtold's methods: the shortness of the time limit, the humiliating demands, and the infringements upon Serbia's sovereignty. By the time the German ambassador, Count Friedrich von Pourtalès, called on Sazonov in support of his Austrian colleague, the Russian foreign minister had worked himself into a towering rage. His fury was such that Pourtalès expressed the fear that he was blinded by his hatred of Austria. "Hate," replied Sazonov, "is foreign to my nature. I do not hate Austria; I despise her." And then he exclaimed: "Austria is seeking a pretext to gobble up Serbia; but in that case Russia will make war on Austria." [22]

General Sukhomlinov, too, had no doubt that Austria would invade Serbia after the expiration of the time limit. He felt that a war between Austria and Serbia would mean a war between Austria and Russia and therefore between Germany and Russia. As one of his aides put it: "One does not send such an ultimatum except when the cannons are loaded." [23] These Russian perceptions of Austrian intentions produced the next logical step for Russia: mobilization.

In conjunction with its declaration of war against Serbia, Austria-Hungary had mobilized eight out of a total of sixteen army corps. By this action, Berchtold hoped not only to administer a decisive military defeat to Serbia but also to frighten off Russia from intervening. Sazonov, however, viewed this partial mobilization as directed against Russia and, as a result, decided to order a partial mobilization of his own. He hoped that quick Russian action would deter Austria from attacking Serbia in the first place. Thus, both the Austrian and Russian decisions to mobilize a part of their armies were, in essence, bluffs designed to deter the other side.

When the Kaiser was informed of the Austrian declaration

of war and of the partial Russian mobilization, his indifference gave way to growing panic. The implications of his
blank check policy now became painfully clear. He decided
to make a determined effort to localize the Austro-Serbian
war and to act as mediator between Austria and Russia. In
this attempt he was encouraged by Sir Edward Grey, the
British foreign secretary, who was becoming increasingly nervous as tensions grew with every passing hour.

The Kaiser took the most direct possible route: he sent a
telegram to his cousin Czar Nicholas II. The following excerpt reveals his conciliatory intent:

> It is with the gravest concern that I hear of the impression
> which the action of Austria against Serbia is creating in your
> country. . . . With regard to the hearty and tender friendship
> which binds us both from long ago with firm ties, I am exerting
> my utmost influence to induce the Austrians to deal straightly
> to arrive at a satisfactory understanding with you. I confidently
> hope you will help me in my efforts to smooth over difficulties
> that may still arise.
>
> Your very sincere and devoted friend and cousin.
>
> Willy [24]

In the past, direct personal messages of this kind had been
helpful in steering the Russian and German ships of state
through troubled waters. At the same time, on the Kaiser's
instructions, another telegram was dispatched by Bethmann to
Berchtold asking him to halt the Austrian armies in Belgrade
and not spread the war.

The Russian leadership, too, was eager to prevent the
Austro-Serbian conflict from escalating into a Russo-German
war. Sazonov told General von Chelius, the German military
plenipotentiary in St. Petersburg, that "the return of the
Kaiser has made us all feel easier, for we trust in His Majesty

and want no war, nor does Czar Nicholas. It would be a good
thing if the two Monarchs should come to an understanding
by telegraph." [25] Accordingly, Nicholas sent to his German
cousin the following telegram which crossed on the wires that
sent by Wilhelm:

> Am glad you are back. In this most serious moment, I appeal
> to you to help me. An ignoble war has been declared on a
> weak country. The indignation in Russia shared fully by me
> is enormous. I foresee that very soon I shall be overwhelmed
> by the pressure brought upon me and be forced to take extreme
> measures which will lead to war. To try and avoid such a
> calamity as a European war, I beg you in the name of our old
> friendship to do what you can to stop your allies from going
> too far.
>
> Nicky [26]

Wilhelm's response to this telegram was another wire asking
his cousin not to take military measures that "would be looked
upon by Austria as threatening." [27] Nicholas wired back the
following message:

> Thank you heartily for your quick answer. The military mea-
> sures which have now come into force were decided five days
> ago for reasons of defense on account of Austria's preparations.
> I hope from all my heart that these measures won't in any way
> interfere with your part as mediator which I greatly value. We
> need your strong pressure on Austria to come to an understand-
> ing with us. [28]

This last communication which was received by the Kaiser on
July 30 destroyed his sense of balance completely. In growing
panic, he wrote the following comments in the margins of the
czar's wire:

According to this the Czar has simply been tricking us with his appeal for assistance and has deceived us. . . . Then I must mobilize too. . . . The hope that I would not let his mobilization measures disturb me in my role of mediator is childish, and solely intended to lure us into the mire. . . . I regard my mediation action as brought to an end.[29]

In short, the Kaiser believed that the czar had used the German mediation effort as a way to get a five days' head start in his own military preparations behind Wilhelm's back. The "Willy-Nicky" telegrams had simply bought time for the Russians. By the afternoon of July 30, the Kaiser's panic took on a quality of paranoia. At 1 P.M., a telegram had arrived from Lord Grey who warned that "if war breaks out, it [would] be the greatest catastrophe that the world has ever seen."[30] Wilhelm's response to this was to scribble in the margin: "This means they will attack us; Aha! The common cheat."[31] In the Kaiser's view, England was combining threat with bluff "to separate us from Austria and to prevent us from mobilizing, and to shift responsibility of the war."[32]

Wilhelm's response to both Austrian and Russian general mobilization was to place the blame on England. At the precise moment that Lord Grey desperately attempted to avert a general war, the Kaiser saw the British at the head of a plot to attack and destroy Germany. In an extraordinary and revealing marginal comment on one of Lord Grey's diplomatic notes, Wilhelm wrote:

The net has been suddenly thrown over our head, and England sneeringly reaps the most brilliant success of her persistently prosecuted, purely anti-German world policy, against which we have proved ourselves helpless, while she twists the noose of our political and economic destruction out of our fidelity to Austria, as we squirm isolated in the net.[33]

This British plot, which included Russia and France, to exterminate Germany was absolutely real in the Kaiser's view. The time to strike back had come. "This whole business must now be ruthlessly uncovered," the Kaiser exclaimed to Bethmann, "and the mask of Christian peaceableness publicly and brusquely torn from its face in public, and the pharisaical hypocrisy exposed on the pillory."[34] The entire world must unite against "this hated, lying, conscienceless nation of shopkeepers; for if we are to be bled to death, England shall at least lose India."[35]

This was the basis on which Kaiser Wilhelm made his decision to strike first. On July 31, the Kaiser proclaimed a "state of threatening danger of war" and issued a twelve-hour ultimatum to Russia demanding demobilization. When the Russian leadership refused to comply, Wilhelm promptly ordered full mobilization. The "iron dice" had begun to roll.

The Iron Dice

As emperors and statesmen on all sides gradually lost control over the deepening crisis, generals and military staffs increasingly began to dominate the scene. During the final phase before the outbreak of general war, one appalling fact became terrifyingly clear: the unrelenting rigidity of military schedules and timetables on all sides. All these had been worked out in minute detail years before, in case war should come. Now that it was about to happen, each general was terrified lest his adversary might move first and thus capture the initiative. Everywhere, then, military staffs exerted mounting pressure on their chiefs of state to move schedules ahead to be able to strike the first blow. What each plan lacked to an astonishing degree was even a small measure of flexibility. In the words of the chief of the mobilization section of the Russian general staff, for example, "the whole plan of mobilization is worked out ahead to its final conclusion and in all its detail . . . once the moment is chosen, everything is settled; there is no going back; it determines mechanically the beginning of war." [36] This was not only an accurate description of the situation in Russia, but also in Austria, France, and, most particularly, in Germany.

In Russia, the czar vacillated between full mobilization which would make retreat very difficult and partial mobilization which left some room for maneuver. When he was informed of the Austrian bombardment of Belgrade during the afternoon of July 29, he decided to order full mobilization. That evening, however, Wilhelm's telegram arrived in which he pleaded with the czar not to take the military measures that would precipitate a calamity. Pondering the telegram, the czar now felt that he had made a mistake in signing the ukase for general mobilization. He decided to cancel the order and substitute another one for partial mobilization. At this point the Russian generals became extremely alarmed. Minister of War Sukhomlinov, Chief of Staff General Ianushkevich, and Chief of Mobilization General Dobrorolski all were convinced that a suspension of general mobilization would give the enemy the opportunity to mobilize more quickly than Russia. The czar, nonetheless, remained firm, and toward midnight of July 29 the order for partial mobilization was released.

The three generals, however, refused to yield. On the following morning, they won Sazonov over to their point of view. The foreign minister, in turn, promised to win over the czar. The chief of staff asked Sazonov to inform him at once by telephone from Peterhof whether or not he had succeeded. If Sazonov's news was positive, the chief of staff would convert the partial mobilization into a general one and immediately thereafter "retire from sight, smash my telephone and generally take all measures so that I cannot be found to give

any contrary orders for a new postponement of general mobilization." [37]

It took Sazonov approximately one hour to convince the
czar. The arguments he used were essentially those of the generals. The foreign minister telephoned the chief of staff as
promised and added: "Now you can smash the telephone.
Give your orders, General, and then—disappear for the rest
of the day." [38]

We have already seen Berchtold's role in persuading Emperor Francis Joseph of Austria-Hungary to agree to partial
mobilization against Serbia. Berchtold, in turn, was under the
influence of Austria's chief of staff, Conrad von Hötzendorff.
The chief of staff hoped to deter Russia through a quick military victory, and thus to keep the war localized. He was ready,
however, to risk the danger that Russia might intervene and
thus insisted on the mobilization of eight army corps, com-
prising approximately half of the Austrian armed forces. He
also worked out a plan to convert partial into full mobilization
with a minimum of delay, which in fact he did when the
news of Russian general mobilization reached Vienna. Encouraged by a telegram from the German chief of staff, Helmuth
von Moltke, urging general mobilization, von Hötzendorff
decided to push the button on July 31 instead of on
August 1, as had been agreed upon in an audience with Emperor Francis Joseph. As the head of Austria's militarist party,
von Hötzendorff had great faith in the ability of his army to
deliver a crushing blow to Serbia and, if necessary, to capture
the initiative in a military campaign against Russia.

In Germany, the Kaiser waited anxiously for a Russian reply
to his ultimatum. When the deadline of twelve noon on
August 1 passed without word, Wilhelm's remaining balance
collapsed and paranoia again took over. Upon hearing the
news of the Russian mobilization, Wilhelm burst into a tirade
that no longer had any connection with reality:

The world will be engulfed in the most terrible of wars, the ultimate aim of which is the ruin of Germany. England, France, and Russia have conspired for our annihilation . . . that is the naked truth of the situation which was slowly but surely created by Edward VII. . . . The encirclement of Germany is at last an accomplished fact. We have run our heads into the noose. . . . The dead Edward is stronger than the living I! [39]

A short time before he decreed general mobilization at 5 P.M. on August 1, the Kaiser confided to an Austrian officer: "I hate the Slavs. I know it is a sin to do so. We ought not to hate anyone. But I can't help hating them." [40]

Wilhelm's hatred of the Slavs attuned his mind to a war with Russia. His general staff, however, in particular its chief, Helmuth von Moltke, thought differently. For several years, the German generals had been committed to the Schlieffen Plan—the product of Count Alfred von Schlieffen—one of the most illustrious disciples of the nineteenth-century Prussian strategic thinker Karl von Clausewitz. The Schlieffen Plan envisaged a German attack upon France through Belgium as the most promising first strike in the eventuality of the outbreak of a general European war. The fact that such a move would violate the neutrality of Belgium hardly bothered the German generals. Caught between his personal desire to begin a military campaign with a devastating blow against Russia and the plan of his general staff to invade Belgium and France, the Kaiser, like Bismarck before him, began to dread the specter of a two-front war. In the meantime, however, mobilization had been ordered and the gigantic German war machine, prepared for years for the coming of this day, had begun to roll. Barbara Tuchman paints a vivid picture of this machine:

Once the mobilization button was pushed, the whole vast machinery for calling up, equipping, and transporting two million men began turning automatically. Reservists went to their designated depots, were issued uniforms, equipment, and arms, formed into companies and companies into battalions, were joined by cavalry, cyclists, artillery, medical units, cook wagons, blacksmith wagons, even postal wagons, moved according to prepared railway timetables to concentration points near the frontier where they would be formed into divisions, divisions into corps, and corps into armies ready to advance and fight. One army corps alone—out of the total of 40 in the German forces—required 170 railway cars for officers, 965 for infantry, 2960 for cavalry, 1915 for artillery and supply wagons, 6010 in all, grouped in 140 trains and an equal number again for their supplies. From the moment the order was given, everything was to move at fixed times according to a schedule precise down to the number of train axles that would pass over a given bridge within a given time. Confident in his magnificent system, Deputy Chief of Staff General Waldersee had not even returned to Berlin at the beginning of the crisis but had written to Jagow: "I shall remain here ready to jump; we are all prepared at the General Staff; in the meantime there is nothing for us to do!" It was a proud tradition inherited from the elder, or "great" Moltke who on mobilization day in 1870 was found lying on a sofa reading *Lady Audley's Secret*.[41]

With the momentum of mobilization directed toward the French frontier, the Kaiser's fear of a two-front war rose to a frenzy. Desperately, he looked for a way out and indeed it seemed that, at the last minute, the opportunity was offered to him. A colleague of Theobold von Bethmann-Hollweg's suggested that the possibility of autonomy for the province of Alsace be suggested to France in exchange for a pledge of French neutrality. With France neutral, England would remain neutral as well and the Kaiser could turn his forces against Russia. Prince Karl Max Lichnowsky, the German ambassador in London, did indeed report that England would observe neutrality if Germany refrained from attacking France.

The Kaiser grasped at this chance for a one-front war and immediately sent for Moltke who had just put the mobilization order into effect. The trains had already begun to roll toward France as a car, specially sent out to fetch Moltke, brought the perplexed chief of staff to the imperial palace. Wilhelm quickly explained the situation and then announced to Moltke: "Now we can go to war against Russia only. We simply march the whole of our army to the East." [42]

Moltke, the successor of Schlieffen, had planned for this day for a decade. In 1914, at the age of sixty-six, he was still living in the shadow of his illustrious uncle, the victor over France in 1870. This burden had taken its toll: the younger Moltke tended toward melancholy, was a poor horseman, and was a follower of Christian Science. Introspective by nature, he carried Goethe's *Faust* in a pocket of his military tunic, and was an ardent reader of contemporary literature. Military decisions were horrendous burdens for him and he reached them only after searing self-doubt. The emotional cost of making them was so great that he found it next to impossible to alter, let alone reverse them. In short, he totally lacked flexibility.

When the Kaiser told Moltke of his plan, the chief of staff was aghast. "Your Majesty," he exclaimed, "it cannot be done." When pressed for a reason, Moltke explained:

> The deployment of millions cannot be improvised. If Your Majesty insists on leading the whole army to the East it will not be an army ready for battle but a disorganized mob of armed men with no arrangements for supply. Those arrangements took a whole year of intricate labor to complete and once settled, it cannot be altered. [43]

The vision of 11,000 trains wrenched into reverse was simply too much for Moltke to bear. He refused the Kaiser point blank. "Your uncle would have given me a different answer," Wilhelm said bitterly. This statement, Moltke wrote afterward, "wounded me deeply," but did not change his opinion that the job "could not be done." [44] In fact, it could have been done, as Barbara Tuchman reveals in *The Guns of August*: "the German General Staff, though committed since 1905 to a plan of attack upon France first, had in their files, revised each year until 1913, an alternative plan against Russia with all the trains running eastward." General von Staab, the chief of the German Railway Division, was so stung by Moltke's "it cannot be done," that he wrote a book about it after the war. In this work, von Staab attempted to show painstakingly that, given notice on August 1, he could have turned most of the armed forces around and deployed them against Russia by mid-August.

Be that as it may, Moltke convinced the Kaiser on that fateful August 1 that the German machine that had begun to roll toward the West could no longer be stopped, let alone reversed. The Kaiser made one final effort: he dashed off a telegram to King George of England informing him that due to "technical reasons" mobilization could no longer be countermanded; he also stated that if both France and England would remain neutral, he would "employ [his] troops elsewhere." Simultaneously, Wilhelm ordered his aide-de-camp to telephone German headquarters at Trier near the Luxembourg border where German troops were scheduled to cross the frontier at any moment. Moltke, according to his memoirs, thought that his "heart would break." [45] The railways of Luxembourg were essential to his timetable since they ran into Belgium and from there into France. He "burst into bitter tears of abject despair," and refused to sign the order countermanding the invasion of Luxembourg. While he was sulking, another call came from the Kaiser, summoning him to the palace. Upon his arrival there, Wilhelm informed him that a negative response had been received from Prince Karl Max Lichnowsky about the prospects of English neutrality. "Now you can do what you like," the Kaiser said to Moltke. The chief of staff later reported that he "never recovered from the shock of this incident. Something in me broke and I was never the same thereafter." [46]

As it turned out, the Kaiser's final effort had been made too late. His phone order to Trier had not arrived in time. German soldiers had already crossed the border into Luxembourg and had entered a little town named *Trois Vierges*. The three virgins that were the symbols of this small border community stood for faith, hope, and charity.

At the same time, the German ambassador at St. Petersburg, Count Pourtalès, presented the Kaiser's declaration of war to Sazonov. According to Maurice Paléologue, the French ambassador, Sazonov responded by exclaiming: "The curses of the nations will be upon you!," to which the German replied: "We are defending our honor." [47] The night before, Admiral von Tirpitz had wanted to know why the Kaiser found it necessary to declare war on Russia at all since no immediate invasion of Russia was planned and the entire thrust of the German strategy was directed westward. To this question the naval minister never received a satisfactory answer. Nor can the question of what would have happened if Moltke had acquiesced to the Kaiser's order to turn the army around and march toward the East be answered with certitude. At the very least, however, valuable time would have been gained. Quite possibly, the outbreak of general war might have been postponed or even averted. But the unrelenting logic of a military schedule foreclosed that possibility.

In France, a similar confrontation between a statesman and a general occurred. Premier René Viviani, haunted by the fear that war might erupt by accident, through "a black look, a brutal word, a shot," took the extraordinary step on July 30 of ordering a 10-kilometer withdrawal along the entire French-German border, from Switzerland to Luxembourg. In Viviani's words, France took a chance "never before taken in history." The French commander in chief, General Joseph Joffre, agreed, but reached the opposite conclusion. Trained to take the offensive, he regarded the withdrawal as a catastrophe and pleaded with the premier to mobilize. By the morning of August 1, he declared that each twenty-four-hour delay before general mobilization would mean a 15- to 20-kilometer loss of territory, and he would refuse to take the responsibility as commander. Several hours later, he had his way and the premier authorized full mobilization.

England was the only major European power that had no military conscription. The cabinet hoped to keep the nation out of war, but it also realized that England's national interest was tied to the preservation of France. As Sir Edward Grey put it in a typical understatement: "If Germany dominated the continent, it would be disagreeable to us as well as to others, for we should be isolated." [48] As the tension mounted, the cabinet became increasingly divided. The man who most clearly saw the imminent outbreak of war on the Continent was First Lord of the Admiralty Winston Churchill. On July 28, Churchill ordered the fleet to sail to its war base at Scapa Flow, and thus prepared it for possible action and probably saved it from a surprise torpedo attack. When, on August 1, Germany declared war on Russia, Churchill asked the cabinet to mobilize the fleet instantly. Encountering no opposition, he went to the Admiralty and promptly issued the order to activate the fleet.

Thus, in every European capital involved in a military alliance, chiefs of state were pressed by their general staffs to mobilize. The generals, under the relentless pressure of their self-imposed timetables, stridently demanded action for fear that even one crucial hour be lost to the enemy. The pressure on the brink was such that, finally, the outbreak of war was experienced not as a world tragedy but as a liberating explosion.

Conclusions

It is my conviction that, during the descent into the abyss, the perceptions of statesmen and generals were absolutely crucial. For the sake of clarity and precision, I should like to consider the following dimensions of this phenomenon: (1) a leader's perception of himself; (2) his perceptions of his adversary's character; (3) his perceptions of the adversary's intentions; (4) his perceptions of the adversary's power and capabilities; and (5) a leader's capacity for empathy with his counterplayer on the other side.

All the participants suffered from greater or lesser distortions in their images of themselves. They tended to see themselves as honorable, virtuous, and pure and the adversary as diabolical. The leaders of Austria-Hungary probably provide the best illustration of this. Berchtold and von Hötzendorff perceived their country as the bastion of European civilization. They saw an Austria-Hungary fighting not only for its national honor but for its very existence against an enemy who had it "by the throat." The possibility of losing prestige and of sinking to the status of a second-class power was anathema to the two Austrian leaders. Hence, they perceived as essential the need for a firm and fearless stand that, in their minds, would make a potential enemy back down. The fact that not only Serbia, but Russia too, perceived the Austrian action as aggression never seriously occurred to either Berchtold or his chief of staff. If aggression is defined as the use of force against the territory of another nation against the wishes of that nation's people, then indeed the Austrian move against

Serbia fits that definition. Yet the Austrians never saw their
action in that light and charges of aggression were simply ignored. In their zeal to defend Austria's honor and to secure
her status as a major power, Berchtold and von Hötzendorff
stepped over the edge of a precipice. They were so fixated on
their goal that they failed to pay attention to the world around
them; they virtually ignored the reactions of their ally Germany and those of their potential adversaries, Russia, England, and France. In their eagerness to vindicate the image
of Austria as a virile nation, they led their country to destruction.

Diabolical enemy images were rampant during the crisis,
but probably the clearest and most destructive of these was
that entertained by Kaiser Wilhelm. Before the crisis had
reached the boiling point, the Kaiser's efforts to mediate between Austria and Russia were carried out in a fairly rational
and constructive manner. But when the czar decided to mobilize, Wilhelm's deep-seated prejudices against the Slavic
peoples broke through and sent him into a frenzy. As tensions
mounted, this frenzy assumed paranoic proportions and was
finally redirected, of all things, against England which, at
that very moment, was exerting every effort to preserve the
peace. Wilhelm saw devils in both Russia and England and
this perception, more than any other, led to his decision to
strike first.

All the nations on the brink of the disaster expected the
worst from their potential adversaries. The Russian leadership
provided a case in point. The czar and his generals perceived
themselves threatened by Austria and thus Sazonov, who "did
not hate Austria, but despised her," responded with threats of
hostile action. As Berchtold and von Hötzendorff, and later
the Kaiser, perceived the Russians' hostility, they, too, escalated
their hostile behavior. These acts convinced the Russians that
their initial perceptions had been correct. Thereafter, the dip-

lomatic exchanges became increasingly negative and threatening and not even the "Willy-Nicky" telegrams were able to save the situation. If a nation perceives another nation to be its enemy, and does so hard enough and long enough, it will eventually be right.

Perceptions of power during the crisis were particularly revealing. During the early phases, leaders notoriously tended to exaggerate their own power and to perceive their enemies as weaker than they really were. Wilhelm's pledge to Austria, for example, betrayed a fundamental contempt for Russia's military power and an exaggerated confidence in the impact of his own appearance on the Russian leadership. Similarly, the Austrians had contempt for Russia's military machine, which they perceived as more cumbersome and weaker than it actually was. As stress mounted, however, these perceptions gradually changed, and were soon replaced by acute fears of inferiority. These fears, interestingly enough, did not deter any of the participants from actually going to war. At the boiling point, all leaders tended to perceive their own alternatives as more restricted than those of their adversaries. They saw their own options as limited by necessity or "fate," whereas those of the adversary were characterized by open choices. This may help explain the curiously mechanistic quality that pervaded the attitudes of statesmen everywhere on the eve of the outbreak: the "we cannot go back now" of Francis Joseph; the "iron dice" of Bethmann-Hollweg; and the unrelenting determinism and enslavement to their timetables of the military leaders who perceived the slightest advantage of the enemy as a catastrophe.

Everywhere, there was a total absence of empathy. No one realized how the situation looked from another point of view. Berchtold did not see that, to a Serbian patriot, Austria's action would look like naked aggression. He did not see that, to the Russian leadership, war might seem to be the only alternative to intolerable humiliation, nor did he see the fateful swing of the pendulum in the mood of his ally, the German Kaiser, from careless overconfidence to frenzied paranoia. Wilhelm's growing panic and total loss of balance made any empathy impossible. And the Russians' contempt for Austria and fear of Germany did likewise.

Finally, one is struck with the overwhelming mediocrity of the personalities involved. Each of the leaders, diplomats, or generals was badly flawed by arrogance, stupidity, carelessness, or weakness. There was a pervasive tendency to place the preservation of one's ego before the preservation of the peace. There was little insight and no vision whatsoever. And there was an almost total absence of excellence and generosity of spirit. It was not fate or Providence that made these men fail so miserably. It was their own evasion of responsibility. As a result of their weakness, the flower of Europe's manhood was destroyed. The sins of the fathers were truly visited upon the sons who forfeited their lives. Of all the cruelties that men have inflicted upon one another, the most terrible has always been that of the weak against the weak.

Notes

1. F. H. Hinsley, *Power and the Pursuit of Peace* (London: Cambridge University Press, 1963), p. 296.
2. See, for example, Sidney Bradshaw Fay, *The Origins of the World War*, 2 vols. (New York: 1928–1930); Luigi Albertini, *The Origins of the War of 1914*, 3 vols. (London: 1952–1957); or Fritz Fischer, *Griff nach der Weltmacht* (Hamburg: 1961).
3. René Recouly, *Les Heures Tragiques d'Avant Guerre* (Paris: 1923), p. 19.
4. Fay, *op. cit.*, Vol. 2, p. 126.
5. Grand Admiral von Tirpitz, *My Memoirs* (London: Hurst and Blackett, 1919), pp. 241–242.
6. Fay, *op. cit.*, Vol. 2, p. 209.
7. Joachim von Kürenberg, *The Kaiser* (New York: Simon & Schuster, 1955), p. 293.
8. *Ibid.*, p. 295.
9. *Ibid.*, p. 430.
10. Fay, *op. cit.*, Vol. 2, p. 253.
11. *Ibid.*, pp. 185–186.
12. Fay, *op. cit.*, Vol. 1, p. 469.
13. *Les Pourparlers Diplomatiques* (Serbian Blue Book) 16/29 juin– 3/16 août (Paris: 1914), p. 37.
14. Freiherr von Margutti, *Vom Alten Kaiser* (Vienna: 1921), p. 404.
15. Karl Kautsky (ed.), *Die Deutschen Dokumente zum Kriegsausbruch* (Berlin: 1919), p. 271.
16. *Ibid.*, p. 293.
17. Barbara Tuchman, *The Guns of August* (New York: Macmillan, 1962), pp. 59–60.
18. Pourtalès to Bethmann, August 23, 1910, cited in Fay, *op. cit.*, Vol. 1, p. 265.
19. Mühlberg, German ambassador in Rome, to Bülow, June 11, 1909, cited in Fay, *ibid.*
20. *Diplomatische Aktenstücke zur Vorgeschichte des Krieges* (Austrian Red Book of 1919) (Vienna: 1919), p. 16.
21. *Ibid.*, p. 19.
22. *Ibid.*
23. Kautsky, *op. cit.*, p. 291.
24. *Ibid.*, p. 335.
25. *Ibid.*, p. 337.
26. *Ibid.*, p. 366.
27. *Ibid.*, p. 359.
28. *Ibid.*, p. 390.

29. *Ibid.*
30. *Ibid.*, p. 321.
31. *Ibid.*
32. *Ibid.*
33. *Ibid.*, p. 354.
34. *Ibid.*, p. 350.
35. *Ibid.*
36. S. Dobrorolski, *Die Mobilmachung der russischen Armee, 1914* (Berlin: 1921), p. 9.
37. Cited in Fay, *op. cit.*, Vol. 2, p. 470.
38. *Ibid.*, p. 472.
39. Cited in Tuchman, *op. cit.*, p. 75.
40. *Ibid.*, p. 74.
41. *Ibid.*, pp. 74–75.
42. *Ibid.*, p. 78.
43. *Ibid.*, p. 79.
44. *Ibid.*
45. *Ibid.*, p. 81.
46. *Ibid.*
47. *Ibid.*, p. 83.
48. *Ibid.*, p. 91.

Selected Bibliography

CHURCHILL, WINSTON. *The World Crisis, 1911–1914*. New York: Scribner, 1928.

EARLE, EDWARD M. (ed.). *Makers of Modern Strategy*. Princeton: Princeton University Press, 1943.

FAY, SIDNEY B. *The Origins of the World War*. 2 vols. New York: Free Press, 1966.

GOERLITZ, WALTER. *History of the German General Staff*. New York: Praeger, 1955.

HERMANN, CHARLES F. (ed.). *International Crisis: Insights from Behavioral Research*. New York: Free Press, 1972.

HOLSTI, OLE R. *Crisis, Escalation, War*. Montreal and London: McGill-Queen's University Press, 1972.

KÜRENBERG, JOACHIM VON. *The Kaiser*. New York: Simon & Schuster, 1955.

TUCHMAN, BARBARA T. *The Guns of August*. New York: Macmillan, 1962.

2.

Barbarossa: Hitler's Attack on Russia

> *You will never learn what I am thinking. And those who boast most loudly that they know my thought, to such people I lie even more.*
>
> Adolf Hitler, to Lieutenant-General Franz Halder, August 1938
>
> *The most distrustful persons are often the biggest dupes.*
>
> Cardinal de Retz, Seventeenth Century

Sigmund Freud once remarked that if a little child had the physical strength to do so, it would smash everything in its path that aroused its displeasure. The key to an understanding of Hitler's invasion of Russia is more likely found in the realm of psychology than in the fields of political science or strategic thought. Hitler was not interested in just defeating Russia; it was not even important to him to conquer and incorporate her into the grand design of his Third Reich that was to last for a thousand years. What he really yearned to

33

do with all the passion of his demonic nature was to destroy Russia altogether, to crush her government, to pulverize her economy, to enslave her people, and to eliminate her as a political entity. His determination to destroy Russia was unalterable regardless of Stalin's policy toward Germany; thus, the German assault would be unleashed sooner or later.

It was this childlike single-mindedness that made Hitler's attack on Russia so utterly destructive and so difficult to comprehend. Stalin was indeed afraid that Hitler might attack some day, but he believed that the Führer would first present him with an ultimatum to which a rational response might be possible. It did not occur to the Soviet leader that Hitler would attack no matter what, and he was not alone in this belief. The great majority of world leaders and intelligence services had misperceived Hitler's intentions quite as badly.[1] Thus, Hitler achieved almost complete strategic and tactical surprise in his attack on Soviet Russia. Stalin, that least trusting, most cunning and devious of men, had actually placed his trust in the rationality of Hitler, the least rational of men. The mystery of this war lies therein. What led Hitler to this utterly self-destructive decision to invade? What was the basis of Stalin's trust in a man who had broken every promise and violated every pledge? What was the psychological interplay between these two evil geniuses that pitted them against each other in mortal combat? The answers to these questions unlock some of the mysteries that continue to surround the outbreak of one of the bloodiest and most terrible wars in modern history.

Hitler and Russia

The conquest of Russia had been on Hitler's agenda ever since he wrote *Mein Kampf* in 1924, the year of Lenin's death. Already he had expressed the ambition to acquire *Lebensraum* in the East:

> We terminate the endless German drive to the South and West of Europe, and direct our gaze towards the lands in the East. . . . If we talk about new soil and territory in Europe today, we can think primarily only of Russia and its vassal border states. The colossal empire in the East is ripe for dissolution, and the end of the Jewish domination in Russia will also be the end of Russia as a state.

To understand Hitler's growing hatred for Russia, one must appreciate that he paved his road to power with Communist blood. As the German population became increasingly polarized between Right and Left, as a result of the deepening economic crisis and a growing wave of unemployment, Hitler began to perceive the Communists as his only serious obstacle and, next to the Jews, as his worst enemies. His storm troopers confronted them in innumerable street battles, beer hall skirmishes, and fistfights in crowded meeting halls. Since Russia was the citadel of the Communist movement, Hitler's fury against the Soviet Union became an unreasoning obsession. His desire merely to conquer Russia changed over the years to a deep emotional need to destroy her. As a young artist in Vienna, Hitler had accumulated a fair amount of knowledge about English, French, and Italian history and culture, but there is no evidence that he had the slightest acquaintance with Russian civilization or that he ever read a book by a Russian writer. To him, Russia was a vast land beyond the pale of civilization, inhabited by ignorant peasants and their savage Bolshevik masters. Shortly after the beginning of the invasion of Russia, he said: "The Bolsheviks have suppressed everything that resembles civilization, and I have no feeling at all about wiping out Kiev, Moscow, and St. Petersburg." [2] This attitude crystallized during the years of his struggle for power. By the time he became chancellor, it had congealed into an idée fixe.

Hitler's first years in power brought him into gradually escalating conflict with the Soviet Union. With every confrontation his fury against Bolshevism soared to greater heights. One of his first acts as chancellor in 1933 was to abrogate a long-standing mutual rearmament agreement that had strengthened both the German and the Soviet armies. Three years later, Hitler persuaded Japan to sign the Anti-Comintern Pact that contained a number of secret military provisions directed against Russia. Late in 1936, Hitler confronted Stalin on the field of battle for the first time, albeit indirectly, by sending thousands of airmen, artillerymen, and tank crews, thinly disguised as volunteers, to fight in the Spanish Civil War. But it was the annexation of Czechoslovakia in 1939 that revealed, for the first time, Hitler's mindless hatred for the Slavic peoples in all its relentless brutality.

In Operation Green, the blueprint for the invasion of Czechoslovakia, Hitler had written: "It is my unalterable decision to smash Czechoslovakia in the near future." To his generals, he explained this move as the first step toward a larger "reckoning with the East." Much has been written about Hitler's interview with Dr. Emil Hácha, the hapless president of Czechoslovakia, shortly before the German armored columns entered Prague. Hácha fainted during the conversation and had to be revived with a hypodermic needle. What many historians have failed to dwell upon, however, was the fierce intensity of Hitler's rage against the Czechoslovak statesman. Dr. Paul Schmidt, the interpreter who was present at the time, was struck by Hitler's ferocious hatred and commented on it afterward.[3] This hatred seems not to have been artificially manufactured just for the purpose of intimidating Hácha; it evidently sprang from deep and genuine emotional wellsprings. Its very intensity apparently had a profound psychological impact on Hácha and contributed to his political capitulation.

Arthur Schopenhauer, in his *The World as Will and Idea,* advanced the argument that blind, unreasoning will was the most powerful force in man. Reason was simply a "light that the will had kindled for itself" in order better to attain the object of its drive. Perhaps this may explain the paradox of Hitler's decision in 1939 to ally himself temporarily with Stalin's Russia, the country that, above all others, he so passionately wanted to destroy. After the conquest of Czechoslovakia, the next Slavic country on his timetable of destruction was Poland. But in order to crush Poland quickly and without risk, Hitler needed the acquiescence of Stalin. An alliance with Stalin would also permit Hitler to complete his conquest of Western Europe without the fear of a two-front war. With the resources of all Europe at his command, the task of annihilating Russia would then be simple. In short, Hitler allied himself with Stalin in order to crush him more effectively later in a war of total annihilation.

In August 1939, Hitler instructed his foreign minister, Joachim von Ribbentrop, to explore with Stalin the possibility of a nonaggression pact, complete with a "supplementary protocol" that would divide up Poland between the two dictators. When, after a week, no response was forthcoming from the Kremlin, Hitler took the initiative personally and wrote a letter to Stalin in which he, in effect, asked the Soviet leader to hurry since a German invasion of Poland was imminent:

> The tension between Germany and Poland has become intolerable. . . . A crisis may arise any day. Germany is at any rate determined from now on to look after the interests of the Reich with all the means at her disposal.[4]

On August 21, in a letter addressed to "The Chancellor of

the German Reich, A. Hitler," Stalin replied that he would receive Ribbentrop in Moscow on August 23. On the following day, in a state of euphoria, Hitler addressed his generals and announced his plans for the imminent destruction of Poland:

> I shall give a propagandist cause for starting the war. Never mind whether it is plausible or not. The victor will not be asked, later on, whether we told the truth or not. In starting and waging war, it is not Right that matters but Victory. Have no pity. Adopt a brutal attitude. . . . Complete destruction of Poland is the military aim. To be fast is the main thing. Pursue until complete annihilation. The start will be probably ordered for Saturday morning.[5]

Saturday was August 26 and the attack on Poland was to take place only two days after the signing of the Nazi-Soviet pact. Hitler was in no mood to lose time in his plans to destroy another Slavic country.

The Hitler-Stalin pact was duly signed in Moscow on August 23. The attached Secret Additional Protocol divided up Poland and assigned to the Soviet sphere of influence Finland, Estonia, Latvia, and part of Rumania. Nine days later, Hitler invaded Poland, and England and France declared war on Germany. Stalin now hoped that his three enemies would exhaust each other in a long and bloody war and that he would simply sit by and watch their death agonies.

To Stalin's growing dismay, however, Hitler's armies made short shrift of most of Western Europe. The goal of annihilating Russia lay in Hitler's mind like bedrock and never for a moment did he consider abandoning it. In fact, a mere three months after signing the nonaggression pact with Stalin, Hitler informed a group of high military officers that he would move against the Soviet Union immediately after the conquest of Western Europe. General Franz Halder who kept a copious diary recorded on October 18, 1939, that Hitler had instructed his generals to regard conquered Poland as "an assembly area for future German operations."

As Hitler observed that Stalin's attitude toward territorial conquest increasingly began to resemble his own, his rage against Bolshevik Russia gradually assumed frantic proportions. Stalin's attack on Finland in late 1939 sparked an emergency meeting in Berlin at which Hitler demanded that his generals be ready for an attack on Russia by the autumn of 1940. The desperate protestations by the entire General Staff to the effect that such a forced schedule would pose insuperable logistical problems made Hitler postpone the projected assault until the spring of 1941. To make matters worse, while Hitler was busy conquering Denmark and Norway in the spring of 1940, Stalin imposed Red Army bases on the three Baltic states of Estonia, Latvia, and Lithuania. In June, he took the provinces of Bessarabia and Bukovina away from Rumania and one month later, on July 21, he simply annexed the three Baltic states. That same day, in a raging speech to his generals, Hitler ordered immediate feasibility studies for the conquest of Russia.

Hitler's obsession with the Soviet Union now began to color his view of Britain. So desperate was he to destroy Russia that he told his generals in July 1940 that Britain's stubborn determination to continue the war could only be explained by her hope that Russia would enter the war. Hence, Hitler argued, Russia had to be destroyed first, since the road to London passed through Moscow: "If Russia is smashed, Britain's last hope will be shattered. . . . In view of these considerations Russia must be liquidated, spring 1941. The sooner Russia is smashed, the better." [6] In early August, Hitler ordered *Aufbau Ost* (Buildup East), his plan "to wipe

out Russia's very power to exist."[7] The destruction of the
Soviet Union came first. Operation Sea Lion, the planned invasion of Britain, had to wait.

Thus, Hitler's hatred of Russia blinded him completely
to the strategic realities that prevailed in the summer of 1940.
Stalin had absolutely no intention of helping Britain in her
plight. It is quite conceivable that Hitler could have dealt
Britain a fatal blow had he not been mesmerized by his own
need to annihilate the Soviet Union at all costs. Winston
Churchill realized this only too well when he wrote to
Franklin D. Roosevelt at the time that the continuation of
the war "would be a hard, long, and bleak proposition." Thus,
Hitler's boundless hatred for the Slavic peoples was respon-
sible for one of the greatest blunders of his career.

In the autumn of 1940, Hitler issued a directive to transfer
large segments of the Wehrmacht to the East. Strict orders
were given to keep these transfers secret in order not to arouse
Stalin's suspicions. Accordingly, the German military attaché
in Moscow was instructed to inform the Soviet government
that the massive troop transfers were merely efforts to replace
older men who were being released to industry. In the words
of General Alfred Jodl, "these regroupings must not create
the impression in Russia that we are preparing an offensive in
the East."[8]

Hitler was so infuriated by Stalin's annexation of the two
Rumanian provinces that, in late August 1940, he ordered
five panzer and three motorized divisions plus airborne troops
to seize the Rumanian oil fields. Moscow was not consulted
and, in late September, Soviet Foreign Minister Vyacheslav
Molotov warned Hitler that the Soviet Union still had interests in Rumania. He also complained that the Germans had
sent reinforcements to Norway via Finland which he considered to be in the Soviet sphere of influence. In October,
Ribbentrop asked Stalin to send Molotov to Berlin so that "the

Führer could explain personally his views regarding the future molding of relations between the Reich and the Soviet Union." He hinted that Hitler intended to propose a scheme that would in effect divide up the world among the four leading dictatorships. As he put it euphemistically: "It appears to be the mission of the Four Powers—The Soviet Union, Italy, Japan, and Germany—to adopt a long-range policy by delimitation of their interests on a world-wide scale." [9] Stalin accepted the invitation on behalf of Molotov and on November 12, the Soviet foreign minister, eager for a more advantageous division of the spoils, and apparently quite unaware of *Aufbau Ost*, arrived at Berlin's main railroad station, which was decorated for the occasion with the hammer and sickle flying side by side with the swastika. It was this meeting between Hitler and Molotov that provided the final spark to Operation Barbarossa, the invasion of Russia.

Dr. Paul Schmidt, Hitler's interpreter, has left a vivid account of the Berlin meeting. It seems that during the morning of November 12 Ribbentrop was given the task of explaining Hitler's conception of the "new order" to Molotov. The Führer, he said, had concluded that all four allies should expand in a southerly direction. Japan and Italy had already done so and Germany would seek new *Lebensraum* in Central Africa. The Soviet Union, too, might "turn to the South for the natural outlet to the open sea which was so important to her." "Which sea?" Molotov asked laconically. Ribbentrop had no answer. In the afternoon it was Hitler's turn. In Schmidt's words, "the questions hailed down upon Hitler; no foreign visitor had ever spoken to him in this way in my presence." [10] The precise Bolshevik with the pince-nez wanted to know what Hitler was up to in Finland and demanded that German troops be pulled out. In addition, he wanted clarification regarding Soviet interests in Bulgaria, Rumania, and Turkey. Hitler was too taken aback to answer and proposed to adjourn the meeting until evening. At the dinner meeting, the Führer did not put in an appearance. It was left to Ribbentrop to entertain the Russian. This he did by expounding at length about the imminent collapse of Britain and the great opportunity, in which the Soviet Union would share, to divide up the remnants of the British Empire. At almost exactly that moment, according to Dr. Schmidt, the air-raid sirens began to sound and Ribbentrop and his guest were forced to run for shelter somewhat unceremoniously. British bombers had appeared over Berlin. When Ribbentrop, sitting in the air-raid shelter, repeated again that the British were finished, Molotov asked: "If that is so, why are we in this shelter, and whose are these bombs which fall?" [11]

The next day, after Molotov's departure, Hitler was beside himself with rage. "Stalin is clever and cunning," he told his generals. "He demands more and more. He is a cold-blooded blackmailer. A German victory has become unbearable for Russia. Therefore: she must be brought to her knees as soon as possible." [12] On December 18, Hitler dictated the secret directive that became the basis for Operation Barbarossa:

> The German Armed Forces must be prepared, even before the conclusion of the war against England, to crush Soviet Russia in a rapid campaign. . . . I shall issue orders for the deployment against Soviet Russia eight weeks before the operation is timed to begin. Preparations . . . will be concluded by May 15, 1941. It is of decisive importance that our intention to attack should not be known. [13]

Thus, May 15 was set as the date for the destruction of Russia. Throughout the winter, Hitler was preoccupied with the military planning for Barbarossa. He decided to penetrate the Soviet Union with two gigantic armies, one to conquer Leningrad in the north and the other to attack Kiev in the south. Moscow, in Hitler's view, would inevitably fall once the rest of Western Russia had been conquered. Only nine copies of this directive were made, one for each of the three armed services and the others to be guarded at Hitler's headquarters. The Führer demanded that the number of officers privy to the secret be kept as small as possible. "Otherwise the danger exists that our preparations will become known and the gravest political and military disadvantages result." [14] There is no evidence whatsoever that any of the generals who were taken into Hitler's confidence objected to Barbarossa. Halder, the chief of the General Staff, noted in his diary in December 1940 that he was full of enthusiasm for the Russian campaign. Several weeks later, in February 1941, Halder submitted such an optimistic assessment of German chances to annihilate the Red Army in short order that Hitler exclaimed jubilantly: "When Barbarossa commences, the world will hold its breath and make no comment." [15] He then called for the operation map in order to put the finishing touches on his plans for the massacre that was to begin on May 15.

During this crucial period two events took place that prompted Hitler to postpone the invasion of Russia by five weeks. It is of the utmost importance to consider these events at least briefly since the postponement of the invasion probably spelled the difference between victory and defeat.

In October 1940, Mussolini, eager for martial glory of his own, decided to invade Greece in a surprise attack. When Hitler visited his fellow dictator in Florence on October 28, Mussolini met him at the railroad station and announced triumphantly: "Führer, we are on the march! Victorious Italian troops crossed the Greco-Albanian frontier at dawn today!" [16] According to Schmidt, who was present, Hitler managed to control his rage. Shortly thereafter, however, the Italian campaign turned into a rout and by January 1941 Mussolini had to ask Hitler humbly for military assistance. Hitler complied and by April 1941 Nazi tanks rattled into

Athens and the swastika flew from the Acropolis. The price
of this diversionary maneuver, however, amounted to twelve
German divisions which now were mired down in Greece.

Even more crucial was a coup d'état that took place on
March 26, 1941, in Yugoslavia. During that night the government of the regent, Prince Paul, who had come close to being
a puppet of Hitler, was overthrown. The young heir to the
throne, Peter, was declared king, and the Serbs made it quite
clear on the following day that Yugoslavia's subservience to
Germany had ended.

According to William Shirer, the Belgrade coup threw
Hitler into one of the wildest rages of his entire life.[17] He
took it as a personal affront from a Slavic nation that existed
only at his whim. His generals were called into immediate
session. Hitler announced that "no diplomatic inquiries
[would] be made, and no ultimatum presented."[18] Yugoslavia would be crushed with "unmerciful harshness." He ordered Goering to "destroy Belgrade in attacks by waves" and
also ordered the immediate invasion of Yugoslavia. Then he
announced to his generals the most fateful decision: "the beginning of the Barbarossa operation will have to be postponed
by up to four weeks."[19]

Once again, none of the generals present objected. But six
months later, when German troops were hit by deep snows
and Arctic temperatures in front of Moscow, three or four
weeks short of what General Halder thought they needed for
final victory, the chief of staff was to recall with deep bitterness that the postponement of Barbarossa was probably the
most catastrophic military decision of the entire war. In order
to vent his personal revenge on a small Slavic nation, the Nazi
leader had thrown away the opportunity to annihilate the
Soviet Union. Hitler, too, realized this shortly before his
death. Like the Roman Emperor Augustus, shouting into a
pitiless sky, "Varus, give me back my legions," Hitler, in the

underground bunker of the Reich chancellery with the Russians only several blocks away, was supposed to have screamed in anguish at a portrait of Frederick the Great: "Give me back my four weeks!"

On March 30, 1941, the number of Wehrmacht officers fully apprised of Barbarossa suddenly jumped to approximately 250. The occasion was a long speech delivered by Hitler in the new Reich chancellery in Berlin. The subject was the coming massacre of the Soviet Union, now rescheduled to begin on June 22, 1941. The basic purpose of the speech was to prepare the generals for a war of total annihilation. Hitler described the coming campaign as a war to the death between two opposing ideologies. The struggle would be conducted with merciless harshness and no quarter would be given. Breaches of international law would be excused since Russia had not participated in the Hague Conference and thus had no rights under it. Soviet commissars who surrendered were to be executed. In conclusion, Hitler stated, "I do not expect my generals to understand me, but I shall expect them to obey my orders." [20] None of the generals in Hitler's audience asked any questions, nor was there any discussion. Five years later at Nuremberg, when the question of the notorious Commissar Order was brought up, several generals confessed that they had been horrified but had lacked the courage to object.

During the final weeks before the invasion, Hitler alternated between detailed military planning and indulging himself in fantasies of what he would do to the hated Russians. "In a few weeks we shall be in Moscow," he declared, "there is absolutely no doubt about it. I will raze this damned city to the ground and I will make an artificial lake to provide energy for an electric power station. The name of Moscow will vanish forever." [21] Historical Russia would cease to exist. Her culture would cease to exist. No Russian books except perhaps agricultural handbooks would be printed and Russian children would be given just enough instruction in their schools to understand the orders of their German masters. All Russian Jews would perish and the population of Russia would be drastically reduced through starvation and mass executions. On the morning after the summer solstice, the German army would smash into Russia. Long before the winter solstice, Russia would disappear from the map.

Hermann Goering was placed in charge of the economic exploitation of the Soviet Union. On May 23, 1941, Goering issued a directive in which he announced that most of Russia's food production would go to Germany and the Russian population would be left to starve:

> Any attempt to save the population from death by starvation . . . would reduce Germany's staying power in the war. As a result, many millions of persons will be starved to death if we take out of the country the things necessary for us. This must be clearly and absolutely understood.[22]

Once again, there is no evidence that any of Goering's subordinates who prepared the spoliation of Russia during that pleasant German spring of 1941 voiced any protest.

When the order to invade the Soviet Union was finally given at 3 A.M. on June 22, Hitler was the absolute master of the most formidable fighting machine the world had ever seen: 154 German divisions, not to mention Finnish and Rumanian detachments, were massed on the Russian border; 3,000 tanks and 2,000 airplanes were ready for battle; generals fresh from a succession of victories were in command of the Wehrmacht. It seemed that nothing could prevent Hitler's entry into Moscow before the end of the summer.

In addition, the attack was a complete surprise, not so much through Hitler's own discretion, but through Stalin's stubborn refusal to believe that a surprise attack was imminent. During the night of the invasion, Moscow slept peacefully. As dawn broke, the commander of a small Soviet frontier post was awakened by artillery fire. He called the general in command and reported that he was being fired upon. "You must be insane," was the reply. By this time, the Germans had overrun the post and advanced deep into Russia.

In looking back on these events, one is struck by the private and personal nature of Hitler's war against Russia. The need to destroy the hated Slavic nation weighed upon him like an oppressive presence and blinded him completely to the strategic realities in Russia, both before and after the invasion. Perhaps the most revealing document on this subject is a letter that Hitler wrote to Mussolini on June 21, a few hours before the German troops poured into Russia. In this document, Hitler said:

> Since I struggled through to this decision, I again feel spiritually free. The partnership with the Soviet Union . . . was nevertheless often very irksome to me, for in some way or other it seemed to me to be a break with my whole origin, my concepts and my former obligations. I am happy now to be relieved of these mental agonies.[23]

Thus, German soldiers, sure of a summer victory, entered Russia. They came in their light uniforms. No provisions had been made to procure winter clothing should it be needed and no preparations had been made to cope with the Russian winter. Men and machines were tooled to perfection, but only for another *Blitzkrieg*. The lessons of Charles XII of Sweden and of Napoleon Bonaparte, who had met their doom in the snows of Russia, were ignored. Yet, Hitler chose two symbols whose murky significance is strange indeed. Barbarossa, after whom he named his greatest military venture, had been a crusader of the Holy Roman Empire who had failed in his mission to the East and drowned. His corpse and the site of his burial were lost. More strangely still, while Hitler never mentioned the fate of the Grand Armée in its retreat from Moscow in 1812, he chose June 22 as the day of reckoning. It has never been established whether or not he knew that this was the exact anniversary of Napoleon's invasion of Russia almost a century and a half before.

Stalin and Germany

When one thinks of the Russo-German war today, the images that are conjured up most readily are the Soviet victory at Stalingrad and the ultimate triumph of Soviet arms in Berlin in 1945. What is not so readily remembered, however, is the fact that "the scale of the disaster wrought by the German invaders in the first hours, days, weeks, and months of the war can be considered unprecedented in the history of modern warfare." [24] One month after the beginning of the invasion, the German Army Group Center was within 200 miles of Moscow; Army Group North was moving toward Leningrad; and Army Group South was approaching Kiev, the capital of the Ukraine. Most of the Soviet air force had been destroyed, much of it on the ground during the first five days. More than half a million prisoners had been taken by the advancing German armies. By mid-summer of 1941, German troops controlled Soviet territory amounting to more than twice the size of France. While there can be no doubt about the determined resistance and dogged fighting spirit of the Red Army, it is likely that, in the last analysis, the Soviet Union was saved by her immense space, manpower, resources, and, perhaps most important, by the Russian winter.

The haunting question that arises when one contemplates

the disaster of June 1941 is: How was it possible for Hitler to achieve such complete strategic and tactical surprise when Stalin was warned of the imminent attack through an abundance of intelligence information? Without a doubt, Stalin "received more and better information on the approaching danger, even on specific details of date and hour of invasion, than did any other leadership of an attacked country in the history of modern warfare." [25] Winston Churchill, who personally warned Stalin several times, was so appalled by this incongruity that he reached the conclusion that "Stalin and his commissars showed themselves to be the most completely outwitted bunglers." [26] Soviet prewar predictions of the likely course of a Nazi-Soviet war were separated from reality by a limitless gulf. In the summer of 1939, there appeared in the Soviet Union a novel by N. Shpanov, entitled *The First Strike—The Story of a Future War,* in which a Fascist air attack on Russia was repulsed by Soviet fighters within half an hour. Ten hours later, the Soviet air force reported the destruction of the entire German war-making potential. Considering that this military science fiction seems to have been widely believed in the Soviet Union, the reality of the summer of 1941 took on the dimensions of a colossal nightmare and produced a "mental vacuum and a terror of the unexplainable." [27] Yet an explanation must be sought in the personality of the absolute ruler of the Soviet Union—Joseph Stalin.

The first, and probably the most important, single reason for the disaster was the Great Purge of the 1930s. While this unprecedented terror that was unleashed by Stalin after the death of Sergei Kirov in 1934 crippled all sectors of Soviet society, it virtually decimated the officer corps of the Red Army. The last-known execution of the senior military officer prior to the Nazi invasion took place a mere two weeks before the German assault. The victim was General Shmushkevich, chief of the Soviet air force.

It is likely that, even if Stalin had heeded the numerous intelligence warnings that pointed to the Nazi attack, he could not have averted the disaster completely. The Great Purge was a horrible bloodletting. Many more senior officers were killed during those years than during four years of war against Nazi Germany.[28] Arrests of senior officers in 1936 commenced the assault. In 1937, a group of the highest ranking officers of the Red Army, including General Tukhachevsky, were arrested, tried as "foreign agents," and shot. A crescendo of executions was reached under the head of the Secret Police, N. I. Yezhov, until that "lord high executioner" was himself executed in 1939 and replaced by Lavrenti Beria. During these years, the Soviet military establishment sustained terrible and irreplaceable losses. Moreover, the professional competence of the Red Army, not to speak of its morale, deteriorated disastrously. By 1940, about one-fifth of the positions of unit and subunit commanders were vacant; military schools could neither fill vacancies nor provide reserves.[29] At the time of the invasion, only 7 percent of all Soviet officers had received higher military education, and 37 percent had not even completed military training; 75 percent had occupied their posts for less than a year.[30] Careers were broken and made with dizzying speed, and inexperienced men often reached the apex of command, not because of professional competence but because of political favor and the personal whim of the supreme commander, Joseph Stalin. The atmosphere of overwhelming fear generated by the purge and the knowledge of the possible consequences of a single misstep resulted in a situation in which decisions on grave as well as trivial matters gravitated to the ultimate center of all power—Stalin. By 1941, military policy had, in effect, been reduced to preparing proposals for Stalin, asking permission from Stalin, appealing for help to Stalin, and, above all, to executing the orders of Stalin.[31] Even after the invasion, the Soviet generals feared

Stalin more than they feared the Germans. Top field commanders, responsible for the lives of close to 700,000 troops faced with almost certain annihilation in the trap at Kiev in 1941, refused to risk Stalin's anger by requesting permission to withdraw. Very much like Field Marshal Friedrich von Paulus at Stalingrad, who feared Hitler's anger more than Soviet guns, the Russian generals preferred to take their chances with the Nazis rather than face the risk of Stalin's wrath. The Soviet leader's control over the Red Army in 1941 was just as complete as that of Hitler over the Wehrmacht.

What in Stalin's nature led to these purges that almost broke the backbone of Russia's fighting forces in her hour of supreme trial? The evidence suggests that Stalin placed the security of his power within the Soviet state above all else, including the security of the nation from foreign attack. In essence, the purges were a cleansing process to eliminate not only all actual but also all potential opposition to Stalin's absolute rule. Conveniently enough, many victims of the purge, some of whom were made to testify at the notorious Moscow Trials, were depicted as "paid agents of the capitalist powers." The attention of the Russian people was thus deflected from their real domestic problems to imaginary dangers that lurked outside Soviet borders. Stalin started the engine of destruction and only when it threatened, in its mad momentum, to get out of hand completely did he stop it, but not before it had almost torn apart the very fabric of society.

Nikita Khrushchev, in his famous "secret speech" to the Twentieth Party Congress in 1956, accused Stalin of empty boasts about Russia's fighting ability in 1941 and chastised him for failing to heed the numerous clear warnings of Nazi intentions in word and deed that were made available to him before the invasion. He challenged Stalin's qualifications as a military commander and stressed his nervousness and hysteria. He alleged that, for two weeks after the invasion, Stalin

suffered a nervous collapse and "ceased to do anything whatever" except sulk. But he reserved his strongest words for
Stalin's disastrous annihilation of military cadres during the
years of the Great Purge. This, he said, almost cost the Soviet
Union its national existence.

Stalin's role as war leader was elevated after Khrushchev's
ouster in 1964. But condemnation of the Stalin purge has
remained official Soviet policy. As a more balanced picture of
the man who ruled Russia for a quarter of a century slowly
begins to emerge, it seems that his role in the "Great Patriotic
War" will remain controversial. The Great Purge, however,
will probably continue to be regarded, both inside and outside
of the Soviet Union, as Stalin's greatest crime and greatest
blunder.

A second major cause for the disaster of June 1941 was
Stalin's decision to ally himself with Hitler in 1939. Stalin
justified the pact on the occasion of his first broadcast to the
Soviet people after the invasion. In this message, which he
delivered on July 3, Stalin said:

> We secured peace for our country for one and a half years, as
> well as an opportunity of preparing our forces for defense if
> fascist Germany risked attacking our country in defiance of the
> pact. This was a definite gain for our country and a loss for
> fascist Germany.[32]

In short, Stalin argued that his deal with Hitler had given
Russia the same breathing spell that Czar Alexander had
secured from Napoleon at Tilsit in 1807 and Lenin had
wrested from Germany at Brest-Litovsk in 1917. This argument merits detailed and objective consideration.

During the early 1930s, Stalin began to cast about for
allies against the rising threat of Hitler. He sought mutual
security pacts and promoted popular front alliances between

Communist parties and other anti-Fascist groups within other nations. By 1938, however, Stalin felt increasingly insecure in his temporary alliance with Britain and France. He may even have suspected that Britain aimed at encouraging Hitler to strike to the East to promote a death struggle between the Soviet Union and Germany. At any rate, the Anglo-French fiasco at Munich confirmed for the Soviet leader his suspicion that an alliance with Hitler might yield great advantages. Stalin calculated that such a pact would safeguard the Nazi dictator's eastern flank and thus give him the green light to launch an offensive against the West. Since, in Stalin's view, Nazi Germany and Western Europe were approximately equal in strength, a mutually exhausting war would give the Soviet Union an opportunity to grow stronger in peace and ultimately to absorb both adversaries. In addition, a pact with Hitler would buy time and, since the Great Purge had seriously weakened the Soviet military machine, time was of the essence. Moreover, the Soviet Union would at last be able to make some territorial gains: half of Poland and the three Baltic states of Latvia, Lithuania, and Estonia. Thus, in 1939, Stalin decided to sacrifice Marxism-Leninism on the altar of Machiavelli. As it turned out, Stalin's hopes were premised on a great miscalculation: it took Hitler not years but weeks to conquer most of Western Europe. By 1940, therefore, Stalin was dismayed to see himself confronted with a Nazi colossus with the resources of most of Western Europe to draw upon. Throughout 1941, 1942, and 1943 Stalin was to complain bitterly that there was no second front in Europe against Hitler and that Russia was forced to bear the sole burden of containing the German army. In 1939, there was still a Western front in Europe that could have drawn off the German forces. Poland, too, would not have been overrun in two weeks if Stalin had supported her instead of carving her up with Hitler. And most important, there might not have been any war if Hitler had known that he would have had to face the Soviet Union in addition to England and France. Even his timid generals had warned him at the time that Germany's chances of winning were slim against such a formidable coalition.

Stalin's pact with Hitler was also the result of his contempt for the policies of Britain and France. He argued that he had only done what the two capitalist powers had done the year before at Munich: bought peace and the time to rearm at the expense of a small state. Chamberlain had bought time by sacrificing Czechoslovakia and Stalin did the same by sacrificing Poland.

By the time Ribbentrop visited Moscow on August 23, 1939, to sign the pact, Stalin had become so anti-British that he exchanged confidences with his German guest. "The British military mission in Moscow," he told Ribbentrop, "had never told the Soviet government what it really wanted." Ribbentrop responded by saying that Britain had always tried to disrupt good relations between Germany and the Soviet Union. "England is weak," he declared, "and wants to let others fight for her presumptuous claim to world dominion." Stalin eagerly concurred and added: "If England dominated the world, that was due to the stupidity of the other countries that always let themselves be bluffed." [33] After the signing of the pact, Stalin spontaneously proposed a toast to Hitler: "I know how much the German nation loves its Führer. I should therefore like to drink to the Führer's health." [34] As Ribbentrop was leaving, Stalin took him aside and said: "the Soviet Government takes the new pact very seriously. I can guarantee on my word of honor that the Soviet Union will not betray its partner." [35] Stalin, in short, wanted to convey to Hitler that he trusted him more than he had ever trusted the British and French. Less than four weeks later, he absorbed his share of Poland.

The Soviet population seems to have been utterly confused by Stalin's *volte-face*. In the following excerpt, a pilot in the Soviet air force, writing after the war, looked back on those "twenty-two strange and incomprehensible months" when the pact was in force:

> The fascists were no longer called fascists—one could not find any trace of this word in the press or in official reports and speeches. Things which we had become accustomed to seeing as hostile, evil, and dangerous . . . had somehow become virtually neutral. This was not stated directly in words but rather crept into our consciousness from the photograph showing Hitler standing beside Molotov, from reports of Soviet oil and Soviet grain flowing from us to fascist Germany, and even from the introduction of the Prussian parade step at that time. Yes, it was difficult to understand what was what! [36]

At the time the pact was signed, there is little doubt that Stalin had more faith in Hitler than in "Anglo-American capitalism." In this exaggerated trust in his fellow dictator and his equally exaggerated suspicion of Britain and the United States there is yet another key to the riddle of the disaster of June 1941.

During the year preceding the invasion, eighty-four separate warnings about Barbarossa were conveyed to the Soviet Union.[37] Presumably, a great number of these were brought to Stalin's attention. The strongest of these, however, emanated from British and American sources. Stalin, instead of considering the information on its merits, discounted it in most cases because of its source. He received with suspicion, or even rejected outright, all information about Hitler's actions that came from the English or the Americans. Since he believed that Britain wanted him to go to war with Germany, he was convinced that all English intelligence about the possibility of war in the near future was a fabrication designed

to provoke a Russo-German war. When the veracity of these
"capitalist" sources finally dawned upon him, the time for
effective countermeasures had almost passed. A fair sample of
these warnings will suffice to demonstrate the depths of
Stalin's self-delusion.

The British government attempted to warn Stalin on six
separate occasions. On June 25, 1940, Churchill wrote a personal letter to Stalin in which he pointed out that Hitler's
insatiable lust for conquest posed a common problem. Ambassador Stafford Cripps delivered Churchill's note and added
his own concurring remarks. Stalin, who, according to Cripps,
was "formal and frigid," never bothered to reply to Churchill's
note. In late February 1941, Cripps, on his own initiative,
again warned Molotov, stating that he was convinced that
Hitler would attack the Soviet Union before the end of June.
Stalin not only dismissed the warning but passed it on privately to the German ambassador. On June 13, a TASS release branded Cripps as an *agent provocateur*. On March 30,
1941, Churchill was struck by the growing eastward deployment of German forces and again instructed Cripps to warn
Stalin with an urgent personal message. Once more, there
was no reply from the Kremlin. On June 10, British intelligence had become convinced that Hitler was about to attack
and that an explicit warning to Stalin was in order. Accordingly, on that day Under-Secretary Sir Alexander Cadogan
asked Soviet Ambassador Ivan Maisky to see him at the Foreign Office. There he proceeded to dictate from documents a
detailed inventory of Germany's recent eastward deployment,
giving specific dates and places of movement of division after
division.[38] He then announced that "the Prime Minister
asked that these data be communicated immediately to the
Soviet Government."[39] Maisky recalls in his memoirs that he
conveyed this warning to Moscow immediately, adding his
own impression to the effect that the report "should give

Stalin serious food for thought and lead him urgently to check it and, in any case, give strict instructions to our Western frontier to be on guard." [40] Maisky further recalls his "extreme amazement" when the only apparent response to his own warning was a TASS communiqué issued on June 14 publicly denouncing "the British and foreign press rumors about the imminence of war between the USSR and Germany." [41] On June 13, Anthony Eden, together with Victor Cavendish-Bentinck, the chairman of Britain's Joint Intelligence Committee, saw Maisky once again to warn him. Cavendish-Bentinck added that "he would put his money on 22 June." [42] Finally, at 1 P.M. on Saturday, June 21, Cripps telephoned Maisky to inform him that he now had reliable information that the attack would take place on the following day. Maisky sent a telegram to Moscow and nervously awaited the outcome. By daybreak he had his answer.

No wonder that Churchill, on his first wartime trip to Russia, August 15, 1942, asked Stalin why he had chosen to ignore these repeated warnings. Stalin shrugged and replied: "I did not need any warnings. I knew war would come, but I thought I might gain another six months or so." [43] We know from the memoirs of General Georgi Zhukov, however, who worked closely with Stalin at the time, that the Soviet leader was "strongly prejudiced against information coming from imperialist circles, particularly from Churchill." [44] Ideological blinders prompted Stalin to trust Hitler rather than Churchill.

The Americans, too, were generous with their intelligence information. On March 1, 1941, Cordell Hull and Sumner Welles tried to warn Soviet Ambassador Konstantin Umansky in Washington. According to Hull, Umansky "visibly blanched, averred that he fully realized the gravity of the message and promised to forward it to Moscow immediately." [45] Instead of heeding the warning, however, Molotov instructed Umansky to inform the German ambassador in

Washington that the Americans had evidence of a German plan to attack Russia. Stalin was so fearful of "Anglo-American provocations" that he decided to tattle to the Nazis in order to maintain the precariously balanced Russo-German relationship. What he did not know was that Hitler had already decided to end the entire balancing act.

Britain and the United States, of course, were not the only sources from which Moscow received its information. Stalin had his own man in Tokyo, Dr. Richard Sorge, who conveyed repeated warnings about the imminence of Barbarossa. Leopold Trepper, *"le grand chef"* of Soviet espionage in Europe, also communicated vital information. In addition, countless flights by German reconnaissance planes over Soviet territory and unmistakable firsthand reports about German troop movements toward the Soviet border finally disturbed even Stalin's monumental complacency. His response, however, was not to take military defense measures but to engage in special demonstrations of friendliness toward Hitler, to bribe history as it were, in order to postpone what he now began dimly to feel would be a catastrophe. On April 13, 1941, for example, Stalin threw his arm around the German military attaché, Colonel Krebs, at the Moscow railroad station, and said to him: "We will remain friends with you—through thick and thin!" [46] Two days later, Stalin unconditionally accepted Hitler's proposals for the settlement of the border between the two countries. In addition, Stalin continued to supply grain, petroleum, manganese ore, and rubber to blockaded Germany. This compliant attitude struck Hitler as "very remarkable," and indeed it was. As a supreme conciliatory gesture, Stalin closed the legations of countries conquered by Hitler and proceeded to recognize the pro-Nazi government of Iraq.

On the very day that Hitler convened his final military conference for the planning of Barbarossa, June 14, 1941, Stalin authorized TASS to broadcast a communiqué stating that "rumors of Germany's intention to break the pact and open an attack on the USSR are devoid of all foundation; the recent transfer of German troops is . . . it must be assumed, connected with other reasons which have no bearing on Soviet-German relations."[47] Thus, one week before the invasion, Stalin still refused to face squarely the accumulating evidence.

The above material suggests the following conclusions about Stalin's failure to prepare for the disaster. First, he perceived British and American warnings as "capitalist provocations" and simply dismissed them. In no case did he bother to examine the evidence on its own merits. When, however, under the weight of irrefutable facts coming in from Soviet sources, Stalin began to realize in early 1941 that Hitler might indeed attack, the terror of this realization was too much for him. He then began to engage in appeasing Hitler. As Admiral N. G. Kuznetsov of the Soviet navy recounts:

> Stalin acted so as to avoid giving Hitler the slightest pretext for an attack in order not to provoke a war. As a result, when German planes photographed our bases, we were told: Hold your fire! When German air intelligence agents were caught over Soviet fortifications and made to land at our airports, the order was: release them at once![48]

Finally, Stalin believed that if Hitler would decide to attack, he would first present the Soviet Union with an ultimatum. What he did not perceive at all was Hitler's childlike, single-minded determination to destroy Russia no matter what the Soviet leader would or would not do. Thus, Stalin erred in three fundamental ways: he was too blinded by his own ideological biases to credit the veracity of truthful Anglo-American information; he attributed to Hitler a basically rational view of Russo-German relations and was unable to understand the nature of Hitler's irrational and mindless hatred for

Russia. And, finally, when the dreadful truth began to become clear to him, Stalin found its implications so horrendous that he was simply unable to face the consequences.

Thus, when Hitler struck, Stalin became paralyzed and suffered a nervous breakdown. According to Khrushchev's "secret speech," as well as the memoirs of leading Soviet military men, it took repeated proddings by members of the Politburo to shake Stalin out of his lethargy. But he did finally emerge and, on July 3, with his élan restored, broadcast his first war speech to the Russian people. In the end, despite the horrors of the purges, the blunders of the pact with Hitler, and his blindness toward Hitler's true intentions, Stalin triumphed over Nazi Germany. His hold on reality, while precarious at times, nevertheless remained firm on the field of battle. Hitler, on the other hand, like a compulsive gambler unable to cut his losses, lived more and more in fantasy until, when overtaken by reality, he was face to face with doom.

Conclusions

How was it possible for Hitler to inflict himself upon the German people, to mesmerize them, and to take them with him to disaster in the wastes of Russia?

I am convinced that the secret of Hitler's charismatic grip on Germany had its roots in the authoritarian structure of the German family. Erik Erikson paints a convincing portrait of the German father whose frequent remoteness and tyranny over his children made the maturation process excessively difficult:

When the father comes home from work, even the walls seem to pull themselves together. . . . The children hold their breath, for the father does not approve of "nonsense"—that is, neither of the mother's feminine moods nor of the children's playfulness. . . .

. . .

Later, when the boy comes to observe the father in company, when he notices his father's subservience to superiors, and when he observes his excessive sentimentality when he drinks and sings with his equals, the boy acquires the first ingredient of *Weltschmerz*: a deep doubt of the dignity of man—or at any rate of the "old man." . . .

. . .

The average German father's dominance and harshness was not blended with the tenderness and dignity which comes from participation in an integrating cause. Rather, the average father, either habitually or in decisive moments, came to represent the habits and ethics of the German top sergeant and petty official who—"dress'd in a little brief authority"—would never be more but was in constant danger of becoming less; and who had sold the birthright of a free man for an official title or a life pension.[49]

This kind of father, of course, creates for the son an unusually difficult adolescence, a period of "storm and stress," in Goethe's words, that becomes a strange mixture of open rebellion and submissive obedience, of romanticism and despondency. For each act of rebellion the boy suffers profound pangs of guilt, but for each act of submission he is punished by self-disgust. Hence, the search for identity frequently ends in stunned exhaustion, with the boy's "reverting to type" and, despite everything, identifying with his father. The excessively severe superego implanted by the father in his son during childhood has entrenched itself like a garrison in a conquered city. The boy now becomes a "bourgeois" after all, but with an eternal sense of shame for having succumbed.

During the 1930s, the catalytic agent that offered the possibility of escape from this vicious circle was Adolf Hitler. In the Führer's world the adolescent could feel emancipated. "Youth shapes its own destiny"—the motto of the Hitler Youth—was profoundly appealing to a youth whose psychological quest for identity was often thwarted. Erikson points out that Hitler did not fill the role of the father image. Had he done so, he would have elicited great ambivalence in the German youth. Rather, he became the symbol of a glorified elder brother, a rebel whose will could never be crushed, an unbroken adolescent who could lead others into self-sufficiency —in short, a leader. Since he had become their conscience, he made it possible for the young to rebel against authority without incurring guilt. Hermann Goering echoed the sentiments of the Hitler Youth when he stated categorically that his conscience was Adolf Hitler. It was this complete official absolution from guilt that made the German pattern of authoritarianism unique among nations. Parents were to be silenced if their views conflicted with the official doctrines of the Third Reich: "All those who from the perspective of their experience and from that alone combat our method of letting youth lead youth, must be silenced." [50] The young Nazi was taught that he was destined by Providence to bring a new order to the world. Young Nazi women, too, felt a surge of pride when they were told that childbirth, legitimate or illegitimate, was a meaningful act because "German women must give children to the Führer." I recall how, on numerous occasions, large groups of young women would march the streets chanting in chorus: "We want to beget children for the Führer!" National socialism made it possible for the young to rid themselves of their profound personal insecurities by merging their identities into the image of a superior and glorious German nation. This image of a common future was well expressed in the famous Nazi marching song, sung by the German soldiers as they advanced into Russia: "Let everything go to pieces, we shall march on. For today Germany is ours; tomorrow the whole world!"

Gregor Strasser summed up Hitler's appeal concisely:

> Hitler responds to the vibrations of the human heart with the delicacy of a seismograph . . . enabling him, with a certainty with which no conscious gift could endow him, to act as a loudspeaker proclaiming the most secret desires, the least permissible instincts, the sufferings, and personal revolts of a whole nation.[51]

It seemed that Hitler had the gift to suspend the critical faculty in others and to assume that role for himself alone. He appealed to the deepest unconscious human longings. With his premium on harshness and brutality and his rejection of all things civilized and gentle, those who were victimized by him constantly strove to be what they were not and tried to exterminate that which they were. In the end, in fighting for Hitler in Russia, his soldiers and his generals were fighting unconsciously for what appeared to them to be their own psychological integrity. To face themselves and what they had done honestly and without rationalization would have meant the collapse of an entire *Weltanschauung* and complete psychological disintegration. The only way for the German people to break this fatal bond with Hitler was to drink the cup of bitterness to the end and go down with him to destruction.

What about Stalin's role in the Soviet recovery from the initial disaster? No doubt, the Soviet leader received a great deal of help from Hitler. The Nazi leader's policy of treating Russians as subhumans to be shipped as *Ostarbeiter* to the German Reich soon encountered fierce resistance. Early Russian defections to the German side quickly ceased and the Nazi invaders found themselves confronted by a people fighting for its national existence.

Even more important, Stalin immediately perceived that the Russian soldier would not give his life for Communism, the party, or its leader, but that he would fight to the death for his Russian homeland. In his first broadcast after the invasion on July 3, Stalin appealed to "Comrades, citizens, brothers and sisters, fighters of our Army and Navy" to repel the invaders in a "great patriotic war." This was something new. Stalin had never spoken like this before. He conjured up the memories of Napoleon and Wilhelm II who, also, had been smashed by a people fighting for their motherland. This war, Stalin said, was not an ordinary war between two armies; it was a war of the entire Soviet people fighting against the Nazi hordes. In short, Stalin appealed to the national loyalties, rather than to Communist loyalties, of the Russian population. It was going to be 1812 all over again.

The effect of this speech was electric. Until that time there had always been something artificial in the adulation of Stalin. After all, he had been associated with forced collectivization and the terror of the Great Purges. But now, after this patriotic appeal, which greatly resembled Churchill's famous "blood, sweat and tears" speech after Dunkirk, the Russian people felt that they had a strong and able war leader. Konstantin Simonov, in his novel *The Living and the Dead*, gave a poignant description of the impact of Stalin's address on soldiers in a field hospital:

> There was a discrepancy between that even voice and the tragic situation of which he spoke; and in this discrepancy there was strength. People were not surprised. It was what they were expecting from Stalin. They loved him in different ways, wholeheartedly, or with reservations; admiring him and yet fearing him; and some did not like him at all. But nobody doubted his courage and his iron will. And now was a time when these two qualities were needed more than anything else in the man who stood at the head of a country at war.[52]

This passage is particularly remarkable since it was written in 1958, at the height of Khrushchev's "de-Stalinization" drive. But evidently the author was unwilling to distort the truth on this cardinal point. Most Western observers who heard the speech also testified to its critical, even decisive, importance.

After the story of the outbreak of this terrible war is told, one final truth emerges with striking clarity: Hitler ultimately lost the war because he despised everything and everybody including the German people whom he professed to love. In the end, Stalin emerged triumphant despite his blunders and his purges because he was able to convince the Russian people that he loved them and was committed to their homeland. Hitler never learned from his mistakes when the fortunes of war began to go against him in Russia. He compounded them again and again until disaster became a certainty. Stalin, on the other hand, did learn from his initial disaster and thus was able to turn a rout into a final victory. The war in Russia became the supreme character test for both men and stripped them naked to the core. In Stalin, madness never gained the upper hand; in Hitler, madness conquered.

Notes

1. Barton Whaley, *Codeword Barbarossa* (Cambridge, Mass.: MIT Press, 1973), p. 7.
2. Robert Payne, *The Life and Death of Adolf Hitler* (New York: Praeger, 1973), p. 430.
3. *Ibid.*, p. 336.
4. Documents on German Foreign Policy, Files of the German Foreign Office, VII, pp. 156–157.
5. Cited in Payne, *op. cit.*, p. 361.
6. Cited in William L. Shirer, *The Rise and Fall of the Third Reich* (Greenwich, Conn.: Fawcett, 1960), p. 1047.
7. *Ibid.*
8. *Ibid.*, p. 1048.
9. *Ibid.*, p. 1053.
10. Paul Schmidt, *Hitler's Interpreter* (New York: Heinemann, 1951), p. 212.
11. Shirer, *op. cit.*, p. 1061.
12. *Ibid.*, p. 1062.
13. *Ibid.*, p. 1063.
14. *Ibid.*, pp. 1064–1065.
15. *Ibid.*, p. 1078.
16. Schmidt, *op. cit.*, p. 220.
17. Shirer, *op. cit.*, p. 1080.
18. *Ibid.*
19. Oberkommando der Wehrmacht (OKW), Minutes of the Meeting, *Trials of War Criminals Before the Nuremberg Military Tribunals,* Vol. 4 of 15 vols. (Washington, D.C.: Government Printing Office, 1951–1952), pp. 275–278.
20. Payne, *op. cit.*, p. 419.
21. *Ibid.*, p. 431.
22. Shirer, *op. cit.*, p. 1093.
23. Cited in *ibid.*, pp. 1114–1115.
24. Severin Bialer (ed.), *Stalin and His Generals* (New York: Pegasus Press, 1969), p. 181.
25. *Ibid.*, p. 180.
26. Winston S. Churchill, *The Second World War* (London: Cassell, 1950–1955), Vol. 3 of 6 vols., p. 316.
27. Bialer, *op. cit.*, p. 179.
28. *Ibid.*, p. 63.
29. *Ibid.*
30. *Ibid.*
31. *Ibid.*, p. 89.

32. Cited in Shirer, *op. cit.*, p. 721.
33. *Ibid.*, p. 718.
34. *Ibid.*, p. 719.
35. *Ibid.*
36. Cited in Bialer, *op. cit.*, pp. 128–129.
37. Whaley, *op. cit.*, pp. 24–129.
38. *Ibid.*, p. 107.
39. *Ibid.*, p. 108.
40. Ivan Maisky, *Memoirs of a Soviet Diplomat: The War, 1939–1943* (New York: Scribner, 1968), p. 149.
41. *Ibid.*
42. Whaley, *op. cit.*, p. 115.
43. Churchill, *op. cit.*, Vol. 4, p. 493.
44. Georgi K. Zhukov, *Memoirs* (New York: Delacorte Press, 1971), p. 224.
45. Cordell Hull, *Memoirs* (New York: Macmillan, 1948), p. 968.
46. Cited in Shirer, *op. cit.*, p. 1100.
47. Whaley, *op. cit.*, p. 207.
48. Bialer, *op. cit.*, pp. 199–200.
49. Erik Erikson, *Childhood and Society* (New York: Norton, 1950), p. 289.
50. *Ibid.*, p. 300.
51. Cited in Walter C. Langer, *The Mind of Adolf Hitler* (New York: Basic Books, 1972), p. 205.
52. Alexander Werth, *Russia at War* (New York: Avon Books, 1964), pp. 173–174.

Selected Bibliography

BIALER, SEVERIN (ed.). *Stalin and His Generals.* New York: Pegasus Press, 1969.

ERIKSON, ERIK. *Childhood and Society.* New York: Norton, 1950.

IRVING, DAVID. *Hitler's War.* New York: Viking, 1977.

LANGER, WALTER C. *The Mind of Adolf Hitler.* New York: Basic Books, 1972.

PAYNE, ROBERT. *The Life and Death of Adolf Hitler.* New York: Praeger, 1973.

WAITE, ROBERT G. L. *The Psychopathic God: Adolf Hitler.* New York: Basic Books, 1977.

WERTH, ALEXANDER. *Russia at War.* New York: Avon Books, 1964.

ZHUKOV, GEORGI K. *Memoirs.* New York: Delacorte Press, 1971.

3.

The Temptations of Victory: Korea

This was the toughest decision
I had to make as President.

Harry S Truman, June 26, 1950

The outbreak of the Korean War remains shrouded in mystery. We can only speculate about the motivations for the North Korean attack of June 1950. Four possibilities, in descending order of probability, suggest themselves.

The most likely explanation is that it was a probing action by Stalin against the West. With the establishment of the North Atlantic Treaty Organization (NATO) in 1949, Soviet advances into Western Europe had begun to meet determined resistance. It seemed that the absorption of Czechoslovakia in 1948 might be Stalin's final European triumph. Thus, the time had arrived to turn to Asia. Conveniently enough, Secretary of State Dean Acheson, in a speech before the National Press Club in Washington on January 12, 1950, had outlined the "military defense perimeter" of the United States. There was one notable omission: Korea. It is reasonable to assume that Stalin, thus encouraged, ordered the North Koreans to attack the South.

A second possibility is that Stalin sought to create problems not for the United States but for China. Mao Tse-tung had come to power in China without the help of Stalin and since, at the time, the Soviet leader was engaged in major purges of Communist parties everywhere, it is not likely that he was untroubled by Mao's ascendancy. Perhaps, it might be argued, Stalin's pact with Mao in February 1950 was merely a façade and Stalin's order to absorb South Korea an attempt to place China in a Soviet nutcracker. In short, Stalin might not have told the Chinese about the imminent attack. It might have come as much of a surprise to them as it did to the Americans. And if the war did involve the United States, then Stalin would succeed in ruining any possibility of reconciliation between mainland China and America. A Machiavellian plan indeed, but certainly not one that was beyond the Soviet leader's ken.

A Chinese initiative in North Korea presents a third, though unlikely, possibility. Mao Tse-tung had been in power for less than a year and was fully occupied with problems of domestic consolidation. Besides, North Korea was clearly in the Soviet orbit and China had little, if any, influence there. Finally, it is most improbable that the North Korean attack was an internal affair, as has been contended by the Soviet Union: that it was precipitated by an independent decision of Premier Kim Il Sung. Kim had been placed in power in Pyongyang by Stalin. He had come to Korea with the Soviet army and had lived in Russia for years. His government in 1950 was, for all practical purposes, a dependency of Moscow; independent North Korean action was almost impossible.

What does seem certain is that Stalin was behind the North Korean attack. His motives seem less certain. At any rate, he was sure of a speedy military victory. The North Korean leadership announced that it would win the war before V-J Day in September. Once again a war was to be brought to a victorious conclusion before the leaves had fallen from the trees.

In this chapter the focus will be on the response to the North Korean assault by the United States and the United Nations. The evidence here is abundant and empirical analysis is quite possible. The following crucial phases of the American and United Nations responses will be examined: (1) President Truman's decision in June 1950 to commit American forces and the role of the United Nations in initiating the "police action"; (2) General MacArthur's crossing of the thirty-eighth parallel; (3) his drive toward the Chinese border at the Yalu River that precipitated China's military intervention; and (4) the significance of the Korean War in the larger perspective of recent history.

President Truman's Decision

At 4 A.M., Korean time, on Sunday, June 25, 1950, more than 100,000 North Korean troops charged across the thirty-eighth parallel into South Korea. This event presented the United States with two classical challenges of a genuine crisis: danger and opportunity.

At the time of the North Korean attack, Harry S Truman was sixty-six years old and had served as president for more than five years. Truman had always admired "strong liberal Presidents," and had singled out for his particular affection Thomas Jefferson, Andrew Jackson, Abraham Lincoln, Theodore Roosevelt, and Franklin D. Roosevelt. He saw himself as the champion of the common man and was deeply committed to the liberal tradition in American politics.

Perhaps most significant for the Korean decision was Truman's belief in a strong chief executive. In his view, whenever a president weakly deferred to the Congress, the public interest was the real loser. A decade of experience as senator had made Truman wary of the power of special interests in the passage of legislation. Certain decisions, in particular those pertaining to foreign policy, could only be made by the president in a strictly bipartisan manner. His readiness to accept full responsibility for crucial decisions was expressed by the motto inscribed on the triangular block that was always prominently displayed on his desk: "The buck stops here."

Harry Truman was blessed with the capacity to make extremely tough decisions without tormenting afterthoughts. As he wrote in a letter to his mother shortly after he assumed office: "I have to take things as they come and make every decision on the basis of the facts as I have them and then go on from there; then forget that one and take the next." [1] At the time he made the decision to drop the atomic bomb on Japan, he wrote to his sister: "Nearly every crisis seems to be the worst one, but after it's over, it isn't so bad." [2] Critics of President Truman have never asserted that his "resolution [was] sicklied o'er with the pale cast of thought." His advisors admired his readiness to accept full responsibility; historians, however, will regard most of the Truman foreign policy decisions as controversial for decades to come. Finally, Truman was deeply committed to the United Nations: "As long as I am President," he declared on May 10, 1950, "we shall support the United Nations with every means at our command." [3]

Secretary of State Dean Acheson, fifty-seven years old at the time of the Korean crisis, had been in office for almost a year and a half. His relationship with the President was excellent. He thought of himself as "the senior member of the Cabinet" and was completely loyal to the President. Truman, in turn, had great confidence in Acheson's judgment and, in case of disagreements between the secretary of state and other members of the cabinet, almost always ruled in Acheson's favor.

The secretary of state, too, admired his President's ability to make difficult decisions. "The decisions are his," he wrote, "the President is the pivotal point, the critical element in reaching decisions on foreign policy. No good comes from attempts to invade the authority and responsibility of the President."[4] A secretary of state, in Acheson's view, should be the "principal, unifying, and final source of recommendation" on foreign policy matters to the president. Acheson's admiration for Truman was rooted in his belief that the more difficulty a problem presented, the rarer was the capacity for decision. As he put it:

> The choice becomes one between courses all of which are hard and dangerous. The "right" one, if there is a right one, is quite apt to be the most immediately difficult one. . . . In these cases the mind tends to remain suspended between alternatives and to seek escape by postponing the issue.[5]

Acheson saw it as his duty to give the President the "real issues, honestly presented, with the extraneous matter stripped away."[6] The decision was the President's: "Ultimately, he must decide."[7] Finally, like his chief, Acheson was committed to the United Nations. On June 22, 1950, only two days before the North Korean attack, he had declared before a Harvard commencement audience that the United States would give its "unfaltering support to the United Nations."[8]

At 11:20 p.m., Saturday night, June 24, Dean Acheson telephoned President Truman at his home in Independence, Missouri, where he was spending a quiet weekend with his wife and daughter. "Mr. President, I have very serious news," the secretary of state reported, "the North Koreans have invaded South Korea."[9] He explained that, a few minutes earlier, a cable had been received from John J. Muccio, the United States ambassador in South Korea, advising that North

Korean forces apparently had launched "an all-out offensive against the Republic of Korea." [10]

Acheson recommended that an emergency meeting of the United Nations Security Council be called immediately. The President concurred and expressed his strong conviction to bring the issue of the invasion before the United Nations. A few minutes later, Assistant Secretary John D. Hickerson telephoned the home of Ernest A. Gross, the United States deputy representative to the United Nations and, failing to reach him, telephoned the home of the secretary-general of the United Nations, Trygve Lie.

Trygve Lie, the first secretary-general, had been active in Norwegian labor politics for many years before his election to the UN post. He was known to be a man of strong convictions who did not hesitate to take positions on explosive issues. Only a few months before the Korean crisis he had provoked the extreme displeasure of the American government by publicly supporting the application of the People's Republic of China for membership in the United Nations. By summer, his relations with the host country had deteriorated even further because of Senator Joseph McCarthy's probe for disloyal Americans in the United Nations Secretariat.[11] Now the other superpower was reproached. "My God," Lie exclaimed on learning the news, "that's a violation of the United Nations Charter!" [12] He decided to cable immediately a request for full information to the United Nations Commission on Korea whose observers were actually on the scene. In the meantime, Acheson and a small group of State Department officials in Washington considered possible courses of action.

The most striking observation to be made about these early American responses was the unanimous agreement that the United States would have to respond to the North Korean challenge through the United Nations. As Ambassador Philip C. Jessup summarized these first reactions: "We've got to do something, and whatever we do, we've got to do it through the United Nations." [13] At 2 A.M. on Sunday, Secretary Acheson again telephoned the President and informed him that a group of officials in the State Department had drafted a resolution that charged North Korea with a "breach of the peace" and an "act of aggression" and asked the UN Security Council to end the fighting. President Truman approved the draft, and, at 3 A.M., Ambassador Gross telephoned Secretary-General Lie requesting a meeting of the Security Council by early afternoon.

During the early hours on Sunday morning, top officials at the United States Mission to the United Nations, under the guidance of Ambassador Gross, planned the American strategy for the Security Council meeting. Gross, greatly worried about a possible Soviet veto that would paralyze the council, made contingency plans for initiating an emergency session of the General Assembly within twenty-four hours. The delicate problem of whether the operative paragraph of the resolution should take the form of an "order" or of a "recommendation" to the Security Council was sidestepped when Gross suggested that the phrase "call upon" be employed. This language was diplomatically strong, but kept the precise legal status of the resolution somewhat in doubt. Another problem was resolved by midmorning when a message from the United Nations Commission on Korea became available. The commission reported a "serious situation which [was] assuming the character of full-scale war." Since sole reliance on American sources might have created difficulties in the Security Council, this United Nations source provided a most welcome basis for factual information. By noon, the Americans were ready for the meeting.

Shortly after 11 A.M., Dean Acheson arrived coatless at the State Department. For Acheson, who had been named "Best-Dressed Man of the Year" in 1949, this was unusual behavior.

Reporters deduced from it that the situation was most serious. Acheson, indeed, had just learned from military intelligence sources at General Douglas MacArthur's headquarters in Tokyo that the North Korean attack seemed like an "all-out offensive" and that "the South Koreans seemed to be disintegrating." [14] At 2:45 P.M. he telephoned the President who now decided to return to Washington without delay. At the Kansas City airport, the President was described by reporters as "grim-faced" and one of his aides privately told a reporter: "The boss is going to hit those fellows hard." [15]

According to his *Memoirs,* the President spent most of the journey to Washington alone in his compartment, reflecting on the "lessons of history." The North Korean attack, in his view, was the latest link in a chain of aggressive acts unleashed by the German, Italian, and Japanese military adventurers that had led to World War II. There was no doubt in the President's mind that a Soviet probing action was behind the North Korean invasion. Unless Communist belligerency was deterred promptly and effectively, a third world war between Communist and non-Communist states would inevitably ensue. Finally, the principles of the United Nations, ratified with such high hopes in 1945, would have to be affirmed through a collective response to aggression. [16] He would act through the United Nations if possible, but without it if necessary. While still in flight, the President sent a message to his secretary of state instructing him to arrange a dinner conference at Blair House to which leading State and Defense Department officials were to be invited. At that very moment, the UN Security Council was beginning its emergency session. Present in the council chamber were the representatives of China, Cuba, Ecuador, Egypt, France, India, Norway, the United Kingdom, the United States, and Yugoslavia. The Soviet Union, conspicuous by its absence, was boycotting the

Security Council in order to express its opposition to the presence of Nationalist China.

Secretary-General Lie informed the council that, on the basis of information submitted by the United Nations Commission on Korea, it was his belief that North Korea had violated the charter. He then went on to say that he considered it "the clear duty of the Security Council to take steps necessary to re-establish peace and security in that area." [17] Immediately after the secretary-general had made his statement, Ambassador Gross proceeded to read the American draft resolution to the assembled delegates. He "called upon" North Korea to cease hostilities and to withdraw to the thirty-eighth parallel; he also "called upon" all member states "to render every assistance to the United Nations in the execution of this resolution." [18] While no mention was made of the Soviet Union, American officials were convinced that it was behind the North Korean move. As Edward W. Barrett, assistant secretary of state for political affairs, put it, "the relationship between the Soviet Union and the North Koreans [was] the same as that between Walt Disney and Donald Duck." [19] At 5:30 P.M., the council was ready to vote on the American draft resolution. The final vote would have been unanimous save for a single abstention: Yugoslavia. Several delegates, believing that the United Nations was fighting for its very life, actually risked their political futures by deciding to vote in the absence of instructions from their governments.[20] Independent voting of this nature was most unusual.

Despite strong UN support, neither President Truman nor his secretary of state had any illusions about the situation. Both men knew that the United States would have to take unilateral military initiatives if the North Korean attack was to be successfully stemmed.

President Truman landed in Washington "in a grim mood."

"That's enough," he snapped at reporters who crowded around him to take pictures, "we've got a job to do!" [21] Before departing for Blair House, he stated that he was not going to let the North Korean attack succeed and that he was going to "hit them hard." [22] Thirteen of the nation's top diplomatic and military leaders, including the Joint Chiefs of Staff, awaited the President at Blair House and by dinner time, Truman and Acheson were in complete agreement on the main proposals to be presented at the meeting.

After dinner, the President opened the discussion by calling upon the secretary of state to advance suggestions for consideration by the conference. He encouraged all those who were present to voice their opinions freely. Acheson then proceeded to make four specific recommendations: (1) that General MacArthur be authorized to furnish South Korea with generous supplies of military equipment; (2) that the air force be authorized to cover and protect the evacuation of American civilians; (3) that consideration be given to strengthening the role of the UN Security Council; and (4) that the Seventh Fleet be interposed between Formosa and the Chinese mainland. [23]

There was complete agreement on Acheson's first recommendation. As General Omar Bradley put it: "This is the test of all the talk of the last five years of collective security." [24] In view of the sparsity of information from the battle area, however, no one recommended that American ground forces be committed at that moment. "No one could tell what the state of the Korean army was on that Sunday night," the President later noted in his *Memoirs*. [25] Accordingly, as an interim measure, General MacArthur was authorized to give the South Koreans whatever arms and equipment he could spare. There was no disagreement whatsoever over the second recommendation which was Ambassador Muccio's main concern. As Defense Secretary Louis A. Johnson put it, the

measure was more of an "assumption" than a "decision." So
far as the role of the United Nations was concerned, the
President emphasized that, in this crisis, the United States
was "working for" the world organization. He added that he
would wait for the Security Council resolution to be flouted
before taking any additional measures. He instructed the
Chiefs of Staff, however, to "prepare the necessary orders" to
make American forces available should the United Nations
request them.[26] Finally, there was full agreement to use the
Seventh Fleet in order to restrain the Chinese Communists as
well as the Chinese Nationalists from military operations that
might widen the theater of war. The conference closed with
a strong sense of resolve that the United States was prepared,
under the United Nations banner, to take whatever measures
were required to repel the invasion.

On Monday morning, Ambassador Gross reported from
the United Nations that there seemed to be growing support
among the delegates for sterner measures to enforce North
Korean compliance with the Security Council Resolution of
June 25. In Washington, President Truman pointed out
Korea to reporters on a large globe in his office and said to an
aide: "This is the Greece of the Far East. If we are tough
enough now, there won't be any next step."[27] Members of
the White House staff commented upon the President's mood
of grim resolution. By 2 P.M., the military situation in Korea
had grown so desperate that President Syngman Rhee placed
a personal telephone call to Washington to plead with President Truman to rescue his government from complete disaster.
The President and secretary of state met in seclusion during
the afternoon in order to plan the next steps. By evening they
had agreed that the situation had become serious enough to
warrant another full-scale conference at Blair House at 9 P.M.

"There was no doubt! The Republic of Korea needed help
at once if it was not to be overrun," President Truman re-

called in his *Memoirs* about the second conference.[28] Unless such help was immediately forthcoming, no further decisions regarding Korea would be necessary. Accordingly, the President proposed that the navy and air force be instructed to give the fullest possible support to the South Korean forces south of the thirty-eighth parallel. In addition, the President recommended stepped-up military aid to the Philippines and the French forces engaged in fighting Communist Vietminh troops in Indochina. No mention was made of ground troops in Korea, but it was clear that American sea and air cover were logical preludes to such a commitment. That strong naval and air support would give the South Koreans sufficient superiority to render a ground commitment unnecessary was deemed unlikely. Ambassador Gross believed that the Security Council resolution could be "stretched" to cover the President's recommendations. The problem of possible Soviet or Chinese countermoves was discussed and the conclusion reached that neither the Soviet Union nor China was likely to intervene directly in Korea. Once again, the conferees drew historical analogies, this time from the Greek crisis of 1947 and the Berlin crisis of 1948. There, too, resolute American resistance had been successful. Support for the President's position was unanimous. As Defense Secretary Johnson was to recall later:

> If we wanted to oppose it, then was our time to oppose it. Not a single one of us did. There were some pointing out the difficulties . . . and then the President made his decision which . . . I thought was the right decision.[29]

Ambassador Jessup recalled that he "felt proud of President Truman" and General Bradley explained that "we did it so we wouldn't have one appeasement lead to another and make war inevitable."[30] The President confided to Acheson that "everything I have done in the last five years has been to try to avoid making a decision such as I had to make tonight." [31] In his *Memoirs,* he later recalled that "this was the toughest decision I had to make as President." [32]

By Tuesday, June 27, General MacArthur had been notified of the President's decision. His reaction was one of pleasant surprise since he had not expected such forceful action. At noon, the President and Acheson briefed a group of congressional leaders on the most recent developments. The responses in both the Senate and House were overwhelmingly favorable. While a few congressmen and senators questioned the President's authority to make these decisions without prior congressional approval, not a single legislator directly opposed the wisdom of the decision.

During the afternoon, attention shifted from Washington to the United Nations. At 3 P.M., the Security Council met in one of the most dramatic sessions of its short history. There was considerable apprehension in the United States Mission that Ambassador Yakov A. Malik of the Soviet Union would be present in order to cast a veto. A great deal of thought had been given to this possibility and various contingency procedures that would mobilize the General Assembly were under active consideration. Just before the Security Council meeting, Ambassadors Gross and Malik were lunching with Secretary-General Lie and other UN delegates. As the delegates rose from the table, Lie approached Malik and told him that the interests of the Soviet Union demanded his participation in the meeting. "No, I will not go there," the Soviet delegate replied. Outside the restaurant Ambassador Gross heaved a huge sigh of relief.[33]

The Soviet absence from the council on that fateful afternoon has been the subject of a great deal of speculation. Most likely, it was a blunder. The cumbersome Soviet processes for reaching decisions probably had left Malik without instructions on what to do in the Security Council. Hence, his only option was to be absent from the council altogether.

The American position was stated by chief delegate Warren R. Austin. The text of the resolution had been approved personally by President Truman. Its operative paragraph recommended "that Members of the United Nations furnish such assistance to the Republic of Korea as may be necessary to repel the armed attack and to restore international peace and security in the area." [34] The council had before it another report from the United Nations Commission on Korea that stated that the North Korean regime was carrying out a "well-planned, concerted, and full-scale invasion of South Korea." [35] The council postponed a vote twice because the delegates of India and Egypt were waiting for instructions. Finally, just before midnight, the Security Council passed the American-sponsored resolution with the United Kingdom, France, China, Cuba, Ecuador, and Norway supporting the United States, Egypt and India abstaining, Yugoslavia in opposition, and the Soviet Union absent. The Security Council had recommended military measures in order to stem the North Korean assault. At almost precisely the time of the voting, Seoul, the capital of South Korea, was taken by the North Korean army.

On the following morning, President Truman chaired a meeting of the National Security Council in Washington. The council had before it a report from General MacArthur stating that "the United States would have to commit ground troops if the thirty-eighth parallel were to be restored." [36] The President signed a bill to extend the Selective Service Act, but stopped short of ordering American ground forces into combat in Korea. That afternoon, amid loud acclaim by the press, General MacArthur flew to Korea to conduct a personal reconnaissance of the military situation. *The New York Times* commented editorially that:

> Fate could not have chosen a man better qualified to command the unreserved confidence of the people of this country. Here is a superb strategist and an inspired leader; a man of infinite patience and quiet stability under adverse pressure; a man equally capable of bold and decisive action.[37]

The President decided to wait for the general's report from the scene of battle before taking the crucial step of committing ground forces.

MacArthur, with a small group of advisers, surveyed "the dreadful backwash of a defeated and dispersed army" during a convoy ride toward Seoul. Thousands of southbound refugees clogged the roads, probably unaware that MacArthur was passing by. The South Korean army seemed to be in a state of complete and disorganized rout.[38] During his flight back to Tokyo, the general drafted a report to the President in which he made his position absolutely clear:

> The only assurance for holding the present line and the ability to regain the lost ground is through the introduction of United States ground combat forces into the Korean battle area. . . . Unless provision is made for the full utilization of the Army-Navy-Air team in this shattered area, our mission will at best be needlessly costly in life, money and prestige. At worst, it might even be doomed to failure.[39]

Specifically, the general declared that, if the President gave the authorization, he could "hold Korea with two American divisions."[40]

At the same time that MacArthur was drafting his report, the President held a press conference in Washington. One reporter wanted to know whether the United States was at war or not. "We are not at war," the President replied. When another reporter queried the President whether "it would be possible to call the American response a police action under the United Nations," Truman responded that this was exactly what it was. The action was being taken to help the United Nations repel a raid by a "bunch of bandits."[41] Later that evening, President Truman and Acheson considered an offer by President Chiang Kai-shek to send 33,000 Chinese Nationalist troops to Korea. The President was not inclined to accept the offer but delayed making a final decision.

General MacArthur's urgent recommendation to commit American ground forces in Korea reached Washington at dawn on June 30. "Time is of the essence and a clear-cut decision without delay is essential," the general insisted. At 5 A.M., Secretary of the Army Frank Pace, Jr., communicated MacArthur's recommendation to the President. Truman, without hesitation, approved the commitment of one regimental combat team. During the morning he met with the secretary of state and top military officials. At that conference it was decided to decline politely the Chinese Nationalist troop offer and to give General MacArthur "full authority to use the troops under his command."[42]

On the afternoon of June 30, Ambassador Austin informed the UN Security Council of the latest American decision. He emphasized again that the American action was being taken under the United Nations banner. Other members, however, would have to contribute if the Korean police action was going to be a genuine collective security measure. The United States had taken the lead in protecting the UN Charter. Now it was up to the others to assume their share of the responsibility.

In response to the Security Council Resolution of June 27, Secretary-General Lie had sent a cable to all member states asking for information on the nature and amount of assistance each member state was prepared to give. Of the fifty-nine replies, he felt fifty-three were generally favorable.[43] In concrete and specific terms, however, actual military contributions were slow in arriving. Within two weeks of the request, naval and air units from the United Kingdom, Australia, and New Zealand were actively involved and units from the Netherlands and Canada were on their way. By the middle of September, Lie reported that fourteen members other than the United States had contributed ground forces. From the beginning, the United States bore the main brunt of the fighting, with the Republic of Korea in second place. By services, the American contribution was 50.32 percent of the ground forces, 85.89 percent of the naval forces, and 93.38 percent of the air forces. The respective contributions of South Korea were 40.10 percent, 7.45 percent, and 5.65 percent.[44] From these figures it is evident that the contributions of other UN members remained small indeed. While the military contributions were disproportionate throughout the Korean War, it must be noted that thirty governments decided to render supplementary assistance in the form of field hospitals, blood plasma, rice, and soap. Iceland, for example, made a contribution of codliver oil for the troops.

In view of the predominant role played by the United States, the Security Council, on July 7, decided to establish a "Unified Command" under the leadership of the United States, and authorized this command to use the United Nations flag. On the following day, President Truman designated General MacArthur as supreme commander of the United Nations forces. The general, however, also retained his title of Commander in Chief of United States Forces in the Far East. MacArthur viewed his connection with the United Nations as nominal and continued to receive his instructions directly from the President. On August 1, when Yakov Malik, the Soviet representative, returned to the Security Council and assumed the presidency of that body, the council went into eclipse. On September 6, the Soviet Union cast its first veto on the Korean problem and thus removed any further possibility of using the Security Council to direct the UN action in Korea.

When the UN General Assembly met in mid-September, it was confronted with a dramatic change in the military situation in Korea. On September 15, General MacArthur had executed a daring amphibious landing at Inchon which took the North Koreans by complete surprise. Two weeks later, the North Koreans were in full retreat and the United Nations forces, in hot pursuit, had reached the thirty-eighth parallel. The question that now confronted the United States and the UN General Assembly was whether the UN forces should cross into North Korea. A desperate crisis had suddenly been resolved and an attractive new possibility had arisen: the invader was on the run and could now be taught a lesson. This possibility, however, raised serious questions of tactics as well as of policy which had to be quickly resolved. The relationship between the United States and the United Nations had to be clarified, especially the role of the supreme commander, General MacArthur. The possible responses of the two great Communist powers, China and the Soviet Union, to a UN crossing of the parallel had to be weighed. The sudden successes of MacArthur's forces, in short, presented entirely new challenges. But only a few weeks later, these events were to precipitate a massive military intervention by China and—in General MacArthur's words—an "entirely new war."

General MacArthur's Gamble

Two explosive events brought the United Nations forces face to face with China on the battlefields of Korea: first, the crossing of the thirty-eighth parallel in October and, second, the drive toward the Chinese border at the Yalu River in November. Crucial to both events was the personality of General MacArthur, who was widely acclaimed as, and probably believed himself to be, America's greatest living soldier. The startling success of his Inchon landing had made the general's confidence in his own military genius unshakable. President Truman and his secretary of state had full confidence in America's most honored soldier and believed the armed might of the United States to be invincible. Despite all this, the United Nations Unified Command was badly mauled in its first encounter with Chinese troops, and MacArthur suffered the worst defeat in his entire military career. An analysis of the outbreak of this "entirely new war" may help explain this paradox.

As the United Nations forces approached the parallel, the problem of whether to cross it or not presented the Unified Command with an acute dilemma. On the one hand, it was impossible to achieve total defeat of the North Korean invaders if the United Nations forces were not allowed to cross the parallel. It could be argued that the North Korean attack had destroyed whatever sanctity the thirty-eighth parallel had as a boundary and that the "hot pursuit" of the invader was therefore perfectly in order. On the other hand, if the mission of the Unified Command was merely to "repel the armed attack," then it could be argued that the UN forces should not be permitted to cross into territory that was not a recognized part of the Republic of Korea before the North Korean attack occurred. Moreover, there was the important question: Who was to decide whether United Nations forces should cross the parallel, and, if so, for what purpose and within what limits? Finally, there was on record an explicit warning that had been made by Indian Ambassador K. M. Panikkar in Peking. If United Nations forces would cross the parallel, China would probably enter the war.[45]

In view of these conflicting considerations, there was considerable initial confusion over the matter. President Truman's first response on September 22 was to let the United Nations make the decision.[46] Less than a week later, however, he apparently changed his mind and instructed Secretary Acheson to declare that the resolutions passed by the Security Council in June and July gave the Unified Command the necessary authority to cross the parallel. This was also the view held by General MacArthur and the Joint Chiefs of Staff. MacArthur, in particular, was of the opinion that the resolution of June 27 gave ample authority to cross the parallel. He felt that he required broad and flexible powers and that the safety of his troops rendered impractical any restrictions placed upon him. This view evidently impressed the President and his top advisers. As it turned out, it was never seriously disputed by most other member states at the United Nations.

When the UN General Assembly met in late September, most delegations were quite willing to follow the leadership of the United States. In view of the fact that the United States had been the first to come to the assistance of South Korea, and had now apparently reversed the scales of battle in favor of the UN forces, this willingness to accept the American lead was considered quite natural. Ambassador Austin set forth the American position in a major speech before the General Assembly on September 30. He argued the case for crossing the parallel in the strongest possible terms:

> The artificial barrier which has divided North and South Korea has no basis for existence either in law or in reason. Neither the United Nations, its Commission on Korea, nor the Republic of Korea recognizes such a line. Now, the North Koreans, by armed attack upon the Republic of Korea, have denied the reality of any such line.[47]

The United States took the lead in drafting an eight-power resolution calling for the taking of appropriate steps "to insure conditions of stability throughout Korea" and "the establishment of a unified, independent and democratic Government in the sovereign State of Korea." [48] Apart from the Soviet bloc, there was little opposition, and the final vote on October 7 was 47 in favor, 5 opposed, and 7 abstentions.[49] The UN General Assembly had now placed its seal of approval on the twin American objectives of destroying the North Korean forces and of unifying the entire country under the flag of the UN command.

On October 8, General MacArthur, speaking as United Nations commander in chief, called upon the North Korean army to surrender and to "cooperate fully with the United Nations in establishing a unified, independent, democratic government of Korea." [50] He informed the North Korean authorities that, unless a favorable response was forthcoming immediately, he would "at once proceed to take such military action as may be necessary to enforce the decrees of the United Nations." The ultimatum was drafted personally by MacArthur and the style and phraseology were unmistakably his own.

There is no evidence to suggest that President Truman's position on the question of crossing the thirty-eighth parallel differed from that of the general. The President and his top aides felt that by its aggression North Korea had forfeited any right that it might previously have had to prevent the execution of the UN's decree by force. Neither the fact that the UN General Assembly lacked the legal authority to legislate decrees nor that its recommendation of October 7 had only been partially accepted deterred the American leadership from declaring its own military objectives as identical with those of the United Nations. And neither the fact that the Soviet Union had advisers with the North Korean army down to the battalion level nor that China had issued a stern warning deterred General MacArthur from crossing the parallel and initiating a rapid advance toward the Chinese border at the Yalu River.

South Korean troops crossed the parallel into the North on October 1 and the first American forces, the United States First Cavalry Division, followed suit on October 7. Ambassador Panikkar issued his warning on October 2, and, on October 10, China's Foreign Minister Chou En-lai announced that "the Chinese people [would] not stand idly by in this war of invasion." These warnings received only passing attention in Washington and Tokyo. The tendency among American government officials was to dismiss them as Chinese bombast.

On October 15, however, President Truman and General MacArthur met on Wake Island. As a result of the increasing frequency of Chinese warnings, the President had become sufficiently concerned to ask the general for a professional assessment about the possibility of Chinese intervention. MacArthur considered this possibility remote:

Had they interfered in the first or second month, it would have been decisive. We are no longer fearful of their intervention. We no longer stand hat in hand. The Chinese have 300,000 men in Manchuria. Of these, probably not more than 100 to 125,000 are distributed along the Yalu River. They have no Air Force. Now that we have bases for our Air Force in Korea, if the Chinese tried to get down to Pyongyang, there would be the greatest slaughter.[51]

Four days later, when MacArthur's forces entered Pyongyang, the State Department also came to the conclusion that Chinese intervention in Korea was "unlikely." In the opinion of one leading authority:

This assessment was by no means confined to the department

over which Acheson presided. It was shared alike by the President, the Joint Chiefs of Staff, members of the National Security Council, General Walter Bedell Smith, Director of Central Intelligence, prominent senators, congressmen, and political pundits of all hues. If questioned, that amorphous character "the man in the street" would have expressed the same opinion.[52]

Nevertheless, at the very time that the American leadership denied the possibility of Chinese intervention, the Chinese Fourth Field Army crossed the Yalu and penetrated the ragged mountain terrain of North Korea.

Truman and MacArthur were convinced that China neither would nor could intervene in Korea and relied on frequent pronouncements of America's nonaggressive intentions to reassure the Chinese leaders. On November 16, the President declared that the United States had "never at any time entertained any intention to carry hostilities into China."[53] He added that, "because of the long-standing American friendship for the people of China, the United States [would] take every honorable step to prevent any extension of the hostilities in the Far East."[54] Thus, American policy makers chose to view the tension between America and China as a passing phenomenon and felt that assurances of good will toward China would suffice to insulate the Korean conflict from Chinese intervention. Operating upon the assumption of long-standing Sino-American friendship, both Truman and MacArthur were deeply astonished at the rising tone of violence in Chinese statements during the month of October. They simply did not see the intervention coming. That the illusion of a firm Sino-American friendship underlying a Communist veneer persisted in the face of growing evidence to the contrary suggests that the United States was not yet prepared to take the new China seriously. Her statements were not as yet considered credible. So far as Ambassador Panikkar's warning was concerned, neither Truman nor MacArthur took it seriously. Truman viewed it as "a bold attempt to blackmail the United Nations" and later observed in his *Memoirs* that "Mr. Panikkar had in the past played the game of the Chinese Communists fairly regularly, so that his statement could not be taken as that of an impartial observer."[55]

On the other side of the Yalu, the Chinese leaders regarded the United States as the heir to Japan's imperialist ambitions in Asia. They became increasingly convinced that only a powerful intervention in Korea would prevent the United States from invading China. As one scholar of Chinese-American relations has noted:

> While Secretary Acheson was talking about the traditional friendship of America, the Chinese Communists were teaching their compatriots that from the early nineteenth century onward the United States had consistently followed an aggressive policy toward China which culminated in her support for Chiang Kai-shek in the civil war and her present actions in Korea and Taiwan. The Chinese people were told to treat the United States with scorn because she was a paper tiger and certainly could be defeated.[56]

Truman, MacArthur, and the State Department perceived a China that no longer existed. The conviction that China would not intervene represented an emotional rather than an intellectual conclusion, an ascription to the enemy of intentions compatible with the desires of Washington and Tokyo.[57] This misperception prepared the ground for a military disaster of major proportions.

If the Americans misperceived Chinese intentions by refusing to take them seriously, the Chinese erred in the opposite direction. The world as viewed from Peking presented a picture of implacable American hostility. Not only were American troops marching directly up to the Chinese border at the Yalu River, but the United States was protecting the hated Nationalist regime on Taiwan and was aiding the French against the revolutionaries in Indochina. In addition, the United States was rehabilitating and rearming Japan. With this kind of outlook, it was hardly surprising that the Chinese leaders regarded verbal protestations of good will on the part of the United States as a mockery.

Most basic to an understanding of MacArthur's drive to the Yalu was his peculiar perception of China's power. Despite the fact that the general characterized China as a nation lusting for expansion, he had a curious contempt for the Chinese soldier. He equated the highly indoctrinated and well-disciplined Communist soldier of 1950 with the demoralized Nationalist soldier of 1948. To be blunt, he did not respect his enemy, and this disrespect was to cost him dearly.

Far from regarding the Chinese as military equals, MacArthur insisted that "the pattern of the Oriental psychology [was] to respect and follow aggressive, resolute and dynamic leadership, to quickly turn on a leadership characterized by timidity or vacillation." [58] This paternalistic and contemptuous view of the military power of the new China led directly to disaster in October and November 1950. The story is worth examining in some detail.

On October 26, to the accompaniment of fierce bugle calls, shrill whistles, and blasts on shepherds' horns, the Chinese launched a surprise attack on South Korean and American forces some 50 miles south of the Chinese border. The results were devastating. Several United Nations regiments were virtually decimated. Nevertheless, Major General Charles A. Willoughby, MacArthur's main intelligence officer, still voiced the opinion on the following day that "the auspicious time for Chinese intervention [had] long since passed" and that "there [was] no positive evidence that Chinese Communist units, as such, [had] entered Korea." [59] On November 1, the Chinese initiated a massive attack against the United States Third Battalion and virtually tore it apart. Then, after shattering the United States Eighth Cavalry, the Chinese abruptly broke contact and withdrew.

MacArthur's reaction to these events demonstrates how difficult it is for an old, but stubbornly entrenched, misperception to yield to the facts. On the day of the Chinese disengagement, his estimate of total Chinese strength in Korea was between 40,000 and 60,000 men.[60] In fact, as of October 31, the Chinese had deployed, in utmost secrecy and within short distances of the American forces they were about to strike, almost 200,000 men.[61] Some of these had crossed the Yalu before the Wake Island meeting between Truman and MacArthur.

The Chinese troops had done what MacArthur had deemed impossible. They had moved by night in forced marches, employed local guides and porters, and used the barren and hostile terrain of the North Korean hills to their advantage. Then they launched their assault on MacArthur's unsuspecting army. When the Chinese temporarily withdrew, MacArthur immediately ascribed this turn of events to the heavy casualties the enemy had sustained. The Chinese needed to rest, in MacArthur's view, and, hence, a golden opportunity was at hand for a second and victorious American drive to the Yalu.

In retrospect, it is clear that:

The Chinese withdrawal in early November was designed to encourage the enemy's arrogance; to lure the UN forces deeper into North Korea, where their tenuous supply lines could be interdicted and where units separated from one another by the broken terrain could be isolated and annihilated. This was the

nature of the deadly trap which P'eng, at his Shenyang headquarters, was setting for the overconfident general in the Dai
Ichi Building in Tokyo.[62]

Thus, MacArthur, believing that he was faced with 40,000
instead of 200,000 Chinese soldiers and believing that these
soldiers were badly in need of rest after their encounter with
the American army, advanced northward again for the "final
offensive." The Chinese watched for three weeks and, finally,
on November 27, attacked in overwhelming force, turning the
American advance into a bloody rout. Thus, a peasant army
put to flight a modern Western military force commanded by
a world-famous American general. In one bound, China had
become a world power, and the image of the Chinese ward,
almost half a century in the making, was finally shattered at
a cost of tens of thousands of battle casualties on both sides.
MacArthur, incredibly enough, did not learn much from the
experience. In the words of his aide-de-camp, Major General
Courtney Whitney, the general "was greatly saddened as well
as angered at this despicably surreptitious attack, a piece of
treachery which he regarded as worse even than Pearl Harbor."[63] The stark truth was that MacArthur had blundered
into the trap of his own misperceptions.

The paternalistic attitude of American leaders toward Communist China died hard. It remained extremely difficult for
the United States to admit that the new China was growing
in power and was fiercely hostile, and that this attitude was
more than a passing phenomenon. Many rationalizations were
invoked to explain this disturbing new presence on the world
scene. Communism was viewed as somehow "alien" to the
"Chinese character." It would pass, leaving the "traditional
friendship" between China and America to reassert itself—although the paternalism implicit in this traditional relationship

was never admitted.[64] At other times, Chinese hostility to the
United States was explained as the result of the evil influence
of the Soviet Union:

> On November 27, immediately following Mr. Vyshinsky's state-
> ment of charges of aggression against the U.S., the United
> States representative in this Committee [one of the United
> Nations], Ambassador Dulles . . . with a feeling of sadness
> rather than anger, said one could only conclude that the Soviet
> Union was trying to destroy the long history of close friendship
> between China and the United States and to bring the Chinese
> people to hate and, if possible, to fight the United States.[65]

One of the more bizarre examples of this attempt to maintain old attitudes in the face of bewildering new facts was the
brief flurry in the press during December 1950 concerning
the possibility of a United Nations military action in China—
directed not against the Chinese people but against the Mao
faction, which was presumed to be their oppressor. A headline in *The New York Herald Tribune* proclaimed "Declaration of State of War Against Mao's Faction Urged" and stated
in the text that "So far as can be determined now, the action
of the UN will not be one of war against China or the Chinese people but against one faction in China, namely the
Communists." [66] How this distinction was to be put into effect
on the battlefield was never made clear, and apparently the
utterly unrealistic nature of the proposal led to its early death.
Nevertheless, the distinction between the Chinese people and
their Communist leaders persisted for some time. On December 29, 1950, in a statement for the Voice of America, Dean
Rusk, then assistant secretary of state for Far Eastern affairs,
accused the Chinese Communists of having plotted the North
Korean assault. The press reported that "As all American officials have done consistently, Mr. Rusk drew a distinction

between the Chinese people, for whom the United States has a long tradition of friendliness, and their Communist rulers." [67] By denying that the new government of China had a power base and a measure of popular support, the United States tried to maintain intact its old illusions about the historical relationship between the two nations. But that relationship had been a predatory one, and it was precisely this that was never admitted.

Indian Ambassador Panikkar detected this blind spot in the American picture of China. He noted that in the early days of the Korean War, the Western military attachés in Peking had been utterly confident that Chinese troops could not possibly stand up to the Americans. The American defeat in late November, he noticed, came as a profound shock to them, and their attitude thenceforth was very different. [68] In a good summation of the problem, he stated: "China had become a Great Power and was insisting on being recognized as such. The adjustments which such a recognition requires are not easy, and the conflict in the Far East is the outcome of this contradiction." [69]

The Chinese intervention in the Korean War provides a good illustration of the practical, operational consequences of divergent perceptions in world affairs. These perceptions are, in effect, definitions of the situation at hand. Once the situation has been defined, certain alternatives are eliminated. One does not conciliate an opponent who is perceived as implacably hostile; hence, the Chinese Communists felt in the end that they had no resort but to intervene in Korea. One does not credit the threats of an opponent whose powers one feels to be negligible; hence, the United States perceived even specific Chinese warnings as bluff. One does not compromise with an opponent whose ideology is perceived as antithetical to one's own values; hence, the United States and China remained poised on the brink of potentially disastrous conflict, neither one accepting the other's perception of its world role as legitimate. This was the central significance of the "entirely new war" that was to ravage the peninsula for another eighteen months.

Conclusions

The outbreak of the Korean War may be divided into three separate and distinct phases: the decision to repel the North Korean attack; the decision to cross the thirty-eighth parallel; and MacArthur's drive to the Yalu River that provoked the Chinese intervention. In my judgment, the first decision was correct, the second dubious, and the third disastrous.

When President Truman made his decision to commit American ground forces in Korea, Stalin was still alive and the global Communist movement still intact. China and the Soviet Union had just concluded an alliance. Korea was a test of whether the Communist movement was able to impose itself through direct invasion upon the territory of another political entity, or whether that attack could be stemmed through collective action led by the United States.

The President's early decisions were firm, yet graduated: a full week elapsed between his initial response and the infantry commitment. During that week, his top advisers were fully heard on several occasions and their support remained virtually unanimous throughout. The North Koreans had ample opportunity to stop their invasion and thus avoid a full-scale collision with American power. Instead, they pressed the attack and escalated the ferocity of the initial encounter. Finally, even though the President "jumped the gun" on the United Nations by twenty-four hours, he quite genuinely perceived his action as taken on behalf of the principle of collective security set forth in the United Nations Charter.

Temptation beckoned when the tide of battle turned deci-
sively in favor of the Unified Command. Initially, neither
President Truman nor General MacArthur contemplated the
seizure of North Korea, but the success of the Inchon landing
provided the opportunity to turn the tables and to invade the
invader. At this critical juncture, the general, now speaking
as a "United Nations commander," insisted on forging ahead,
and the President gave his permission. The United Nations
was treated rather cavalierly, as little more than an instrument
of American policy, and although the UN secretary-general
and most member states accepted their role rather meekly, they
had serious inner doubts. A United Nations victory, had it
occurred, would clearly have been a victor's peace.

Disaster struck at the Yalu, largely because of the *hubris* of
General MacArthur. The UN commander lacked all respect
for the new China and preferred, instead, to base his policies
on hopes and fears rather than on realities and facts. By provok-
ing the Chinese intervention, MacArthur probably prolonged
the war by another eighteen months and turned it into one
of the bloodiest conflicts in recent history. Aside from the
34,000 American dead, South Korea suffered over 800,000
casualties, and North Korea more than 500,000. The Chinese
suffered appalling losses of 1.5 to 2 million men. The war
ended indecisively in a draw, with the two Koreas remaining
fully armed dictatorships, bitterly hostile to one another. The
two truncated states were to menace and confront each other
for another twenty years before the first signs of reconciliation
appeared on the political horizon.

Yet, paradoxically, the violent clash between the United
States and China at the Yalu River might in one sense have
contributed to long-run improved relations between the two
countries, for the effectiveness of China's intervention in
Korea established her as a power to be reckoned with. It shattered once and for all the attitude of patronization that, until

then, had characterized the American view of China. One cannot, of course, answer with certitude the question of whether China and America would have gone to war over Vietnam in the 1960s if they had not fought in Korea. But the probability is strong that the Korean War served as a powerful corrective and thus as a restraining memory.

In the Korean War, the victim of aggression was tempted by aggression and succumbed to the temptation. The United Nations became a party to the war and remained identified with one side in the conflict to the end. Since its identity became fully merged with the American cause, it lost the power to be a truly neutral mediator in Korea. This is perhaps the clearest lesson of the outbreak of this war: as the United Nations was captured by one of the parties to the conflict and made into its instrument, all sides suffered in the long run including, in particular, the United Nations itself. No objective entity could now be called upon to act as referee or buffer. Hence, the fighting stopped only through exhaustion, when both sides finally despaired of victory.

Notes

1. Harry S Truman, *Memoirs* (Garden City, N.Y.: Doubleday, 1955), Vol. 1 of 2 vols., p. 293.
2. *Ibid.*, p. 433.
3. Raymond Dennett and Robert R. Turner (eds.), *Documents on American Foreign Relations* (Princeton, N.J.: Princeton University Press, 1951), p. 4.
4. Dean G. Acheson, "Responsibility for Decision in Foreign Policy," *Yale Review* (Autumn 1954), p. 12.
5. *Ibid.*, p. 7.
6. *Ibid.*
7. *Ibid.*
8. *Department of State Bulletin*, 23, 574 (July 1950), 17.
9. Truman, *op. cit.*, Vol. 2, p. 332.
10. Department of State, *United States Policy in the Korean Crisis*, Far Eastern Series, No. 34 (Washington, D.C.: Government Printing Office, 1950), p. 1.
11. For a full treatment of this subject, see John G. Stoessinger, *The United Nations and the Superpowers*, 3rd ed. (New York: Random House, 1973), Chap. 3.
12. Cited in Glenn D. Paige, *The Korean Decision* (New York: Free Press, 1968), p. 95.
13. *Ibid.*, p. 100.
14. *The New York Herald Tribune*, June 26, 1950.
15. *The New York Times*, July 2, 1950.
16. Truman, *op. cit.*, Vol. 2, pp. 332 ff.
17. United Nations Security Council, Fifth Year, *Official Records*, No. 15, 473rd Meeting (June 25, 1950), p. 3.
18. *The New York Times*, June 26, 1950.
19. *Ibid.*
20. Paige, *op. cit.*, p. 120.
21. *The Chicago Tribune*, June 26, 1950.
22. *Ibid.*
23. Paige, *op. cit.*, p. 127.
24. Truman, *op. cit.*, Vol. 2, p. 334.
25. *Ibid.*, p. 335.
26. *Ibid.*
27. Beverly Smith, "The White House Story: Why We Went to War in Korea," *Saturday Evening Post* (November 10, 1951), p. 80.
28. Truman, *op. cit.*, Vol. 2, p. 337.
29. Cited in Paige, *op. cit.*, p. 179.
30. *Ibid.*
31. Smith, *op. cit.*, p. 80.

32. Truman, *op. cit.*, Vol. 2, p. 463.
33. Paige, *op. cit.*, p. 203.
34. United Nations Document S/1508, June 26, 1950.
35. United Nations Document S/1507, June 26, 1950.
36. Roy E. Appleman, *South to the Naktong, North to the Yalu* (Washington, D.C.: Government Printing Office, 1960), p. 34.
37. *The New York Times*, June 29, 1950.
38. Courtney Whitney, *MacArthur: His Rendezvous with History* (New York: Knopf, 1956), p. 327.
39. *Ibid.*, pp. 332–333.
40. Marguerite Higgins, *War in Korea* (Garden City, N.Y.: Doubleday, 1951), p. 33.
41. Paige, *op. cit.*, p. 243.
42. Truman, *op. cit.*, Vol. 2, p. 343.
43. *United Nations Bulletin* (July 15 and August 1, 1950), pp. 50–53, 95, 99.
44. Leland M. Goodrich, *Korea: A Study of U.S. Policy in the United Nations* (New York: Council on Foreign Relations, 1956), p. 117.
45. K. M. Panikkar, *In Two Chinas* (London: Allen and Unwin, 1955), p. 110.
46. *The New York Herald Tribune*, September 22, 1950.
47. UN General Assembly, *Official Records*, Fifth Session, First Committee (September 30, 1950), p. 39.
48. *Ibid.*
49. The negative votes were cast by Byelorussia, Czechoslovakia, Poland, the Ukraine, and the USSR. Abstaining were Egypt, India, Lebanon, Saudi Arabia, Syria, Yemen, and Yugoslavia.
50. *The New York Times*, October 9, 1950.
51. U.S. Senate, *Military Situation in the Far East*, Hearings before the Committee on Armed Services and the Committee on Foreign Relations, 82nd Cong., 1st Sess. (1951), p. 3483.
52. Samuel B. Griffith II, *The Chinese People's Liberation Army* (New York: McGraw-Hill, 1967), p. 124.
53. *The New York Times*, November 17, 1950.
54. *Ibid.*
55. Truman, *op. cit.*, Vol. 2, p. 362.
56. Tang Tsou, *America's Failure in China, 1941–1950* (Chicago: University of Chicago Press, 1963), p. 578.
57. Griffith, *op. cit.*, p. 124.
58. Douglas MacArthur, Message to Veterans of Foreign Wars, August 28, 1950.
59. *Military Situation in the Far East, op. cit.*, p. 3427.
60. Griffith, *op. cit.*, p. 134.
61. *Ibid.*, p. 129.

62. *Ibid.*, p. 134.
63. Whitney, *op. cit.*, p. 394.
64. Allen S. Whiting, *China Crosses the Yalu* (Stanford, Calif.: Stanford University Press, 1960), pp. 169–170.
65. United States Mission to the United Nations, Press Release No. 1129, February 2, 1951.
66. *The New York Herald Tribune*, December 6, 1950.
67. *The New York Herald Tribune*, December 30, 1950.
68. Panikkar, *op. cit.*, p. 117.
69. *Ibid.*, pp. 177–178.

Selected Bibliography

DE RIVERA, JOSEPH. *The Psychological Dimensions of Foreign Policy.* Columbus, Ohio: Merrill, 1968.

GOODRICH, LELAND M. *Korea: A Study of U.S. Policy in the United Nations.* New York: Council on Foreign Relations, 1956.

PAIGE, GLENN D. *The Korean Decision.* New York: Free Press, 1968.

STOESSINGER, JOHN G. *Nations in Darkness: China, Russia, America.* 3rd ed. New York: Random House, 1978.

TRUMAN, HARRY S. *Memoirs.* 2 vols. Garden City, N.Y.: Doubleday, 1955.

WHITING, ALLEN S. *China Crosses the Yalu.* Stanford, Calif.: Stanford University Press, 1960.

WHITNEY, COURTNEY. *MacArthur: His Rendezvous with History.* New York: Knopf, 1956.

4.

A Greek Tragedy in Five Acts: Vietnam

> *If you look too deeply*
> *into the abyss, the*
> *abyss will look into you.*
>
> Nietzsche

Vietnam has been the Thirty Years' War of the twentieth century. In the course of a single generation, five American presidents misperceived reality in Indochina and substituted their own phantoms, at first called fear and, later on, called hope. These fears and hopes obscured the facts until they conjured up a nightmare with its own reality: the longest war in American history and the most divisive conflict since the Civil War.

I do not believe that history will show that five evil men deceived their people and led them into war in Indochina. I do believe, however, that each of these five men, in his own particular way, made a concrete policy decision that escalated the war and contributed to the disaster. It is for this reason that this chapter will deal with the Vietnam war in five "acts," each to be seen as a "quantum leap"—a virtually new out-break—in a gradually escalating conflict.

In retrospect, the tragedy of the American encounter with Vietnam is plain. But the question remains whether it was an example of Greek tragedy, "the tragedy of necessity," where the feeling aroused in the spectator or historian is "What a pity it had to be this way" or of Christian tragedy, "the trag-edy of possibility," where the feeling aroused is "What a pity it was this way when it might have been otherwise." The main thesis of this chapter is that, in Vietnam, the misperceptions of five presidents transformed a tragedy of possibility into a tragedy of necessity.

Act One: Truman—Asia Was Not Europe

President Truman's perception of Indochina underwent profound changes between 1945 and 1952. In 1945, when hostilities erupted between France and Ho Chi Minh, the President was decidedly sympathetic to the latter. He regarded the war as France's problem and what France deserved for her colonial ambitions. An American OSS officer who had worked closely with Ho Chi Minh for several months prior to V-J Day had described him as an "awfully sweet guy whose outstanding quality was his gentleness." [1] This perception was very much in line with that of President Franklin D. Roose-velt during World War II. Roosevelt had openly opposed the return of French power to Indochina and had advocated some form of international trusteeship for the area. If the fighting in Indochina was a colonial war, it followed that the United States should disapprove of France. This remained American policy under Roosevelt's successor. In 1947, President Tru-man urged France to end the war and resisted all appeals for assistance, insisting, for example, that American-produced propellers be removed from the British aircraft given by Britain to the French troops fighting against Ho Chi Minh.[2]

When President Truman's perception, and that of the American leadership in general, did change, the reversal was not based on actual events in Indochina but on developments altogether outside the area. In 1948, America's concept of its world role changed profoundly. Crisis followed crisis, in Berlin, in Greece, and in Czechoslovakia. The division between East and West crystallized and hardened. The imagery of the "iron curtain" and of "containment" came to pervade the entire American view of foreign affairs. The chasm between the Eastern and the Western camps appeared deeper by the day, and President Truman, architect of the North Atlantic Treaty, began to see himself as the leader of an embattled "free world" resisting the expansion of a ruthless totalitarianism.

The threat in Europe was undeniably real, and President Truman's response to it was, on the whole, not exaggerated. The Truman Doctrine probably saved Greece and Turkey from Soviet conquest and the North Atlantic Treaty in all likelihood stopped Stalin from overrunning Western Europe. The new American definition of the European situation, however, spilled over to encompass the entire globe. Having recognized a mortal threat in the heart of Europe, the American leadership soon came to redefine *all* conflicts throughout the world as part of the same struggle. Truman, in effect, decided to transplant the containment policy from Europe to Indochina.

Inexorably, the United States came to believe that the "frontiers" of the free world included Asia as well. In October 1948, the House Foreign Affairs Subcommittee on World Communism issued a report calling China the active theater in the cold war. The report said that the Communists were

using China as a testing ground for tactics they might employ
to take over the world and recommended a "guarantee of territorial and political integrity" to the Chinese Nationalists.[3]

This shift in outlook implied an American redefinition of
the "true" nature of Ho Chi Minh as well:

> In this country, it is only now beginning to be understood that
> in any Asiatic nationalist movement connected with Moscow
> through its leadership, the totalitarian-imperialist trend must
> inevitably kill native nationalism. . . . His [Ho Chi Minh's]
> Indochinese independence has become the means to another
> end: Russian conquest of the Southeast Pacific.[4]

The New York Herald Tribune, on June 17, 1949, stated
flatly that "Ho Chi Minh is a Comintern agent whom the
French rate as an authentic political genius." This redefinition
did *not* coincide with any objective developments in the Indochinese conflict. It coincided instead with an extraneous event:
the Communist victory in China. The sense of betrayal that
the American public felt over the loss of China intensified the
anxieties arising from the cold war. Thus, peril in Europe,
compounded by betrayal in China, produced a strongly emotional reevaluation of the United States' relationship to Southeast Asia.

Hence, American failure in China was attributed to the
machinations of a world-wide conspiracy. From 1949 onward,
the American press reflected an inexorable trend in which the
perceptual grid of cold war categories was superimposed upon
the older conflict in Indochina. This grid gradually eclipsed
all awareness of the nationalist origins of the Ho Chi Minh in-
surgency. It even erased American recollections of the colonial
conditions that had sparked the revolt, until, finally, the original disapproval of France as an imperial power disappeared
altogether in a redefinition of the French as "defenders of the
West."

One by one the ambiguities disappeared. "Nationalist rebels" were steadily amalgamated with the Communist threat. Bao Dai, once referred to as the "nightclub emperor" and described as a man irretrievably tainted by his close association with the French colonial regime, was now officially considered as "offering more opportunity to the Vietnamese people to develop their own national life than a leader who must obey the orders of international Communism."[5] On February 2, 1950, the *Department of State Bulletin* asserted that the recognition of Ho Chi Minh by the USSR, China, North Korea, and the European nations ended any speculation as to the fate of Vietnam under Ho, who was now described as a lifelong servant of world Communism.

Since the definition of what was going on in Indochina had changed, it was only natural that there should be a related shift in ideas of what should be done. This correlation was, in fact, strikingly close. Now that the deadly enemy was seen at work in Southeast Asia, President Truman was eager to keep the French in Indochina. In May 1950, the Griffin mission recommended an aid program of $23 million in economic assistance and $15 million in military aid to the French in Indochina.[6] A few days after the outbreak of the Korean War, President Truman authorized the first shipments of aircraft to Indochina. In addition, $119 million in military aid was made available to France under the Mutual Defense Assistance Program. This aid increased to $300 million in 1952. Thus, before he left the presidency in 1953, Harry Truman had underwritten the French war effort in Indochina.

By 1951, the American leadership and large segments of the American public perceived France as the free world's front-line ally in the fight against Communism in Southeast Asia. "That the French are making a tremendous effort to hold Indochina for the free world is better understood now than it was a short time ago," stated *The New York Times* in an editorial on September 24, 1951. The reevaluation was even made retroactive: "A bitter and bloody struggle between Communist forces and French Union troops has been racking Indochina for six years," declared the State Department's Office of Public Affairs in 1951.[7] And in March 1952, a State Department official stated that "In this battle to preserve their country from Communism, France is contributing financially and militarily. . . . French soldiers and resources have borne the brunt of this brutal attack."[8]

By early 1952, the cold war grid was firmly in place. No longer was Southeast Asia viewed as the arena of an anticolonial revolt; it had now become part of the global East-West power struggle. On January 25, 1952, the *Christian Science Monitor* stated in an editorial that "no one planned that, after a stalemate in Korea, there should be a new trial of strength in the southward projection of Asia," implying that the Indochinese conflict had begun *after* the outbreak of the Korean War. The editorial concluded by imposing the cold war dichotomy in full force: "Indochina is a place which is bound to be occupied eventually either by East or West. The strategic prizes are so great that the issue must be joined and eventually settled."

While President Truman's attention in Asia was, of course, focused primarily on Korea, by 1950 he believed that the French were fighting for the free world in Indochina just as the United Nations was fighting for it in Korea. He never committed combat troops in Southeast Asia as he did in Korea, but he authorized material aid in 1950 and raised the level of this assistance steadily until he left office in 1953. By that time, the United States was paying almost one-third of the total cost of the French war effort in Indochina. President Truman had transferred his cold war images from Europe to Southeast Asia and based his policies there on facile analogies rather than on specific Asian realities. But Asia was not

Europe and what had worked in Europe would turn out to be a disaster in Indochina.

Act Two: Eisenhower—the Lesson of France Ignored

President Dwight D. Eisenhower and Secretary of State John Foster Dulles were absolutely convinced that China would intervene in the Indochina war on the side of Ho Chi Minh against France, similar to the manner in which she had intervened on the side of North Korea against the United States. To forestall such an intervention, Eisenhower and Dulles had increased American military assistance to France to $500 million by 1953. By 1954, this assistance had reached the $1 billion mark. The United States was now paying over one-half of the cost of the Indochinese war.[9]

The American expectation of a Chinese invasion was so powerful that it defied all evidence to the contrary. Neither the fact that the anticipated invasion failed to materialize nor the lack of evidence that it was actually planned lessened American apprehensions. Instead, the very strength of the expectation produced its own substantiation. Time and again, unfounded rumors were accepted as proof of impending intervention. The result was a recurrent pattern of false alarms. These began as early as April 11, 1951, with a headline in *The New York Times* that reported that a "Chinese Unit [was] said to join [the] Vietminh." Secretary Dulles repeatedly stated that the Chinese were directly engaged in battlefield operations. On April 5, 1954, during the siege of Dienbienphu, he claimed that Chinese troops were actually participating in the battle for the French fortress.[10] President Eisenhower, looking back upon this period in his memoirs, declared that "the struggle . . . began gradually, *with Chinese intervention,* to assume its true complexion of a struggle be-

tween Communist and non-Communist forces rather than
one between a colonial power and colonists who were intent
on attaining independence." [11]

By 1954 then, largely as a result of their perceptions, the
Americans were fighting a proxy war in Indochina. The battle
for Dienbienphu almost changed this into a direct American
war of intervention. Dienbienphu was France's last stand in
Indochina. She had fought for almost a decade and had committed an army of 400,000 men. On March 20, 1954, with
the fortress already under siege, General Paul Ely, commander
of the French forces in Indochina, informed President Eisenhower that unless the United States intervened, Indochina
would be lost. Admiral Arthur W. Radford, chairman of the
Joint Chiefs of Staff, recommended military intervention, and
Vice-President Richard M. Nixon backed him by stating on
April 16 that "if the United States cannot otherwise prevent
the loss of Indochina, then the Administration must face the
situation and dispatch troops." [12] President Eisenhower over-
ruled his vice-president and the chairman of the Joint Chiefs
of Staff and decided not to intervene. He feared that the
French had engendered too much popular antagonism to win
the war and also felt that his administration would get little
backing from the Congress for a military intervention in Asia
so soon after the conclusion of the Korean War. Thus, on the
American side the war remained a war by proxy for a little
while longer, but by a narrow margin.

The facts, in all cases, were strikingly different from Eisenhower's and Dulles' perceptions. So far as Ho Chi Minh's
relations with China were concerned, the North Vietnamese
leader was always somewhat suspicious of China. In Bernard
Fall's words, he was "probably equipped with an instinctive
Vietnamese fear of Chinese domination, no matter what its
political coloration, just as to a Russian, *any* Germany might
be slightly suspect." [13] His policy was essentially one of bal-

ance, of maintaining the independence and integrity of his movement, vis-à-vis both China and the Soviet Union, while accepting as much aid as could safely be accepted from both.

Chinese aid to Ho Chi Minh was at times considerable, but never decisive. It consisted mostly of light weapons, trucks, and radios, largely of American manufacture, that had been captured from the Chinese Nationalists some years before.[14] In view of economic needs at home and the burdens imposed by the Korean War, China could hardly afford to become a bottomless reservoir of military assistance for the Vietminh forces. The best analysis of the Chinese relationship with Ho Chi Minh has probably been provided by Robert Guillain, the front-line correspondent for *Le Monde* in Indochina: "China adheres to a very simple principle: that the balance of power never inclines in any permanent direction toward the French side. There is no need—and this is the difference from what has happened in Korea—of direct intervention, of an invasion."[15] Thus, when France received more American aid following the outbreak of the Korean War, the Chinese stepped up their own aid program just enough to reestablish a rough equilibrium. As Melvin Gurtov put it: "The Indochina campaign eventually became a crude game in which the French could never permanently regain the high ground."[16] Thus, Chinese military intervention on the side of the Vietminh never materialized. Instead, the Chinese used the Vietminh as their proxy.

The Geneva Conference of mid-1954 and the formation, a few weeks later, of the Southeast Asia Treaty Organization (SEATO) marked the end of French military involvement and the beginning of an American military presence in Indochina. The Geneva Conference resulted in the signing of several agreements to cease hostilities in Indochina and to establish three independent sovereign states: Laos, Cambodia, and Vietnam. The accords on Vietnam provided for a "provisional military demarcation line" at the seventeenth parallel. Vietminh forces were to regroup north of the line, while the forces of the French Union were to regroup to the south. The line was to have military significance only, and the political unification of Vietnam was to be brought about through a general election two years hence under the supervision of a neutral three-power International Control Commission consisting of Canada, India, and Poland.

France had little choice, but her exit was made somewhat more graceful. Ho Chi Minh's Vietminh forces were dominant in more than three-quarters of Vietnam and were poised to overrun considerably more. To Ho, the terms of the accords were acceptable, since he was convinced that the general election of 1956 would win him all of Vietnam. From his point of view, the certainty of a military victory was simply replaced by the certainty of a political victory. Both the Soviet Union and China, reflecting their recently adopted line of "peaceful coexistence," applied pressure on Ho to accept the terms of the accords, reassuring him that his victory at the polls was certain.

The United States never signed the Geneva Accords. But, in a unilateral decision at the end of the Geneva Conference, the United States government pledged to "refrain from the threat or the use of force to disturb" the settlement and added that it would view any violation of the accords with grave concern.

The general American position at the conference remained ambivalent, since on the eve of a congressional election campaign, the maintenance of Eisenhower's domestic appeal as peace maker in Asia was of great importance. Moreover, to block a peaceful settlement of the Indochina war would also have jeopardized French participation in European defense plans. These conflicting considerations led the Eisenhower administration to dissociate the United States from the Geneva Accords and to seek another solution that would prevent any further territory in Asia from falling under Communist control. The answer was the creation of SEATO. Secretary of State Dulles declared that now that the war had ended, the United States could make arrangements for collective defense against aggression and build up "the truly independent states of Cambodia, Laos, and South Vietnam." On the day the treaty was signed at Manila, in an additional protocol, its eight members designated the states of Cambodia and Laos and "the free territory under the jurisdiction of the state of Vietnam" to be under SEATO protection. The United States thus created SEATO to offset the results of Geneva. It also decided to consider South Vietnam as a separate state.

The Vietminh, on the other hand, regarded SEATO as a clear violation of the spirit of the Geneva Accords. Ho Chi Minh saw the American position as an effort to deprive the Vietminh in the political arena of what it gained militarily on the battlefield. Nevertheless, Ho withdrew his forces from the South, assuming that he would get enough votes there in 1956 to emerge with a clear national majority at election time. His election in the North would be a certainty, and if only a minority would support the Vietminh in the South, his election would be assured. President Eisenhower, too, thought that elections, if held on the basis of the Geneva Accords, would lead to a Communist victory. As he put it in 1954: "Had elections been held as of the time of the fighting, possibly 80 percent of the population would have voted for the Communist Ho Chi Minh as their leader rather than Chief of State Bao Dai." [17]

In the meantime, Ngo Dinh Diem, an American-backed Roman Catholic from a Mandarin family, began to challenge Emperor Bao Dai in the South. The United States strongly supported Diem in his bid for power, and in October 1955, Diem proclaimed the establishment of a Republic of Vietnam, with himself as president.

Hence, Geneva and the SEATO treaty meant the end of French power in Indochina and the beginnings of the American effort to enter the struggle with its own military presence. As yet, there were no significant military encounters between Vietminh and American forces. But the issue was joined. The Vietminh saw the Americans as following the path of French imperialism, and the Americans perceived Geneva as a well-laid Communist trap to engulf all of Vietnam. The end of a colonial war merely signified the beginning of a war between Americans and Communists.

As the East-West conflict superseded the colonial war, the pace of battle gradually intensified. A pattern of escalation emerged in which every diplomatic failure to achieve negotiations paved the way for yet another upward step on the scale of violence.

The first such discernible moves after Geneva were the American effort between 1954 and 1956 to strengthen President Diem's military establishment and Ho Chi Minh's visits to Moscow and Peking in 1955 to negotiate aid and friendship treaties with the two Communist powers. Diem declared in July 1955 that, since South Vietnam had not signed the Geneva Accords, he was not prepared to permit elections under the conditions specified by them. He also added that there was no freedom in the North to campaign for any opposition to Ho Chi Minh. President Eisenhower supported this view, and July 1956, the date scheduled for general elections in the accords, passed without any elections being held. Ho, in retaliation, began to train Communist cadres for guerrilla warfare in the South.

During the remaining years of the Eisenhower administration, the United States continued to support the increasingly unpopular President Diem with military advisers. .By 1960, almost 1,000 Americans served in South Vietnam in that capacity. Thus, Eisenhower and Dulles, ignoring the terrible lesson of the defeat of France, nevertheless decided to take up the burden of Vietnam. "Communism" had to be stopped, even though, in this particular case, "Communism" was an obscure Asian peasant country that by no stretch of the imagination could have posed a threat to the United States. Once again, fear rather than facts determined policy.

Act Three: Kennedy—the Military

John F. Kennedy, during his brief presidency of 1,000 days, deepened the American involvement in Vietnam considerably. By the time of his death, the United States had greatly increased the number of military advisers in Vietnam, napalm and other antipersonnel weapons had been authorized for limited use against the enemy, and the United States had become identified with the highly unpopular regime of President Diem. The Vietnamese leader's violent death preceded Kennedy's own by only three weeks.

Even though Kennedy felt impelled to demonstrate his toughness in the international arena, especially after the disaster at the Bay of Pigs and his abrasive meeting with Nikita Khrushchev in Vienna, he was deeply skeptical about the possibility of a decisive American victory in Vietnam. In a revealing moment, he exclaimed: "In the last analysis, it is *their* war; it is they who must win it or lose it." He was pressed relentlessly by the military to commit combat troops to Vietnam, but refused to do so to the end. Yet, under his leadership, the United States entered a crucial period of transition, from a marginal commitment to a fateful and direct involvement. The reason for this tragedy was that most of the men around the President, including his secretary of defense and the chairman of the Joint Chiefs of Staff, perceived Vietnam essentially as a military rather than as a political problem. In their view, greater quantities of more sophisticated weapons would guarantee victory in a relatively short period of time. Kennedy's instincts told him that this assumption was probably wrong, but he permitted the facts and figures of the military experts to sway him. Shortly before his death, his doubts prevailed, but by then it was too late. Close to 17,000 Americans were serving as advisers in Vietnam by the end of 1963.

Kennedy's first response to stepped-up Vietcong guerrilla activity in South Vietnam was to emphasize the need for antiguerrilla warfare training in the United States. The result was the creation of the Special Forces which enjoyed the President's special favor. In October 1961, according to David Halberstam, the entire White House press corps was transported to Fort Bragg to watch a demonstration put on by the Special Forces:

> It turned into a real whiz-bang day. There were ambushes, counterambushes and demonstrations in snakemeat eating, all topped off by a Buck Rogers show: a soldier with a rocket on his back who flew over water to land on the other side. It was quite a show, and it was only as they were leaving Fort Bragg that Francis Lara, the Agence France-Presse correspondent who had covered the Indochina war, sidled over to his friend Tom Wicker of the *New York Times*. "All this looks very impressive, doesn't it?" he said. Wicker allowed that it did. "Funny," Lara said, "none of it worked for us when we tried it in 1951." [18]

In 1961, Walt Rostow drew the President's attention to Brigadier General Edward Lansdale. Lansdale had made a reputation for himself by helping Philippine President Ramon Magsaysay defeat the Huk rebellion. He seemed to be just the man to defeat the Vietcong. Lansdale recommended that the number of American military advisers in Vietnam be increased to 3,000 men. Kennedy rejected the recommendation but authorized the dispatch of 400 men from the Special Forces to Vietnam. This would give him the opportunity to see how his favorites would acquit themselves in real action.

In March 1961, Kennedy appointed Frederick E. Nolting, Jr. as ambassador to Vietnam. Nolting had been head of the political section of NATO and had earned a good, solid reputation. However, he had never been to Asia and his ideas about Communism had been filtered through the prism of his European experience. Nolting requested as his deputy William Trueheart who had never been to Asia either. This was the price that Kennedy paid for the past. Most experts on Asia were considered possible security risks since the days of Senator Joseph McCarthy. Specialists on Europe, on the other hand, like Nolting and Trueheart, were above suspicion. The fact that they were totally ignorant about Asian realities did not seem to present a serious problem.

In April 1961, in order to boost President Diem's morale, Kennedy decided to ask Vice-President Lyndon Johnson to visit Vietnam on his Asian tour. Johnson was less than enthusiastic but the President coaxed him into accepting: "Don't worry, Lyndon," he said. "If anything happens to you, Sam Rayburn and I will give you the biggest funeral Austin, Texas ever saw." [19]

Johnson was favorably impressed with Diem. He hailed him publicly as "the Winston Churchill of Southeast Asia." When asked by a reporter for the *Saturday Evening Post* whether he really believed that about Diem, Johnson answered: "Shit, man, he's the only boy we got out there." [20] In his official report to the President, Johnson declared that:

The battle against Communism must be joined in Southeast

Asia with strength and determination to achieve success there.
Vietnam can be saved if we move quickly and wisely. . . . The
most important thing is imaginative, creative American management of our military aid program.[21]

Thus, Johnson committed the President more deeply to
Vietnam, and, in addition, committed himself personally to
the war.

The most crucial single event that escalated the American
commitment during the Kennedy administration was the
Rostow-Taylor Report. In October 1961, the President decided to send two of his own special representatives to Vietnam for an on-site fact-finding trip. He chose Walt Rostow
and Maxwell Taylor because of the interest these two men
had displayed in Kennedy's own favorite approach to the
Vietnam problem: limited antiguerrilla warfare.

The report came as a profound shock to Kennedy. Rostow
and Taylor recommended the introduction of 8,000 American
combat troops into Vietnam, and stated flatly that without
such a commitment, Vietnam could not be saved. They ac-
knowledged that American air power could save Vietnam at
any time. Hanoi and Peking, in their view, would face severe
logistic difficulties if they attempted to counter American
power. So far as fighting conditions for the proposed American combat troops were concerned, Taylor and Rostow declared that they found South Vietnam "not an excessively
difficult or unpleasant place to operate." They thought it com-
parable to Korea where American troops had learned to fight
efficiently and well.

Kennedy's own misgivings about this report were echoed
by George Ball, undersecretary of state for economic affairs.
He had observed the French disaster in Indochina and noted
the parallels. He warned the President that even a small combat commitment of 8,000 men would change the nature of

the commitment and the nature of the war. Within five years, he warned, the commitment would be escalated to 300,000 men. Kennedy, who had his own doubts about the Rostow-Taylor recommendations, nevertheless expressed his belief in the capacity of rational men to control irrational commitments. He was reported to have laughed at Ball's warning and to have said: "George, you are crazier than hell." [22]

In a conversation with Arthur Schlesinger, Jr., the President expressed his own reservations very clearly:

> They want a force of American troops. They say it is necessary in order to restore confidence and maintain morale. But it will be just like Berlin. The troops will march in, the bands will play, the crowds will cheer, and in four days everyone will have forgotten. Then we will be told we have to send in more troops. It's like taking a drink. The effect wears off and you have to take another. [23]

Finally, the President compromised. Instead of 8,000 combat troops, he authorized 15,000 military advisers and support units. In making this crucial decision, he made any future withdrawal from Vietnam that much more difficult. Yet, by doing less than he was called upon to do, the President was under the illusion that he was holding the line rather than taking the United States deeper into the war. The commander of the American advisory and support team was to be Lieutenant General Paul D. Harkins, an officer described by David Halberstam as "a man of compelling mediocrity." [24]

The performance of the South Vietnamese army did not improve despite the presence of the new American advisers. The Vietcong had escalated their own guerrilla activities and by late 1962 the situation had become quite desperate. Generals Taylor and Harkins persisted in transmitting overly optimistic military reports to the President. As one firsthand observer succinctly put it:

It became increasingly a policy based on appearances; Vietnamese realities did not matter, but the *appearances* of Vietnamese realities mattered because they could affect American realities. More and more effort went into public relations because it was easier to manipulate appearances and statements than it was to affect reality on the ground.[25]

Harkins argued fiercely for the unlimited use of napalm and crop defoliation. Kennedy hated these weapons because of their particularly inhuman character. Harkins persisted, however, and finally Kennedy approved the use of napalm in battles where there were no population centers and reluctantly authorized limited defoliation on lines of communications, but not on crops. Again, by authorizing less than Harkins and the military wanted, the President felt that he was limiting, rather than expanding, the use of American power.

Robert McNamara, Kennedy's secretary of defense, too, was certain of an American victory. He visited Vietnam frequently, but was so much the prisoner of his own limited experience that he constantly tried to apply American production techniques to an Asian political revolution. With his relentless emphasis on quantifiable data and statistics, he missed the essential quality of his Vietcong enemy: a total commitment to the task of expelling the Americans who by now had become identified as the successors of French colonialism.

In mid-1963, Kennedy was jarred by reports about the growing unpopularity of President Diem. Increasingly, he felt that the United States would have to disassociate itself from the repressive harshness of the South Vietnamese ruling family. The new United States ambassador, Henry Cabot Lodge, advised that, if a coup d'état materialized against Diem, the United States should not attempt to thwart it. During September and October, the Diem regime resorted to particularly brutal measures to crush Buddhist dissidents. More and more the United States looked like the ally of a reactionary government because that government had the single virtue of being anti-Communist. In November, Diem was killed and three weeks later John Kennedy, too, was murdered. Lyndon Johnson, who admired Diem and always opposed the planned coup against him, allegedly said, in an almost mystical way, after the President's death that "the assassination of Kennedy was a retribution for the assassination of Diem."[26]

Kennedy and his military advisers never took seriously the statement made by many Vietcong soldiers that it was the duty of their generation to die for their country. They believed that the Vietcong, in their "black pajamas," were a fake army and that the South Vietnamese had the real and legitimate army. In reality, the reverse was closer to the truth. Taylor and Rostow, in their crucial report, had compared Vietnam to Korea. They had ignored the all-important difference that Korea had been a conventional war with a classic border crossing by an enemy in uniform while Vietnam was a political struggle conducted by guerrillas feeding on subversion and taking advantage of a jungle terrain where front lines became virtually meaningless.

Thus, President Kennedy—essentially a man of reason with a profoundly skeptical bent—became the victim of that particularly American form of *hubris* that blithely assumed that technology, computer-like efficiency, production, air power, and, above all, competent American management could bring down an army of guerrillas who were quite prepared to die for their cause. They would match the American escalation man for man, if not weapon for weapon, and they were prepared to fight for a generation or more. At the time of President Kennedy's death, 17,000 Americans were in Vietnam, but only 70 of these had died by the end of 1963.

Act Four: Johnson—the Catastrophe

"I can't get out. I can't finish it with what I have got. So what the hell can I do?" [27] Shortly after he made this remark to his wife in March 1965, President Johnson authorized massive combat troops to the war in Vietnam. By taking this step, he involved the United States deeply and consciously in a war that he could not win but that he also felt he could not afford to lose.

The record of the Johnson presidency in Vietnam is a story of self-delusion and misperception on a scale so vast that it turned into a national catastrophe. Despite relentless bombing raids on both North and South Vietnam and the introduction of more than half a million American troops, the enemy was not defeated. Instead, Johnson's ego, stubbornness, and pride destroyed his presidency and divided his people in a spiritual civil war.

At no one single point when he made his decisions to escalate the bombing or the ground commitment did Johnson realize that he had crossed the Rubicon and unleashed a major American land war in Asia. He always hoped that a little more bombing, a few more troops, would bring the enemy to the conference table. In doing this, he misperceived his enemy, misled his people, and, ultimately, deceived himself.

It all began with a memorandum of the Joint Chiefs of Staff to the President in January 1964, urging him to increase the commitment in order to win the war more quickly: "The United States must be prepared to put aside many of the self-imposed restrictions which now limit our efforts, and to undertake bolder actions which may embody greater risks." [28] Specifically, the Joint Chiefs were of the opinion that aerial bombing would bring North Vietnam to its knees. Walt Rostow, in support of this recommendation, stated that "Ho

Chi Minh has an industrial complex to protect; he is no longer a guerrilla fighter with nothing to lose." [29]

In the meantime, Robert Johnson, head of the Policy Planning Council and deputy to Rostow, undertook a careful study of the probable effects of bombing. The study concluded that the bombing would not work and predicted, prophetically, that it would imprison the American government. Economic growth was not a major Hanoi objective, the study said, challenging one of Rostow's favorite theses; rather, it was the unfinished business of throwing the foreigners out of the country. Hanoi had two formidable pillars of strength: the nationalist component of unity and the Communist component of control which made for an organized, unified, modern state. Bombing would not affect such a regime. On the contrary, it might even strengthen it.

This remarkable study was ignored. Rostow, who was totally committed to bombing, never brought it to the President's attention. More and more, the President's advisers, both civilian and military, moved toward a consensus on the bombing policy. Robert McNamara, McGeorge Bundy, Maxwell Taylor, and Dean Rusk—all of them perceived a chain of aggression emanating from China that urged on North Vietnam. Ho Chi Minh, in turn, was the source of the Vietcong aggression in the South. Thus, bombing would stop aggression at the source—in the North—and would convince China of American determination. No more dominoes would be permitted to fall to Communism. In a revealing "Pentagon Papers" memorandum to McNamara, John McNaughton, former Harvard law professor and now assistant secretary of defense, set forth American goals in South Vietnam in terms of the following priorities:

70 per cent—To avoid a humiliating U.S. defeat

20 per cent—To keep South Vietnamese territory from Chinese hands

10 per cent—To permit the people of South Vietnam to enjoy a better, freer way of life.[30]

Thus, the official reason that was given to the American people for the intervention in Vietnam with air power and ground troops made up only one-tenth of the real reason.

The specific incident that triggered the bombing of North Vietnam was the encounter of the two American warships *C. Turner Joy* and *Maddox* with North Vietnamese PT boats in the Gulf of Tonkin. The administration maintained that the ships had been fired upon in neutral waters and retaliation was mandatory. Subsequent studies have cast serious doubts upon this official version. One scholar, in a painstaking study, reached the dramatic conclusion that there had been no attack on the *Maddox* and the *Turner Joy* at all, that the President misled Congress and the people, and through that deception was able to obtain congressional authorization for a war that he had decided on months before while promising the voters peace.[31] Whether this conclusion is too harsh or not, there can be little doubt about the fact that the American retaliation was disproportionate. On August 4, 1964, American bombers destroyed twenty-five North Vietnamese PT boats and blew up the oil depot at Vinh in North Vietnam. McNamara reported to the President that, at Vinh, "the smoke was observed rising to 14,000 feet." Johnson was overheard to say to a reporter: "I didn't just screw Ho Chi Minh; I cut his pecker off." [32]

During the next few days, Senator William Fulbright served as floor manager for the Tonkin Gulf Resolution that would give the President broad authority for military action in Indochina. When Senator John Sherman Cooper wanted to know whether this resolution would enable the President "to use such force as could lead into war," Fulbright answered in the affirmative. Two years later, he remembered this episode with deep regret and bitterness.

During his campaign for reelection in 1964, Johnson tried to keep Vietnam out of the public view as much as possible. When later asked why, he answered: "If you have a mother-in-law with only one eye and she has it in the center of the forehead, you don't keep her in the living room." [33] Vietnam decisions were closely held secrets and were made by half a dozen men. Escalation would proceed covertly, by stealth. Only one man in Johnson's inner circle openly voiced his doubts on Vietnam: George Ball. Ball challenged the assumption made by the others that the United States necessarily controlled the scale and intensity of the war. Once on the tiger's back, one could not be sure of picking the right place to dismount. Moreover, nothing that could truly be effective against North Vietnam could be tried without the risk of a much larger war. Ball did not oppose the war because he was a "dove." He simply did not believe in the dissipation of American power through misuse.

On February 7, 1965, the Vietcong attacked the American barracks at Pleiku. Eight Americans were killed and sixty were wounded. McGeorge Bundy, after a quick visit to Pleiku, recommended a reprisal policy of sustained bombing against the North that would cease only if the Vietcong would end their insurrectionist activities. An old Eisenhower aide, Emmett John Hughes, asked Bundy what he would do if the North Vietnamese retaliated by matching the American air escalation with their own ground escalation. "We can't assume what we don't believe," Bundy replied. [34]

Thus, Lyndon Johnson began the relentless bombing campaign that was to devastate North Vietnam for the next three years. While he probably had his own reservations about its effectiveness, his enormous ego and *machismo* must have

played a considerable role. His inner circle, too, was suppor-
tive: McNamara considered victory through air bombardment
as technologically feasible; Bundy made it intellectually re-
spectable; and Dean Rusk thought of it as historically necessary.

The bombing campaign or "Operation Rolling Thunder,"
as it was referred to in *The Pentagon Papers*, did not produce
the desired effect. Ho Chi Minh did exactly what Bundy had
thought to be impossible: he matched the American air escalation with his own escalation, through infiltration on the
ground. Hence, since withdrawal was unthinkable, there was
now only one possible response: to meet the Vietcong challenge head on with American combat troops on the ground.

In March 1965, General William Westmoreland, the commander of U.S. forces in Vietnam, only requested two marine
corps. By April, the Joint Chiefs were recommending a commitment of 50,000 men. Some senators became a trifle uneasy, but were quickly reassured by Vice-President Hubert
Humphrey who said: "There are people at State and the
Pentagon who want to send three-hundred thousand men out
there. But the President will never get sucked into anything
like that." [35] In May, the figure was revised upward to 80,000.
George Ball was appalled, but could not reverse the trend. He
was alone in his resistance. In June, Westmoreland demanded
200,000 men. This would cross the Rubicon and turn Vietnam
into a major American war. Johnson reluctantly assented,
sensing the terrible trap that was closing in on him. As one
reporter wrote of the occasion:

> The President is a desperately troubled man resisting the awful
> pressures to plunge deeper into the Vietnam quagmire—resist-
> ing them as instinctively as an old horse resists being led to the
> knackers. The President bucks, whinnies and shies away, but
> always in the end the reins tighten—the pressures are too much
> for him.[36]

The White House gradually became a fortress. Doubters became enemies and ultimately traitors. Only unreserved and unquestioning loyalty was acceptable to the President.

Westmoreland demanded, and received, more and more men for Vietnam. Yet, Hanoi met every American escalation with an escalation of its own. In November 1965, Westmoreland projected American troop levels that would reach 600,-000 men by 1967. This, too, was of no avail. A great power of 200 million people fighting a limited war found itself stalemated by a small Asian nation of 17 million fighting a total war.

Failure took its toll. One by one the intellectuals departed. McGeorge Bundy and Robert McNamara left. Walt Rostow remained. Of him, Johnson would say: "I'm getting Walt Rostow as my intellectual. He is not Bundy's intellectual. He is not Schlesinger's intellectual; he is going to be my goddam intellectual." [37] The President refused to give in. "A bombing halt," he would say, "I'll tell you what happens when there is a bombing halt: I halt and then Ho Chi Minh shoves his trucks right up my ass. That's your bombing halt." [38] What became clear in 1967, however, even to a self-deluded Johnson was the fact that Ho Chi Minh did not have to run for reelection in 1968.

Robert McNamara, a few months before he left the Department of Defense, authorized a comprehensive study of all materials pertaining to Vietnam, going back to the 1940s. When he read the first chapters of these "Pentagon Papers," he told a friend that "they could hang people for what's in there." [39] His successor was Clark Clifford, who continued the role unsuccessfully played so far by George Ball. He finally succeeded in making the President face, slowly and in agony, the true dimensions of the catastrophe.

The North Vietnamese Tet offensive which began in January 1968 underscored the disaster. Americans at home were now able to see that, despite three years of bombing and a commitment of half a million men, the enemy was still able to mount offensives. It now became clear that the United States suffered much more from the war of attrition than did the enemy. The North Vietnamese manpower pool was far from depleted and there was always the possibility of an intervention by Chinese "volunteers." There was to be no light at the end of the tunnel for Lyndon Johnson. In March 1968, he announced a bombing halt and withdrew from the presidential race. Vietnam had made the man elected by the largest landslide in American history into a one-term president.

Lyndon Johnson, totally ignorant of Asia in general and of Vietnam in particular, simply superimposed his own misperceptions on Asian reality. In his view, aggression had to be stopped "at the source" and the "source" was Communism in North Vietnam and China. The fact that Communism had broken up into numerous diverse political and ideological fragments seemed to have been lost upon him. He never understood that this was a revolutionary war in which the other side held title to the revolution because of the colonial war that had just ended. Revolution and antirevolution were the real issues, rather than Communism and anti-Communism. That is why the Vietcong were willing to fight and die and the South Vietnamese were not. That is why McNamara's statistics were valueless: they overlooked the fact that even if the ratio was 10:1 in favor of South Vietnam, it had no meaning because the one man was willing to fight and die and the ten were not.

Johnson saw himself, Western-style, locked in a shoot-out with Ho Chi Minh. When force did not work he tried manipulation. But neither bombs nor dollars would tempt Ho Chi Minh. Johnson had never met this kind of man before. And so he plunged forward because he could not lose. He fought the awful truth and isolated himself in his fortress. A credibility gap turned into a reality gap. Finally, he deceived himself.

Perhaps the overarching truth about Lyndon Johnson and the men who made Vietnam policy during his presidency was that they never had the kind of experience in tragedy of which the stuff of empathy is made. These were successful men, their vision limited to the American experience. None of them knew, until it was too late, that states, like men, can die. None of them knew that intelligence alone, without wisdom and an empathy for suffering, is only emptiness.

Act Five: Nixon—Full Circle

The presidency of Richard Nixon brought a painful groping for extrication and for "peace with honor." The formula devised by Nixon and his main architect on foreign policy matters, Henry Kissinger, was "Vietnamization." The war would gradually be turned over to the Vietnamese as American combat troops were withdrawn. The American hope was to leave behind a viable anti-Communist South Vietnam with a friendly government firmly installed in Saigon. Thus, the central issue of the war essentially remained the same: Who should rule in Saigon?

The withdrawal of American ground troops began in June 1969 when the peak figure of 541,500 men was reduced by a first cut of 25,000. As the pace of withdrawal gathered momentum, a serious weakness became increasingly apparent in the "Vietnamization" strategy: Communist forces could attack at a low ebb of American strength to try to topple the South Vietnamese regime, while American prestige was still committed to it. President Nixon's answer to this challenge was twofold: the destruction of Communist sanctuaries by ground incursions into Laos and Cambodia and increasing reliance upon air power through bombing. Thus, as American participation in the ground fighting gradually diminished, the air war reached levels of unprecedented ferocity and violence. This policy reflected the dilemma of a president who still believed in the essential mission of the United States in Vietnam but who wanted to attain his goal without incurring additional American casualties. Henry Kissinger, in response to a question posed by an Asian diplomat as to whether President Nixon was going to repeat the mistakes of the Johnson administration, said, half in jest: "No, we will not repeat their mistakes. We will not send 500,000 men. We will make our own mistakes and they will be completely our own." [40] Quite unintentionally, this proved to be a prophetic statement.

In July 1969, the President announced the "Nixon Doctrine," declaring that, in the future, the United States would avoid entanglements like Vietnam by limiting its support to economic and military aid rather than active combat participation. Peace negotiations had begun in earnest in Paris and a moratorium against the war in Washington drew huge crowds demanding a rapid withdrawal of American troops. In January 1970, however, under the euphemism of "protective reaction" to cover air reconnaissance missions over North Vietnam, the United States renewed the bombing of the North. The Vietcong once again increased infiltration on the ground.

On April 30, 1970, in a nationally televised address, President Nixon announced an American-led South Vietnamese "incursion" into Cambodia in order to demonstrate that the United States was "no pitiful, helpless giant." In the same speech he declared that, since 1954, the United States had "respected scrupulously the neutrality of the Cambodian people." However, the discovery of Vietcong supply depots and sanctuaries had made this latest incursion necessary. It would shorten the war, the President explained. Three years later, in the midst of the Watergate hearings, it was revealed that in more than 3,500 raids, American B-52s had dropped over 100,000 tons of bombs on Cambodia and Laos during 1969 and 1970. In Tom Wicker's words, the April 30 speech was "a deliberate and knowing lie broadcast in person to the American people by their President." [41] The President's spokesman at the Pentagon, Jerry Friedheim, when confronted with this contradiction, said: "I knew at the time it was wrong and I am sorry." [42]

In May 1970, President Nixon announced the end of large-scale bombing raids against the North and, in June, he pronounced the Cambodian incursion a success. The Senate repealed the Tonkin Gulf Resolution and barred future military operations in Cambodia without congressional approval. American combat troops now stood at 400,000 men. The year 1971 saw protracted peace negotiations in Paris, while the fighting in South Vietnam continued between the Vietcong and the dwindling American forces and their South Vietnamese allies. By the end of the year, another 200,000 Americans had returned home.

In March 1972, the North Vietnamese launched a major offensive with massed tanks and artillery in the most impressive show of force since the Tet assault of 1968. The North Vietnamese leadership had decided to make an all-out effort to seize what it could in the South at a time when it was facing the danger of a new form of diplomatic isolation. The latest American overtures to China and the Soviet Union threatened to separate North Vietnam from its two major Communist allies. The offensive began shortly after President Nixon's visit to Peking in February but before his trip to Moscow, scheduled for May.

In April and May of 1972, Nixon took two gambles that escalated the war to new levels of violence. In April, B-52 bombers struck Hanoi and Haiphong in saturation bombings that by far exceeded the ferocity of the Johnson raids. And on May 8, the President took a step that his predecessor had always ruled out as too perilous: he ordered the mining of North Vietnam's harbors to cut off the flow of tanks, artillery, and other offensive weapons supplied to Hanoi by the Soviet Union and other Communist nations. At the same time, however, he offered a total troop withdrawal from South Vietnam four months after an Indochina-wide cease-fire and the return of prisoners of war. The risk of a Soviet-American confrontation at sea dominated world attention for several days, but only verbal denunciations emanated from Moscow and Peking. The Soviet Union by now placed a higher priority on its own vital interests, which it perceived in the growing détente with the United States, than on the interests of North Vietnam. The Soviet-American summit took place on schedule and the President's gamble paid off. North Vietnam now realized that it had been virtually abandoned by its own allies. The United States suddenly found itself in the anomalous position of having reached détente with 1 billion Communists—800 million Chinese and 200 million Russians—while it pursued a relentless war against a small peasant country precisely because it was Communist.

In July, the Paris peace talks resumed and troop withdrawal continued. On October 26, in a dramatic announcement, Henry Kissinger predicted that "peace was at hand." This preelection optimism proved to be premature. Early in December, Kissinger's "final talks" with the North Vietnamese were broken off and he reported a stalemate.

On December 18, President Nixon ordered all-out bombing attacks on Hanoi and Haiphong. Millions of tons of explosives were dropped on the North. The fierce intensity and relentlessness of the attacks produced an outcry of protest against "terror bombings" from many parts of the world. The raids were halted on December 30, and the Paris talks once

again resumed. On January 23, 1973, after almost three decades of war, a cease-fire was reached.

The Paris Accords provided for the withdrawal of all American troops and military advisers, an exchange of prisoners,
consultations between South and North Vietnam on general
elections, new supervisory machinery, and the withdrawal of
all foreign troops from Laos and Cambodia.

In essence, what was achieved in Paris in 1973 was a rever-
sion to the status of Vietnam at the time of the 1954 Geneva
Accords. A guest at a Washington dinner pointed this out to
Henry Kissinger. "What's wrong with that?" [43] Kissinger replied. The United States had come full circle in Vietnam.
The clock was turned back twenty years. There was an Or-
wellian irony to the situation. Progress was regress: 1954 by
1973.

The hope, after the withdrawal of American troops, was
that South Vietnam would be able to defend itself against
the North with military and financial assistance from the
United States. For two years that American hope seemed
justified, but then the dam broke. In the spring of 1975, the
Communist insurgents in Cambodia, the Khmer Rouge,
marched upon the capital, Phnom Penh, and forced Marshal
Lon Nol, Cambodia's American-supported president, to flee
the country. Thus, the American "incursion" of 1970 finally
produced the opposite of what it had intended: a Communist
instead of a neutralist Cambodia. At the same time, the South
Vietnamese army lost its fighting spirit and collapsed entirely.
In a matter of weeks, almost all of South Vietnam fell to the
Communists. In the United States, a test of wills took place
between the administration of President Gerald R. Ford, who
favored continued military aid to Cambodia and to South
Vietnam, and the Congress, which became increasingly reluctant to cooperate. Finally, the United States was left with

the humanitarian responsibility of rescuing terror-stricken refugees who were fleeing from the advancing North Vietnamese armies. In April, Saigon surrendered to the Communists and was renamed Ho Chi Minh City. Twenty years of American effort thus ended in failure. As Dean Rusk, one of the main architects of American Vietnam policy during the 1960s, put it in April 1975:

> Personally, I made two mistakes. I underestimated the tenacity of the North Vietnamese and overestimated the patience of the American people.[44]

By the mid-1970s, both the supporters and the critics of the Vietnam war in the United States tended to regard the second Indochina war as one of the most terrible episodes in the history of American foreign policy. There was a general consensus that it would take a long time for the wounds to heal, both in Indochina and in the United States.

Conclusions

The American involvement in Indochina had begun imperceptibly, almost like a mild toothache. At the end, it ran through Vietnam and America like a pestilence. Each president based his policies on exaggerated fears and, later, on exaggerated hopes. Thus, each president left the problem to his successor in worse shape than he had found it.

The United States dropped more than 7 million tons of bombs on Indochina. This is eighty times the amount that was dropped on Britain during World War II and is equal to more than three hundred of the atomic bombs that fell on Japan in 1945. The bombs left 20 million craters that ranged from 20 to 50 feet wide and 5 to 20 feet deep. After the bombardments much of Vietnam looked like a moonscape. Nothing would grow there for generations.

America, too, was in anguish over the war. Her leadership lost respect in the eyes of an entire generation, universities were disrupted, careers were blighted, and the economy was bloated with war inflation. The metal caskets in which the remains of 55,000 Americans came back from Vietnam were to symbolize the war's ultimate and only meaning.

Five presidents told their people that the involvement in Vietnam was entered into for selfless and idealistic reasons. This myth of false innocence permitted the United States to wreak destruction on an enormous scale in Indochina, all in the name of kindliness and helpfulness. Gradually, the means became so horrible that it became increasingly difficult to justify the ends. The war finally became a lost crusade.

In historical perspective, the great unanswered question over Vietnam will probably be: Which would have been less costly, an earlier Communist victory or the agony of this war? One cannot help but wonder what might have happened if not one single American soldier had ever come to Indochina. History does not reveal its alternatives, and thus one cannot say with certitude where this road not taken would have led. Vietnam might indeed have gone Communist much earlier. It would, however, probably have been a form of Communism of the Titoist variety—with a strong dose of nationalism and a fierce tradition of independence vis-à-vis both Moscow and Peking. The United States could have lived with that, it seems. Certainly, its postponement was hardly worth the sacrifice of more than 56,000 American lives and hundreds of thousands of Vietnamese lives and $150 billion.

As the war cost more and more in blood and treasure, it tended to resolve less and less. Finally, it ended in the stunned exhaustion of defeat. Ironically, despite Vietnam, the United

States had reached a fairly solid détente with the two major Communist powers. The hopes, rather than the fears, of five presidents were borne out by long-range international developments. A calmer world had begun to emerge and the Vietnam conflict, first initiated to combat the spread of Communism, had become a deadening anachronism. This, perhaps, is the bitterest lesson of this terrible and foolish war. It had begun in the world of the cold war and ended, a generation later, in a world of détente. Thus, the reasons for its outbreak had almost become irrelevant. History had simply passed it by. When considered in this perspective, the awesome logic about Vietnam is apparent: it was probably in vain that combatants and civilians had suffered, the land was devastated, and the dead had died.

Notes

1. Bernard B. Fall, *The Two Vietnams* (New York: Praeger, 1964), p. 82.
2. Victor Bator, *Vietnam: A Diplomatic Tragedy* (Dobbs Ferry, N.Y.: Oceana Publications, 1956), p. 206.
3. U.S. House Foreign Affairs Subcommittee on World Communism, *China and U.S. Far East Policy, 1946–1966*, 80th Cong., 2nd Sess. (1967), p. 45.
4. Andrew W. Green, "Are You a Middle of the Roader?" *Plain Talk* (April 1949), p. 35.
5. Policy statement by Ambassador Loy W. Henderson, *Department of State Bulletin* (April 10, 1950), p. 565.
6. Miriam S. Farley, *United States Relations with Southeast Asia with Special Reference to Indochina* (New York: Institute of Pacific Relations, 1955), p. 4.
7. U.S. Department of State, Office of Public Affairs, *Background* (Washington, D.C.: Government Printing Office, October 1951).
8. U.S. Department of State, Statement by Robert E. Hoey, officer in charge of Vietnam-Laos-Cambodia affairs, Press Release No. 178, March 8, 1952.
9. Farley, *op. cit.*, p. 4.
10. John Foster Dulles, cited in Bator, *op. cit.*, p. 210.
11. Dwight D. Eisenhower, *Mandate for Change 1953–1956* (Garden City, N.Y.: Doubleday, 1963), p. 167. Italics added.
12. Richard M. Nixon, quoted in Chalmers M. Roberts, "The Day We Didn't Go to War," *The Reporter*, September 14, 1954.
13. Fall, *op. cit.*, p. 90.
14. Melvin Gurtov, *The First Vietnam Crisis* (New York: Columbia University Press, 1967), p. 14.
15. Robert Guillain, *La Fin des Illusions: Notes d'Indochine* (Paris: Centre d'Etudes de Politique Etrangère, 1954), p. 39.
16. Gurtov, *op. cit.*, p. 15.
17. Eisenhower, *op. cit.*, p. 372.
18. David Halberstam, *The Best and the Brightest* (New York: Random House, 1972), p. 124.
19. *Ibid.*, p. 133.
20. *Ibid.*, p. 135.
21. *Ibid.*
22. *Ibid.*, p. 174.
23. Arthur Schlesinger, Jr., *A Thousand Days* (Boston: Houghton Mifflin, 1965), p. 371.
24. Halberstam, *op. cit.*, p. 183.
25. *Ibid.*, p. 207.

26. *Ibid.*, p. 292.
27. Max Frankel, "The Lessons of Vietnam," in *The Pentagon Papers* (New York: Quadrangle Books, 1971), p. 644.
28. Halberstam, *op. cit.*, p. 350.
29. *The Pentagon Papers, op. cit.*, p. 249.
30. *Ibid.*, p. 263.
31. Anthony Austin, *The President's War* (Philadelphia: Lippincott, 1971), *passim.*
32. Halberstam, *op. cit.*, p. 414.
33. *Ibid.*, p. 424.
34. *Ibid.*, p. 528.
35. *Ibid.*, p. 572.
36. Stewart Alsop, cited in *The Pentagon Papers, op. cit.*, p. 650.
37. Halberstam, *op. cit.*, p. 627.
38. *Ibid.*, p. 624.
39. *Ibid.*, p. 633.
40. *Ibid.*, p. 664.
41. *The New York Times*, July 24, 1973.
42. *Ibid.*
43. *The Washington Post*, January 28, 1973.
44. Interview on ABC Television, April 3, 1975.

Selected Bibliography

FALL, BERNARD B. *The Two Vietnams.* New York: Praeger, 1964.
FITZGERALD, FRANCES. *Fire in the Lake.* Boston: Little, Brown, 1972.
GURTOV, MELVIN. *The First Vietnam Crisis.* New York: Columbia University Press, 1967.
HALBERSTAM, DAVID. *The Best and the Brightest.* New York: Random House, 1972.
JANIS, IRVING L. *Victims of Groupthink: A Psychological Study of Foreign Policy Decisions and Fiascoes.* Boston: Houghton Mifflin, 1972.
MCALISTER, JOHN T. *Vietnam: The Origins of Revolution.* New York: Knopf, 1969.
STOESSINGER, JOHN G. *Henry Kissinger: The Anguish of Power.* New York: Norton, 1976.

5.

Three Battles over God:
India and Pakistan
in 1947, 1965, and 1971

> *Man's body is so small, yet*
> *his capacity for suffering is*
> *so immense.*
>
> Rabindranath Tagore

The most savage religious war in history was neither the Christian Crusades against Islam nor the Thirty Years' War that pitted Catholic against Protestant. It was the war of Hindu against Moslem in the twentieth century.

So long as India remained under the British Crown, the conflict between Hindus and Moslems remained relatively dormant, although the two religions—fearing each other more than they feared their common colonial master—waged their own separate struggles for independence against Britain: the Hindus under Mahatma Gandhi and the Moslems under Mohammed Ali Jinnah. When the time for freedom approached, the Moslems insisted on their own sovereign entity, apart from the Hindu majority of colonial India. Thus, when the transfer of power took place in 1947, two new states were born: India and Pakistan.

Britain had hardly withdrawn when the two new fledgling states turned upon each other with a terrible ferocity. Millions of terror-striken Hindus in Pakistan fled for their lives to India and millions of equally frantic Moslems in India sought refuge in Pakistan. The result was the most massive population exchange in history. It had always been clear to participants and onlookers alike that these two religions agreed on virtually nothing and regarded each other as anathema. The Moslem believed in one god and his prophet while the Hindu worshipped a pantheon of gods. Moslem society was fairly egalitarian while that of the Hindus was stratified into a rigid caste system. Moslems believed in actively making converts while Hindus tended to be more passive and absorptive. Moslems observed strict silence in their mosques while Hindus played music in their temples. Hindus would not eat beef and Moslems were enjoined from eating pork. Each regarded the other as idolatrous and a mortal peril to itself.

The three wars to be examined are the outgrowth of this religious conflict. The fact that the two hostile religions were represented by sovereign states made the conflict even more ferocious. Nationalism and religion now were joined in fateful fusion. The modern nation-state served as a handmaiden to religious warfare. The political forces of the twentieth century were mobilized to fight the battles of an earlier age. And so, three times in short succession, India and Pakistan, each invoking its gods, met on fields of battle under empty skies from which the gods had departed.

Colonialism, Partition, and War

Ancient Hinduism was an austere doctrine subscribing to the view that the cause of all evil in the world was human desire. The path toward redemption, therefore, lay in man's capacity to extinguish desire within himself through an act of will and thus reach a state of Nirvana. Hinduism conceived of life as a never-ending cycle, or karma. Death simply meant passage into another incarnation of life. The form this new incarnation would take depended on performance in the previous one. Hence, it was quite possible for a man to pass into a lower or a higher form of life. The standard of excellence toward which the Hindu was to aspire was the attainment of Nirvana, or renunciation of desire. Since men were by nature unequal, only a few could attain this goal. This concept of the inequality of men was expressed in the social structure of ancient India, the caste system. Society was divided into four rigidly separated castes: the Brahmins, or priests, who had come closest to the Hindu ideal; the warriors who were to defend the society; the merchants; and the laborers. Actually, the social system was even more complex since each caste had numerous subdivisions. At the bottom of the social pyramid were the outcasts, or pariahs, also known as "untouchables."

The great inroads made by Buddhism in ancient India may be explained largely in terms of the austerity of the Hindu doctrine. While Buddhism, too, was directed toward the afterlife, its view of man was much more optimistic. Under its influence, the Nirvana concept gradually changed from a doctrine of extinction and renunciation to a goal not unlike the Christian paradise. The figure of the Bodhisattva entered Indian life—the priest who, though entitled to enter Nirvana, had decided to postpone his own entrance in order to show the way to others. Late Buddhism, in fact, steered away more and more from the austerity of the Hindu faith. Sometimes only a few invocations would suffice to gain entrance to Nirvana, and Bodhisattvas frequently became deities who played the role of "social workers," assisting their less fortunate brethren. Despite this radical transformation of Hinduism, it must be remembered that Buddhism was able to grow out of Hinduism because the latter lent itself to the absorption of new forms of faith quite readily.

The third major religion of ancient India—Islam—stands in striking contrast to the other two. It came to India around 1000 A.D. Unlike Buddhism, Islam was never absorbed by the Hindus. The only attribute that Islam shared with its predecessor was its accent on the hereafter; there the similarity ended. When the Moslems first came to India, they destroyed all the Hindu temples and sculptures they found because they considered them idolatrous. After sections of India in the northeast and the northwest were conquered by Moslems, the Hindus tended to regard them as another caste to be kept rigidly separate. The religious conflict between Hinduism and Islam is thus at the root of the struggle between India and Pakistan. By the time the West arrived there, India was a politically divided society in which two radically different ways of life competed for the allegiance of the population: Hinduism, which was tolerant of dissension and absorptive; and Islam, which was militant, exclusive, and dogmatic.

British rule in India was established in the early seventeenth century through the instrument of the East India Company. In their campaign to gain control of the subcontinent, the British followed a strategy of "divide and rule." The many satraps were played against each other until, by the late eighteenth century, most of India was in British hands.

The administration of British India is a story full of contradictions, harmony, and conflict. The coming of the British added yet another element to the already highly complex Indian society. Christianity was brought to India, and yet the materialism of the Christian colonizers stood in stark contrast to the spiritualism of the Hindu. The individualism of the British differed sharply from the group-centered culture of India, and the democratic ideal of equality seemed strange to the caste-conscious Hindu. The British tried very hard, on the whole, to harmonize these many conflicts, and sometimes succeeded.

In the pattern of indirect rule initiated by the British, a viceroy was put in charge of colonial administration. Local customs were left intact so long as they did not present a direct threat to the British presence or radically offend the British social ethos. Thus, the British did not interfere much with the caste system, although they did insist on the abolition of the Hindu custom of suttee, the immolation of widows on the funeral pyres of their husbands. They also outlawed infanticide and *thuggee,* the practice of sacrificing unsuspecting travelers in lonely mountain passes to the goddess Kali.

The British made every effort to teach the Indians about British democracy, thus planting the seeds of the Indians' demand for self-rule. British law and contractual relationships were often mingled with Indian culture, and efforts were made to use indigenous talent in the civil service, especially in the later colonial period. But the British also exhibited extreme insensitivity. For example, in 1857 a rebellion was started by the rumor that pig and cow fats were being used to grease cartridges in rifles to be employed by Hindu and Moslem recruits in the army. The Sepoy Rebellion of 1857 which was touched off by this incident was crushed by the British with extreme cruelty.

The economic aspects of the Indian colonial experience present a similarly mixed record. The early profits made by the East India Company were enormous. The British flooded India with manufactured goods and, in turn, compelled the indigenous population to concentrate on the production of raw materials, thus causing an imbalance in the economy and a decline in Indian industry. On the other hand, the industrial development of India meant the development of modern roads, telegraphs, harbors, mails, and railroads. Some aspects of this industrialization did not conflict with traditional customs, at times they even helped to revive them. For example, a modern network of railroads made religious pilgrimages easier for many Hindus. Another important by-product of British colonialism was the rise of a whole new class of bankers, traders, educators, and lawyers, who were to play a major role in the rise of the new India.

It is impossible to say whether modern India has benefited or suffered more as a result of its experience with British colonialism. To be sure, colonialism had many unfortunate effects: exploitation of the labor force, overdevelopment of natural resources, and dislocation of the economy through exportation of wealth in the form of raw materials, a condition of economic colonialism that was to last much longer than its political counterpart. On the other hand, the British also did much to prepare India for the modern world: they bestowed upon the country an enlightened health and education program; they provided at least the foundations for a higher standard of living; and they educated an elite of future leaders.

In sum, then, India's experience with Western colonialism was by no means entirely negative. In view of this fact, combined with the tolerant faith of the Hindu religion, it is not surprising that when the nationalist reaction in India came, it followed an essentially nonviolent and democratic path.

The Indian nationalist movement was marked by the overwhelmingly powerful personality of Mahatma Gandhi. Gandhi was the spiritual father of the Indian Congress, the nationalist resistance organization under the British that, without his unifying influence, would have been destroyed by factionalism. Indeed, without the charismatic leadership of Gandhi, Indian nationalism might well have run a different and far more violent course.

Gandhi's nationalism was rooted in the doctrine of *ahimsa*, or noninjury to any living being. This concept was translated into the political doctrine of passive resistance, or civil disobedience, a technique of nationalist assertion that the British found very embarrassing. Gandhi lived most unpretentiously. He used a spinning wheel to produce his few garments, and his example led to a widespread boycott of foreign cloth. He denied himself all comforts and often endured long fasts in order to find support for his causes. When the British imposed a heavy tax on salt in 1930, Gandhi walked 165 miles to the sea to make his own salt. Rather than cooperate with the British, he exhorted the population to go to jail, and he was frequently imprisoned. But he always emphasized the nonviolent character of Indian nationalism. His rejection of bloodshed as a deplorable aberration was, indeed, the movement's basic moral and political principle. The steady advance toward independence made by India between 1900 and 1947 was due in large measure to Gandhi's insistence on spiritual rather than physical power.

It was Gandhi who turned Indian nationalism from an urban, elite movement into a mass movement that reached the smaller towns and captured the popular imagination. But it was also Gandhi who unwittingly magnified the differences between Indian Hindus and Indian Moslems with his emphasis on mass participation, majority rule, and Indian (Hindu) tradition. Moslems became apprehensive that majority rule and Hindu revivalism would undermine their faith and dim their political future.

Thus, despite his enormous influence, Gandhi was unable to forge Indian nationalism into a cohesive whole. The congress was always viewed with suspicion by the Moslems, who feared persecution at the hands of a Hindu majority once India became independent. Though he tried his utmost to do so, Gandhi never succeeded in resolving the differences between the two faiths. In the end, in 1948, he was assassinated by a Hindu fanatic who found his dogged attempts at reconciliation unbearable.

The Moslems developed their own nationalist organization,

the Moslem League. Its leader, Mohammed Ali Jinnah, insisted on the creation of a separate state of Pakistan for the
Moslem minority. The great chasm between Hinduism and
Islam robbed the Indian nationalist movement of much of its
effectiveness. Often the two antagonists feared each other
more than they did the colonial rule of Britain. The depth
of the conflict may be seen from the fact that not even the
unparalleled prestige of Gandhi was able to persuade his
Hindu followers to make common cause with Islam. Nor did
the Moslems feel any less strongly. Their view was expressed
by Jinnah:

> How can you even dream of Hindu-Moslem unity? Everything
> pulls us apart: We have no intermarriages. We have not the
> same calendar. The Moslems believe in a single God, and the
> Hindus are idolatrous. Like the Christians, the Moslems believe
> in an equalitarian society, whereas the Hindus maintain their
> iniquitous system of castes and leave heartlessly fifty million
> Untouchables to their tragic fate, at the bottom of the social
> ladder.[1]

It is quite possible that this intense communal strife would
have enabled the British to maintain control over India for an
indefinite period. But World War II forced the British to
make their peace with the prospect of Indian sovereignty. As
a condition of India's collaboration in the war, Gandhi demanded a promise of immediate independence. When the
British hedged, the Indian leader stated caustically that he
was unwilling to accept "a post-dated check on a bank that
was obviously failing." Even a British guarantee of speedy
independence did not prevent some Indian nationalist leaders,
like Subhas Chandra Bose, from throwing in their lot with
the Japanese. After the conclusion of the war, it fell to the
British Labour government, which had always been severely
critical of Conservative policy toward India, to honor Britain's

pledge. But in 1947, when Indian nationalism finally triumphed, the country was a house divided. In spite of Gandhi's repeated fasts and prayer meetings against it, partition seemed the only practicable solution. Hence, India and Pakistan emerged from British colonial rule as two separate sovereign states.

The triumph of nationalism in India was thus severely marred by the tragedy of partition. Three staggering problems were the direct result of this tragedy. The first aftermath of partition saw a gigantic population exchange, probably the most massive in history. Over 7 million Hindus, fearful of persecution in Pakistan, frantically sought refuge in India, and a similar number of Moslems fled from India to safety on Pakistani soil. A vast amount of violence and bloodshed generated by religious hatred accompanied this population exchange. Millions of people lost their homes in the process and the integration of these refugees presented an almost insurmountable problem to both of the new states.

The second problem was economic in nature. Colonial India had been an economic unit for centuries and now it was suddenly divided into three parts: India, East Pakistan, and West Pakistan. East Pakistan, formerly East Bengal, was separated from West Pakistan by almost 1,000 miles of Indian territory. These two Moslem enclaves, dating from the Moslem conquest, had nothing but their religion in common, not even language. Regional jealousies and economic competition immediately rose to the surface between the two Pakistans. Even worse, however, an economic war broke out between Pakistan and India. India devalued her rupee, but Pakistan refused to follow suit. Jute, an important raw material grown mostly in Bengal, now became prohibitively expensive in India. In short, the three parts of the Indian subcontinent, which for centuries had been operating as one economic entity, were now involved in a destructive economic feud. Overshadowing all other disputes between the two new nations was the struggle over contested territory, especially the princely state of Kashmir. India demanded Kashmir on the ground that its ruler had been a Hindu, but Pakistan claimed the state on the basis that over three-fourths of the population was Moslem.

Kashmir combines extraordinary scenic beauty with great strategic importance. Since ancient times, the beautiful and fertile Kashmir Valley had been the resting place for caravans traveling between the plains of India and the highlands of Central Asia. Both India and Pakistan considered Kashmir to be absolutely vital to their strategic and defense requirements. India's Prime Minister Jawaharlal Nehru asserted that:

> India without Kashmir would cease to occupy a pivotal position on the political map of Central Asia. Strategically, Kashmir is vital to the security of India; it has been so since the dawn of history.[2]

But Pakistan's Prime Minister Liaquat Ali Khan justified his claim with similar emphasis:

> Kashmir is very important, is vital to Pakistan. Kashmir, as you will see from the map is like a cap on the head of Pakistan. If I allow India to have this cap on our head, then I am always at the mercy of India.[3]

To make matters even more complicated, the British left three choices to the so-called princely states after their departure: accession to India; accession to Pakistan; or independence. Lord Mountbatten, as representative of the British Crown, advised the leaders of the 565 princely states that they were free "to accede to one or the other of the two new Dominions as the effective successive Powers to the British Raj, at their discretion, with due consideration to be given to

geographical contiguity and communal composition."⁴ If
neither choice was acceptable, they could form independent
states. Of the 565, whose sizes ranged from that of a European
country to that of a small village, only three opted for independence: Junagadh, Hyderabad, and Kashmir. Of these, the
first two did not present insuperable obstacles. But Kashmir,
larger than England, with an area of almost 85,000 square
miles, now became a vital object of competition, coveted with
equal fervor by both new states.

The Maharajah of Kashmir, Hari Singh, offered to enter
into a "standstill agreement" with both states in order to buy
time and ensure Kashmir a measure of autonomy. By now,
however, communal strife had engulfed much of the subcontinent and Kashmir was drawn in. Moslem tribesmen from the
northwest, enraged by alleged atrocities against the Moslems
of nearby Jammu, invaded Kashmir. They came close to over-
powering Kashmir's defenses and carried out mass killing,
looting, and arson. Pakistan described the situation as a popular revolt by the Moslem majority of Kashmir against the
Hindu ruler's autocratic rule. The Maharajah, in desperation,
asked India for military aid. India, seizing the opportunity,
made military intervention contingent upon Kashmir's formal
accession to India. The hard-pressed Maharajah signed the
Instrument of Accession to India on October 26, 1947. On the
following day, Lord Mountbatten accepted the accession, but
transmitted an accompanying letter in which he stated:

It is my Government's wish that as soon as law and order have
been restored in Kashmir and her soil cleared of the invaders,
the question of the State's accession should be settled by reference to the people.⁵

Indian forces were rushed to Kashmir, just in time to stop
the Moslem invaders a few miles from Srinagar, the capital.

Pakistan immediately dispatched troops in order to forestall the collapse of the Moslem invasion. Thus, by late 1947, the two nations found themselves locked in deadly combat over Kashmir. The war continued inconclusively with neither side able to win a decisive military victory.

In early January 1948, India brought the dispute before the United Nations Security Council, charging Pakistan with aggression. Pakistan, in turn, accused India of genocide and illegal occupation of Kashmir. The Security Council called upon both states to refrain from doing anything "which might aggravate the situation." It also established a UN Commission for India and Pakistan that was to investigate the facts and mediate between the contending parties. In August 1948, the commission recommended a cease-fire which went into effect on January 1, 1949.

Thus came to an end the first phase of a modern religious war that erupted in the aftermath of colonial rule. The human tragedy surrounding the partition of the subcontinent was a grim reminder that turbulence and war had not ended with the passing of the European order in India. On the contrary, with the colonial lid off, Hindus and Moslems were free to turn upon each other with the pent-up ferocity of centuries.

The Kashmir War of 1965

The political structures of Hindu and Moslem nationalism diverged sharply after partition. India, under the leadership of Jawaharlal Nehru, Gandhi's successor, immediately embarked on the ambitious and unprecedented experiment of shaping an overwhelmingly illiterate country into an advanced democracy. The Indian national elections of 1951–1952 were indeed an impressive performance. The new Indian government spared no effort to make this election a truly democratic one and, on the whole, succeeded admirably. The Congress party, now pursuing a policy of gradual socialism patterned after the example of the British Labour party, became the dominant political power, with Nehru as its undisputed leader. Pakistan set out on a totally different road and fashioned its political system along authoritarian lines. After a succession of politicians had demonstrated their inability to govern, the army seized power in 1951. Under the leadership of General Ayub Khan, Pakistan received its first effective government and embarked upon an ambitious economic development program. Pakistan developed a formidable power base, but at the expense of the democratic process.

Far from resolving the Kashmir dispute, the 1949 cease-fire had provided merely a breathing spell. India and Pakistan now continued the struggle by diplomatic means. Their initial involvement in international affairs was determined by their overriding search for security vis-à-vis each other. In fact, their quest for friends and allies may be interpreted quite accurately as an outgrowth, first and foremost, of their fear of one another. All other considerations were secondary.

During the 1950s, the military leadership of Pakistan committed the Moslem nation to the Western alliance system. Believing that meaningful negotiations with India over Kashmir could be undertaken only by making Pakistan a strong military state, General Ayub Khan led Pakistan into two American-sponsored regional alliances: the Southeast Asia Treaty Organization (SEATO) and the Central Treaty Organization (CENTO). In 1962, however, when war erupted between China and India over disputed border territory, Pakistan quickly gravitated toward India's enemy. Relations between China and Pakistan grew increasingly more cordial. By the mid-1960s, Pakistan was in the unique position of being a member of two Western military alliances and, at the same time, enjoying the friendship of the People's Republic of China.

In India, Prime Minister Jawaharlal Nehru labored hard

and long during the 1950s to develop a policy of nonalignment and economic advancement for his country. The decisive defeat inflicted upon India by Chinese forces in the border war of 1962 was a severe setback for Nehru's policy. The Soviet Union, increasingly estranged from China, attempted to exploit the situation by consolidating its ties with India while the American leadership, fearful of Communist expansion, extended large quantities of military aid to both India and Pakistan, ostensibly for defense purposes against Communism. In reality, however, both India and Pakistan used the American military equipment to bolster their strength vis-à-vis each other. It was against this complex background of multidimensional maneuverings that the conflict between Hindus and Moslems erupted once again into open warfare.

The war began in an unlikely spot, the so-called Rann of Kutch, an uninhabited piece of territory of little value which was a virtual desert during the dry season but became a flooded marsh during the monsoon. In the spring of 1965, both India and Pakistan stepped up patrolling activity in that area, and soon serious clashes occurred. Pakistani forces quickly outmaneuvered Indian troops, winning an easy victory. Although a cease-fire was achieved through the mediation efforts of British Prime Minister Harold Wilson, and both parties agreed to a mutual withdrawal of forces, the Rann of Kutch encounter "left Pakistan dangerously overconfident and India dangerously frustrated." [6]

The Pakistani leadership began to feel that the Kutch strategy should be tried in Kashmir. A prominent Urdu newspaper openly recommended that "the Rann of Kutch prescription should be applied on the Kashmir front," [7] and *The Pakistan Times,* in a burst of euphoria, predicted that, "In the event of war with India, Pakistani troops would march up to Delhi, would occupy the Red Fort, and hoist the Pakistani flag on it." [8]

In India, on the other hand, resentment was rampant. To be defeated by China was one thing; to be outfought by Pakistan was something that most Indians were unwilling to accept. Lal Bahadur Shastri, Nehru's successor, came under increasing pressure to redress the Kutch defeat. *The Times of India* warned that "Pakistan has put the fish into the water to measure the temperature and one fine morning Pakistan will present the world with a *fait accompli*—the occupation of Kashmir."[9]

Thus, Pakistan's overconfidence and India's humiliation brought the two nations to the brink of war:

> It was barely credible in 1962 that two great countries should be at the brink of full-scale war, as China and India were, over an almost inaccessible stretch of barren and snow-bound track. It is no more credible today that India and Pakistan should fight over a piece of barren land that spends half its life under water; yet it has happened.[10]

In August 1965, Ayub Khan, convinced that his policy of "leaning on India" was working, made the fateful decision of sending Pakistani-trained guerrillas into Kashmir. The infiltrators blew up bridges, disrupted lines of communication, and raided army convoys and military installations. Not surprisingly, Indian forces in Kashmir rounded up the guerrillas and then proceeded to occupy the three main mountain passes that had served as supply routes for the Pakistanis. Ayub Khan now faced a difficult dilemma. He could hardly sustain a guerrilla campaign in Kashmir with the key mountain passes in Indian hands. He either had to back down or raise the stakes. Calculating that Indian fear of China would deter her from a vigorous response against Pakistan and confident of his own military superiority, the Pakistani leader decided to escalate the conflict.

On September 1, Pakistani forces, supported by ninety

Patton tanks, crossed the cease-fire line into southern Kashmir and advanced so rapidly that they threatened the vital road over the mountains linking Srinagar with the plains of India. If Pakistan captured this road, Indian forces in Kashmir would be encircled. Thus, India was now left with the choice of yielding or expanding the war.

On September 5, India opened a new front and invaded West Pakistan in a massive attack. The two armies were now locked in large-scale combat over a wide area. Despite superior weapons and greater mobility, the Pakistani forces were unable to break through Indian lines and advance on India's cities as their leaders had so confidently predicted. In a number of encounters, the Indians even managed to outmaneuver and outfight their opponents, thus reversing the situation that had prevailed in the Rann of Kutch. The Pakistani leadership was badly shaken and resorted to desperate fighting to hold the line. After several weeks of war, the battlelines became relatively stationary, with both sides having fought each other to a virtual standstill.

The war finally ended through the efforts of Premier Aleksei Kosygin of the Soviet Union, who invited both parties to come to Tashkent to settle their differences. Reasoning that a continued conflict between India and Pakistan would probably benefit China, the Soviet leader decided to assume the role of peace maker. Edward Crankshaw, who was in Tashkent during the Soviet-sponsored negotiations, commented as follows:

> Mr. Kosygin, whose ideology demands the fostering of chaos and disruption in non-Communist lands, finds himself doing his level best to calm down a Hindu under direct threat from China and a Moslem supposed to be on friendly terms with Peking, embroiled in a quarrel over the possession of the mountain playground of the late British Raj. And, except for China, nobody minds.[11]

And so the world was treated to the strange spectacle of a Communist state successfully fashioning a truce between two bourgeois nations. The Kashmir problem was not resolved, of course. Both sides merely agreed to set forth their "respective positions" on the issue. Nor were the deeper animosities removed, or even mitigated. Tashkent merely signified a pause in a protracted conflict that, thus far, had proved inconclusive. The decisive encounter was to come half a decade later when the flames of war burst forth once more with terrible ferocity.

The Bloody Dawn of Bangladesh

New nations are seldom born without great pain. The scale of human suffering that marked the birth of Bangladesh, however, was so vast that it stands out starkly even against the grim and melancholy canvas of the twentieth century. First, a natural disaster of titanic proportions, followed by a fratricidal war, then a flood of refugees, and finally another war—these were the four horsemen of the Apocalypse that ushered into the world the state of Bangladesh in 1971.

In order to understand the outbreak of the war between Moslem and Moslem, one must appreciate that, first and foremost, the two Pakistans had nothing whatsoever in common *but* Islam. For almost a quarter of a century, the two wings of Pakistan stood more than 1,000 miles apart from each other—with Indian territory in between. Aside from this physical, and consequently psychological, distance, the two peoples spoke different languages, had different racial characteristics, and prided themselves on different cultural achievements. As one observer put it rather bluntly: "The only bonds between the diverse and distant wings of their Moslem nation were the Islamic faith and Pakistan International Airlines." [12]

As if this condition was not enough to weaken the union, a

sequence of developments aggravated the situation and eventually plunged the two Pakistans into all-out war. First, the founder of Pakistan, Mohammed Ali Jinnah, died one year after the creation of the state and his successor, Liaquat Ali Khan, was felled by an assassin's bullet two years later. The loss of these two charismatic leaders left a serious void and contributed to the declining popularity of the Moslem League that had provided a semblance of unity throughout Pakistan. Second, and even more serious, was the flagrantly unequal distribution of economic resources between the two Pakistans. From the very beginning, the West Pakistanis were far more generously endowed than their coreligionists in Bengal. West Pakistan, six times the size of East Pakistan, had to support only 40 percent of Pakistan's entire population. Third, and perhaps most important, was the tendency of the West Pakistani leadership to treat the Bengalis as poor relations. The nation's capital was established in the West, first in Karachi and later in Islamabad. As Pakistan became a major recipient of American military and economic aid, the West remained the main beneficiary. Westerners were always richer than Easterners and, between 1950 and 1970, more than doubled this income gap. The Bengali jute and tea supplied between 50 and 70 percent of the nation's revenue, but the Bengalis received only 25 to 30 percent of Pakistan's total income. Thus, there was a parasitic quality to the West's relationship to the East. As a leading Bengali spokesman put it:

> We are only a colony and a market. If the only reason for our ties with West Pakistan is that we are both Moslem, why shouldn't we join some other state, like Kuwait, from which we might get more money? [13]

Finally, the West had a virtual monopoly of Pakistan's power elite: 85 percent of all government positions were held by

Westerners; two-thirds of the nation's industry and four-fifths of its banking and insurance assets were controlled by the West; and only 5 percent of Pakistan's 275,000-man army were Bengalis.

East Pakistanis tried hard to compensate for this condition with cultural arrogance. They were lovers of art and literature and regarded the Westerners' respect for the martial virtues with contempt. But gradually, under the growing pressures of deprivation, pride led to a Bengal nationalism that demanded its case be heard. Still, violence might have been avoided had not nature visited upon Bengal one of the most terrible calamities of the century. In November 1970, a devastating cyclone struck the coast of Bengal and claimed the lives of almost half a million people. Those who survived were subject to starvation and disease. The catastrophe was so awesome that it was described as "a second Hiroshima."

At the time of the disaster, the president of Pakistan was Yahya Khan, a general who had assumed power in 1969 by virtue of his military status. Yahya had promised free elections by the end of 1970. Two weeks elapsed, however, before the president even managed to visit the scene of the catastrophe, and most Bengalis perceived this delay as an example of West Pakistan's callousness and indifference to the calamity that had befallen them. The Bengalis' outrage now vented itself at the ballot box.

The election results turned out to be a bitter surprise for the military leadership as well as for the People's party, headed by Zulfikar Ali Bhutto, a Westerner. To their dismay, Sheik Mujibur Rahaman's Awami League won a sweeping victory in East Pakistan. While Sheik Mujibur had always favored Bengali civil liberties, Yahya Khan's apathy in the wake of the cyclone provoked the Sheik's followers into a genuine nationalist movement. The league's platform of complete regional autonomy for East Pakistan would have left only

foreign affairs and defense problems with the central government. On the basis of the election returns in December 1970,
East Pakistan with its large Bengali population was allotted
169 seats in the National Assembly while Bhutto's People's
party won only 90 seats. The results left no doubt that the
next prime minister of Pakistan would not be Bhutto but the
Bengali leader Sheik Mujibur Rahaman.

The Western leadership found this outcome simply unacceptable. It feared that the Awami League, with its absolute
majority in the National Assembly, would vote itself a program for virtual self-government, thus removing East Pakistan
from the control of the central government. The weeks following the election were marked by a feverish contest for power
that finally erupted into bloody conflict.

President Yahya Khan triggered the crisis when he announced the postponement of the assembly session to a later,
unspecified date. The Awami League, perceiving this as a
deliberate attempt to disregard a popular mandate for Bengali
autonomy, launched a campaign of civil disobedience. The
Bengalis, in turn, defied the central government by calling a
massive strike and managed to bring government operations to
a virtual standstill. In response to this pressure, Yahya Khan
scheduled the date of the assembly session for March 26, but
at the same time made arrangements for a massive airlift of
West Pakistani troops to East Pakistan.

In such a climate, negotiations were doomed from the start.
On March 25, private talks between Yahya and Sheik Mujibur broke down and, upon his return to Islamabad, the president denounced the Sheik's activities as "acts of treason." He
ordered the immediate arrest of Awami League leaders and
directed the army to crush the secessionist movement and restore full authority to the central government. This decision
directly precipitated the civil war and led to the end of a

united Pakistan. In view of its crucial importance in the sequence of events, it is worth examining in some detail.

Yahya's plan was to destroy all Bengali resistance centers in one massive strike, thereby crushing the rebellion once and for all. West Pakistan leaders never doubted their own military superiority nor expected the Bengalis to put up more than token resistance. As one high-ranking army officer put it: "Those little brown buggers won't fight," and another was quoted to have predicted confidently: "A good beating and these chaps will come around." [14]

This attitude was deeply rooted in the culture of West Pakistan. The light-skinned Westerners had always extolled martial virtues and looked down with contempt on the dark-skinned Bengalis who preferred the pen to the sword. Thus, Yahya crucially underestimated the appeal of Sheik Mujibur whom he never regarded as a legitimate spokesman for Bengali aspirations; instead he imprisoned the sheik as a traitor. The sheik's statement, in March, that the Bengalis were "prepared to sacrifice one million people to gain independence" [15] was dismissed as empty rhetoric. Yahya, in fact, was reported to have referred to the Bengalis as "mosquitoes" who could be killed with one determined slap of the hand. He ignored the possibility that the "mosquitoes" might soon become guerrillas. Moreover, he never recognized the charisma of the Bengali leader but dismissed him as a saboteur and mischief maker. And, finally, he never took into account the enormous logistical difficulties of supplying an occupation army from bases that were a thousand miles away. Instead, Yahya Khan preferred a military solution of the most brutal kind that not only alienated the Bengalis from West Pakistan forever but plunged the entire subcontinent into open conflict.

The Western crackdown on Bengal was marked by extreme brutality. Pillage, murder, and rape were so pervasive that, by

April, a powerful guerrilla movement had sprung up that fought the West Pakistanis with a courage born of desperation. On April 17, the Bengali resistance fighters, or Mukti Bahini, as they quickly came to be known, established a provisional government of their own in a mango grove just inside the East Pakistan border. They gave their embryonic state the name of Bangladesh.

In terror, millions of Bengalis fled for their lives from the pitiless West Pakistanis. They chose as their haven the neighboring province of West Bengal which was a part of India. Thus it came about that Moslems, in order to save themselves from other Moslems, sought refuge in the country of their former archenemy, India. The growing influx of these panic-stricken people began to create a terrible burden for the overpopulated and impoverished neighboring Hindu nation. India's meager resources had to be drawn upon in order to provide food, medical assistance, and shelter for the refugees. As a result, India's own economic development plans had to be suspended. To make matters even worse, West Bengal also happened to be one of India's politically most volatile and unstable states, and the flood of refugees, of course, exacerbated this instability.

In view of these developments, India could not remain a passive observer of the civil war in Pakistan for very long. On April 16, the government of Indira Gandhi accused the West Pakistan army of "planned carnage and systematic genocide." [16] By May, Pakistani troops were chasing Bengali guerrillas across the Indian border and armed clashes between Indian and Pakistani border patrols became commonplace.

As the flood of Bengali refugees gathered momentum, the Indian government became increasingly alarmed. Its treasury was being drained of $2.5 million a day. In the spring, Mrs. Gandhi warned the Parliament that the refugee problem was "going to be hell for us; we are not going to allow them to stay here." [17] By November, the Indian estimate of Bengali refugees had reached the 10 million mark. If this figure is correct, then "the mass movement of humanity over eight months of 1971 was the most intensive, regionally concentrated large-scale migration in the history of man." [18]

By mid-July, Mrs. Gandhi had evidence that a war with Pakistan would be cheaper than the economic burden of coping with the refugee problem for a single year. This evidence was supplied by the Institute for Defense Studies and Analysis in New Delhi. The Indians concluded that the refugees would cost their country $900 million within a year, or more than thirteen times the cost of the entire Kashmir war with Pakistan in 1965. This report was widely circulated and resulted in a wave of popular emotion in favor of war. The Indian leadership had to respond forcefully in order to alleviate the pressure.

On August 9, Mrs. Gandhi, with an eye toward Pakistan's friendship with China, abandoned India's traditional policy of nonalignment and signed a treaty of friendship with the Soviet Union. This twenty-five-year treaty had all the earmarks of a military alliance. Reflecting the popular mood, the Indian Parliament hailed the new "realism" in India's foreign policy and praised Mrs. Gandhi for having "put some meat in our vegetarian diet of non-alignment." [19] The pact was intended as a clear warning to Pakistan and as a deterrent against the possibility of Chinese intervention. Several weeks later, Mrs. Gandhi embarked upon a tour of the United States, Britain, and Western Europe in order to underline the gravity of the situation and the need for a political solution. Specifically, she demanded the release of Sheik Mujibur which, she hoped, would result in Bengali autonomy and the return of the refugees to their former homes.

On the home front, Mrs. Gandhi quietly took measures to prepare the Indian army for action in case her diplomatic efforts failed. During the months of October and November 1971, Indian forces began to help the Mukti Bahini more actively. Mrs. Gandhi was still hopeful that a major war could be averted and that the Indians, as discreetly as possible, could secure enough territory within East Pakistan to establish a Bangladesh regime. However, this clandestine support for the Bengali guerrillas turned out to be insufficient. Moreover, another natural calamity forced the Indian government to become even more actively involved.

In early November, another cyclone struck, this time spending its fury on Indian soil. The death of 20,000 Indians sharply increased public pressures on Mrs. Gandhi. The Parliament now demanded that priority be given to the Indian victims and that forceful measures be taken to effect the repatriation of the Bengalis. In response to these pressures, Mrs. Gandhi made a crucial military commitment. She authorized Indian forces to engage Pakistani troops on the East Pakistan border. Her strategy was to hit the West Pakistanis with quick, limited strikes that would tie down the occupation troops and give the Bengali guerrillas more freedom to maneuver. This "hit and run" strategy was greeted with a chorus of approval in the Parliament. The commander of the Indian forces in the area, General Jagjit Singh Aurora, was happy that his troops could now challenge the Pakistanis in open combat. As he put it:

> I had finished building up my force in September, and I really began to retaliate in mid-October, but it wasn't until the third week of November that I got permission to go in and silence their guns by pushing them back and giving them a bloody nose.[20]

Mrs. Gandhi had confidence in her strategy for another reason. She was convinced that China would be deterred from intervening, not only because of India's new alliance with the Soviet Union, but also because the Himalayan passes were already blocked by snow. Her assumption proved to be correct.

On November 30, Mrs. Gandhi ordered a blackout of Calcutta and, on the following day, Indian troops penetrated 5 miles into Pakistan as a "defensive measure." On that day, the United States began its "tilt" toward Pakistan by cancelling an arms shipment to India, and Mrs. Gandhi exploded:

> If any country thinks that by calling us aggressors it can pressure us to forget our national interests, then that country is living in its own paradise and is welcome to it. The times have passed when any nation sitting three or four thousand miles away could give orders to Indians on the basis of their color superiority. India has changed, and she is no more a country of natives.[21]

Tension was also high in Pakistan. By late November, it had become public knowledge that President Yahya Khan had taken to heavy drinking. On November 25, while entertaining a delegation of visiting Chinese, he exclaimed to a reporter:

> If that woman thinks she can cow me down, I refuse to take it. If she wants a war, I'll fight her! In ten days, I might not be here. There might be a war. I'll be off fighting a war! [22]

Indira Gandhi's demand that Yahya Khan release Sheik Mujibur enraged the Pakistani leader so much that he sentenced the Bengali nationalist to death. Not only did he resist all appeals and efforts to change his mind, but on November 26 he outlawed the entire Awami League on grounds of conspiracy against the government. The death sentence against Sheik Mujibur, however, was never carried out.

Yahya Khan also betrayed an increasing tendency to reduce

the conflict between India and Pakistan to a personal test of strength between himself and Mrs. Gandhi. In an interview with a *Time* correspondent, his vanity broke through. Proud of his thick, black hair, he exclaimed to the reporter: "My strength lies in it—like Samson's."[23] And to a *Newsweek* correspondent, who questioned him about the possibility of war with India, he confided: "The worst losers will be the Indians themselves. I hope to God that woman understands."[24] A week later, the same reporter interviewed Mrs. Gandhi who promptly returned the compliment:

> "That woman!" I am not concerned with the remark, but it shows the mentality of the person. He is one man who could not get elected in his own country if there were a fair election. I would say he would not even get elected in his province if there were a fair election. What weight has his judgment on India? It is a world which is quite outside his ken.[25]

On December 1, Mrs. Gandhi issued an ultimatum in which she demanded that Yahya Khan withdraw all his forces from East Pakistan. This was a hard blow under any circumstances, but for a man of Yahya Khan's fragile masculine ego, such an ultimatum from a woman was psychologically unacceptable. Thus, even though he knew that the Indian forces outnumbered his own by a ratio of five to one, the president of Pakistan authorized a massive air strike against India on December 3. The decision was greeted with a chorus of approval. Bhutto, who had just assumed the post of deputy prime minister, exclaimed that "Pakistan is faced with a predatory aggressor who never reconciled itself to the establishment of this country."[26] And Lieutenant-General Niazi, commander of Pakistan's forces in the east, got right to the heart of the matter: "We are Moslems and we don't like Hindus. One Moslem soldier is worth five Hindus."[27]

Yahya Khan's military strategy was based on the example of the Israeli surprise attack of June 1967. He hoped to cripple the Indian Air Force with a single devastating blow and, then, move with impunity into Kashmir, which he could use as a trump card in postwar bargaining.

The execution of the December 3 air attack, however, turned out to be a military disaster. Indian jet planes, unlike Egyptian planes in 1967, were well protected in concrete revetments and were thus virtually immune to the Pakistani assault. Besides, only thirty-two Pakistani planes participated in the attack which made the offensive strike very feeble indeed. India's air marshal claimed that India was hardly bruised, let alone hurt, by the attack, and another military expert commented that "In military terms, no one in his right mind would have attacked with three or four planes at each airfield. It was sheer madness." [28]

The failure of the air attack, far from forcing the Pakistanis to face reality, had precisely the opposite effect. Fervent appeals for a holy war against India increased in frequency. *The Pakistan Times* editorialized:

Plainly Islam is the issue between India and Pakistan. . . . Only those qualify to fight the battle of Pakistan who are prepared to fight the battle of Islam. . . . For us there is no choice but to fight, if need be to the last man.[29]

As the conflict intensified in early December, the elements of a fierce religious war made their appearance. Gradually, all restraint was lost, and the religious basis of the struggle was revealed in all its fanaticism and ferocity. As a Pakistani pilot put it: "Our one god makes our victory certain. The Indians are worshippers of idols, of many gods. Ours is the true strength." [30] And an army colonel drew strength from Jehad, or holy war, when he asserted confidently that there would be no Pakistani casualties on the field of battle since, "in the pursuit of Jehad, nobody dies; he lives forever." [31]

When Pakistan was confronted with dismemberment and defeat in mid-December, the truth was so appalling that it was unacceptable. Even the conquering Indian generals were moved to compassion when they saw their former colleagues from the British colonial army under siege in Dacca. Major-General Gandharv Nagra's appeal to General Niazi, the defender of Dacca, makes poignant reading: "My dear Abdullah, I am here. The game is up. I suggest you give yourself up to me and I'll look after you." [32]

Mrs. Gandhi thus emerged as the undisputed victor. India agreed to a cease-fire at her own convenience, acquired 2,500 square miles of Indian territory in West Pakistan, and detained some 93,000 prisoners of war for almost two years. Pakistan was dismembered and Bengal East emerged as Bangladesh. A bitter political divorce and a bloody war had led to the emergence of a new state in the family of nations.

Conclusions

The elements that produced the three armed conflicts between India and Pakistan constituted a veritable witches brew. When one sorts out these elements, it seems difficult indeed to conceive of a more explosive mixture. The awesome list includes religious conflict, territorial claims, economic imbalance, natural calamity, nationalist aspirations, refugee migration, and personality clashes.

The most basic conflict, of course, was religious in nature. Had it not been for the long-standing and bitter enmity between Hindus and Moslems, a single state would have emerged out of the British colony, instead of two hostile ones. The ambiguous status of Kashmir, whose ruler had been a

Hindu but whose population had been predominantly Moslem, injected the element of territorial conflict into the picture. To make matters even more complicated, Pakistan was not really one state but two, with the Eastern part living in deprivation while the Western part enjoyed relative affluence. A natural disaster in the shape of a cyclone that devastated Bengal with the fury of an atomic bomb highlighted the economic imbalance between the two Pakistans even further and precipitated demands for equality. When these demands for equal rights were denied, they grew into a virulent nationalism that turned the two Pakistans against each other in a ferocious civil war. The result was a gigantic refugee exodus from Bengal into India which probably constitutes the largest single mass migration in human history. When India decided that war with Pakistan was cheaper than the support of 10 million refugees, armed conflict became a distinct possibility. And when personal antagonisms and a fragile male ego were added to the mixture, war became a certainty. The dreadful circle was closed, with Hindu once more pitted against Moslem.

It is not easy, of course, to assess the relative weight of each link in this fateful chain. Yet the evidence suggests, that, of all the chapters in this tragic story, the religious one is the most awful and most desperate. It is not an accident that the conflict began and ended as a religious war. This was always its most basic and most irreconcilable feature. When considered in this light, one must question the confident assertion so often made in Western history books: that the age of religious warfare came to an end in 1648 when Catholics and Protestants made peace and signed the Treaty of Westphalia. In our secular age, more than three centuries later, the battle over God continues unabated, though with more awesome weapons and under bleaker skies.

Notes

1. Quoted in George McT. Kahin, *Major Governments of Asia* (Ithaca, N.Y.: Cornell University Press, 1958), p. 268.
2. Jawaharlal Nehru, *Independence and After* (New Delhi: Government of India Publication Division, 1949), p. 95.
3. M. Gopal, "Considerations of Defence," *Caravan* (New Delhi: February 1967), p. 67.
4. Alan Campbell-Johnson, *Mission with Mountbatten* (London: Robert Hale, 1952), pp. 357–358.
5. P. L. Lakhanpal, *Essential Documents and Notes on the Kashmir Dispute* (New Delhi: Council on World Affairs, 1965), p. 57.
6. William J. Barnds, *India, Pakistan, and the Great Powers* (New York: Praeger, 1972), p. 200.
7. *Nava-I-Waqt* (Lahore), May 9, 1965, p. 4.
8. *The Pakistan Times* (Lahore), July 11, 1965, p. 7.
9. *The Times of India* (New Delhi), July 18, 1965, p. 7.
10. *The Economist* (May 1, 1965), pp. 502–503.
11. *The London Observer,* January 9, 1966, p. 11.
12. Dan Coggin et al., "Pakistan: The Ravaging of Golden Bengal," *Time* (August 2, 1971), p. 26.
13. Khushwant Singh, "Why They Fled Pakistan and Won't Go Back," *The New York Times Magazine,* August 1, 1971.
14. Wayne Wilcox, "Conflict in South Asia," Paper presented at the University of London Institute of Commonwealth Studies, February 1972.
15. "Another War in Asia: Who's to Blame?" *Newsweek* (December 20, 1971).
16. "Bangladesh Is Over the Border," *The Economist* (April 24, 1971).
17. Singh, *op. cit.*
18. Louis Dupree, "Bangladesh" (Part I), *American Universities Fieldstaff Reports,* South Asia Series, Vol. 16, No. 5, p. 2, 1972.
19. Quoted by Sydney H. Schanberg, "Pact Said to Bury India's Non-Alignment," *The New York Times,* August 14, 1971.
20. Robert Shaplen, "The Birth of Bangladesh" (Part I), *The New Yorker* (February 12, 1972), p. 55.
21. *The London Times,* December 3, 1971.
22. Shaplen, *loc. cit.*
23. "Good Soldier Yahya Khan," *Time* (August 2, 1971).
24. "A Talk with Pakistan's President Yahya Khan," *Newsweek* (November 8, 1971).
25. "A Talk with India's Prime Minister Indira Gandhi," *Newsweek* (November 15, 1971).
26. Radio Pakistan Broadcast, December 3, 1971.

27. Shaplen, *loc. cit.*
28. "Another War in Asia: Who's to Blame?" *op. cit.*
29. *The Pakistan Times,* December 4, 1971.
30. Rosanne Klass, "Pakistan's Costly Delusion," *Saturday Review* (February 5, 1972).
31. "Bangladesh: Out of War, a Nation Is Born," *Time* (December 27, 1971).
32. "India: Easy Victory, Uneasy Peace," *Time* (December 27, 1971).

Selected Bibliography

BARNDS, WILLIAM J. *India, Pakistan, and the Great Powers.* New York: Praeger, 1972.

BHATIA, KRISHNAN. *Indira: A Biography of Prime Minister Gandhi.* New York: Praeger, 1974.

ERIKSON, ERIK. *Gandhi's Truth.* New York: Norton, 1969.

JACKSON, ROBERT. *South Asian Crisis: India, Pakistan, and Bangladesh.* New York: Praeger, 1975.

LAMB, ALASTAIR. *The Kashmir Problem.* New York: Praeger, 1967.

SHAPLEN, ROBERT. "The Birth of Bangladesh." *The New Yorker,* February 12, 1972.

6.

The Thirty Years' War in the Holy Land: Israel and the Arabs in 1948, 1956, 1967, and 1973

War can protect; it cannot create.

Alfred North Whitehead

Historical tragedies do not arise from encounters in which right clashes with wrong. They occur when right clashes with right. This is the heart of the conflict between Israel and the Arab states in Palestine. A large number of Jews, responding to the horror of Hitler's systematic policy of extermination, attempted to save themselves by creating a state of their own. They established it in a land that had been occupied by Arabs for centuries, at the precise moment when the Arab peoples were emerging from the crucible of Western colonialism and were rediscovering their own national destinies. Thus, Jewish nationalism clashed head on with Arab nationalism in Palestine.

The four wars between Israel and her Arab neighbors have been the result of this collision. The modern Middle East has been the scene of both irreconcilable hopes and aspirations and bitter hatreds and violent passions. The wars were fought with the deepest emotion. Each contestant regarded his rights as self-evident and firmly based upon the will of God, morality, reason, and law. As passions rose, irrationality became commonplace. Desperate deed was heaped upon desperate deed until right and wrong, responsibility and guilt could no longer be distinguished. Each side had done things that the other could neither forgive nor forget.

This tragic clash between two valid claims and two appeals for justice has not abated much with the passage of time. Nor has it yet been possible to break the impasse through a lasting peace settlement.

All this suggests that, perhaps, there is no solution for the Arab-Israeli problem outside the course of history. In the meantime, it is the scholar's duty to offer a diagnosis even though he may not have a prescription for healing a "sickness unto death." The four Palestine wars were merely massive eruptions of an historical encounter that is nothing less than a protracted war spanning an entire generation. As such, they offer us insight into, but not liberation from, some of the darkest recesses of the souls of nations and men.

The Palestine War of 1948

The Zionist movement was founded in 1897 by Dr. Theodor Herzl, an Austrian journalist, with the publication of a book entitled *The Jewish State* in which he urged the settlement of Jewish agriculturists and artisans in Palestine. These pioneers, Herzl hoped, would realize an ancient Jewish dream —the reestablishment of a Jewish homeland in the Promised Land and the gathering together of the Jewish people from their Diaspora of 2,000 years. Responding to Herzl's vision and reacting to anti-Semitic pogroms in Russia and Poland, 60,000 Jews emigrated to Palestine between 1881 and

1914. The land that was used for the Jewish settlements was purchased from absentee Arab landlords by wealthy philanthropists like Baron de Rothschild of Paris or through funds collected by the Zionists abroad. By 1914, almost 100,000 acres of Palestinian land had been purchased by the Jews.

In 1917, Chaim Weizmann, a scientist of world renown and a fervent Zionist, persuaded British Foreign Minister Lord Arthur James Balfour to issue a proclamation that would convert Herzl's dream into a British pledge:

> His Majesty's Government views with favor the establishment in Palestine of a national home for the Jewish people, and will use their best endeavours to facilitate the achievement of this object, it being clearly understood that nothing shall be done which may prejudice the civil rights of existing non-Jewish communities in Palestine, or the rights and political status enjoyed by Jews in any other country.

In 1922, Britain was given a League of Nations mandate over Palestine.

The Palestinian Arabs, understandably enough, objected to the Balfour Declaration and became increasingly uneasy about the large influx of Jewish immigrants. During the 1930s, when Hitler's persecution of European Jews gathered increasing momentum, Jewish immigration soared dramatically. By 1937, the Jews constituted almost one-third of the total population of Palestine. Between 1928 and 1937, their number had risen from 150,000 to 400,000. As the Zionist movement looked toward Palestine as the last refuge from the impending Nazi holocaust, Arab alarm grew accordingly. It was no longer a question of land purchased by individual settlers but the threat of an alien state in a land that had been inhabited by Arabs for over 1,000 years. The British, caught in a vise between their pledge to the Jews on the one hand, and to Arab oil and strategic interests on the other, tried to temporize, but finally placated the Arabs by imposing a ceiling on Jewish immigration. The Jews, in their plight, tried to run the British blockade. In most cases, the British intercepted the immigrant vessels and shipped the passengers to internment camps in Cyprus. In the particularly tragic case of the immigrant ship *Exodus*, the British sent the helpless Jews back to Germany. As one survivor put it, "The Germans killed us, and the British don't let us live." [1]

Despite the British blockade, tens of thousands of Jewish immigrants landed in Palestine illegally. The Arabs became increasingly more restive, and bitter fighting erupted. The British, caught in the lines of fire, were unable to restore the peace. In 1947, in total frustration, Britain announced her intention to relinquish the mandate over Palestine and decided to place the entire problem before the forum of the United Nations.

The undisputed leader of the more than half a million Jewish settlers in Palestine in 1947 was David Ben-Gurion. Ben-Gurion's commitment to the Zionist ideal was total and unswerving. He had come to Palestine in 1906, had been a leading delegate to the World Zionist Congress and, by 1935, had become chairman of the Jewish Agency which represented the World Zionist Movement. No single leader represented the Arab cause, but the most influential men were Haj Amin el-Husseini, the Grand Mufti of Jerusalem, Azzam Pasha, the secretary-general of the Arab League, King Abdullah of Transjordan, and Glubb Pasha, the commander of the British-trained Arab Legion. The Grand Mufti had been in Germany during the war and had helped the Nazis plan a "final solution" of the Jewish problem. He had designs to rule all Palestine and, for this reason, was distrusted by the other Arab leaders. Azzam Pasha was an Egyptian diplomat with relatively moderate views. King Abdullah of Transjordan, who had a reputation for compassion and humanity, met secretly once with Golda Meir to explore the possibility of an Arab-Jewish compromise. And Glubb Pasha's Arab Legion was the only Arab military force that was truly feared by the Zionists.

In early 1947, a specially constituted United Nations Committee on Palestine (UNSCOP) visited the area and examined the alternatives. After several months of highly charged debate, the committee finally recommended the partition of Palestine, with its population of 1.2 million Arabs and 570,000 Jews, into two states—one Arab and one Jewish—with Jerusalem held as trustee of the UN. The Jewish state would include 55 percent of the land and a 58 percent Jewish population; the Arab state, 45 percent of the land and a 99 percent Arab population. This partition plan was eagerly welcomed by the Jews and denounced with equal fervor by the Arabs.

A number of meetings on the partition plan took place between Arab and Jewish leaders. In one such encounter, Abba Eban, then an official of the Jewish Agency, met with Azzam Pasha to discuss the possibility of a compromise. Eban stated that "the Jews [were] a *fait accompli* in the Middle East and that the Arabs [would] have to reconcile themselves to that fact."[2] He then went on to propose an economic program for joint development of the Middle East. Azzam Pasha conceded that the plan was "rational and logical" but added that "the fate of nations [was] not decided by rational logic." "We shall try to defeat you," he said. "I am not sure we will succeed, but we will try. We were able to drive out the Crusaders, but on the other hand, we lost Spain and Persia. It may be that we shall lose Palestine. But it is too late for peaceful solutions."[3] When Abba Eban interrupted by pointing out that this left no alternative but a test of strength through force of arms, Azzam Pasha replied:

It is in the nature of peoples to aspire to expansion and to fight for what they think is vital. It is possible that I don't represent,

in the full sense of the word, the new spirit which animates my
people. My young son who yearns to fight, undoubtedly represents it better than I do. He no longer believes in the old
generation. . . . The forces which motivate peoples are not
subject to our control. They are objective forces. Nationalism,
that is a greater force than any which drives us. We don't need
economic development with your assistance. We have only one
test, the test of strength.[4]

An eyewitness to this encounter detected no hatred in Azzam
Pasha's tone. He referred to the Jews over and over as "cous-
ins." Not once during the two-hour conversation did he express an unkind thought or use a hostile expression about the
Jews. But he did confirm the character of the position of the
Arab majority—a position based not on logic but "on a blind
fatalism, ungovernable as the wind."[5] Sadly, and without
hatred, the two leaders took their leave of one another.

The lobbying for and against the partition resolution was
the most intense that the United Nations had experienced in
its short history. A two-thirds majority was required for passage of the resolution by the General Assembly. To offset the
votes of just the Arab and Moslem nations, the Zionists
needed twenty-two votes, and for each additional vote against
partition, they needed two in favor. While the Zionists were
by no means certain that they could muster a two-thirds majority, they were encouraged by the fact that the two main
antagonists in the cold war, the United States and the Soviet
Union, both supported them. In the United States, President
Truman was deeply sympathetic to the Jewish cause. Moreover, his political instincts told him that the Jewish vote might
well be crucial during the presidential elections of 1948. Overriding the objections of leading State Department officials over
the Soviet threat and American access to military bases, Truman personally warned the United States delegate to the

United Nations, Herschel Johnson, to "damn well deliver the partition vote or there will be hell to pay." [6] From the Soviet point of view, partition seemed the easiest way to oust Britain from the Middle East and to keep the United States at arm's length while playing the Arabs off against the Jews. Two days before the vote, it became clear that the fate of Zionism rested in the hands of a few small, remote nations, in particular Liberia, Haiti, the Philippines, and Ethiopia. The Zionists persuaded the United States to apply strong pressure on these countries. Nevertheless, on November 29, 1947, the outcome was very much in doubt. Moshe Sharett, the Jewish Agency's "foreign minister," solemnly warned the assembly that the Jewish people would never submit to any attempt to subjugate them to an Arab majority. Jamal Husseini, the acting secretary-general of the Arab League, on the other hand, declared that if the assembly did vote for partition, the Arabs of Palestine would go to war against the Jews as soon as the British left: "the partition line will be drawn in fire and blood." [7]

Two eyewitnesses have left a poignant account of that fateful vote on November 29:

An aide set a basket before Aranha (the President of the General Assembly). In it were fifty-six slips of paper, each bearing the name of one of the nations represented in the hall. Aranha extended his hand and slowly drew from the basket the name of the nation whose vote would begin the poll. He unfolded the piece of paper and stared an instant at the men ranged before him.

"Guatemala," he announced. At his words, a terrible silence settled over the Assembly. Even the press gallery fell quiet. For an instant, the three hundred delegates, the spectators, the newsmen, seemed united in awe of the moment before them, in their awareness of the grave and solemn decision about to be taken.

The delegate of Guatemala rose. As he did, suddenly, from the spectators' gallery, a piercing cry sundered the silence of the Assembly hall, a Hebrew cry as old as time and the suffering of men: "Ana Ad Hoshiya. O Lord, save us." [8]

The partition resolution was adopted by a vote of 33 votes in favor, 13 against, and 10 abstentions. The Zionists were ecstatic, but the Arab delegates walked out of the General Assembly, declaring that their governments would not be bound by the United Nations decision.

Both Ben-Gurion, who had heard of the Zionist victory 6,000 miles away from the UN, and the Grand Mufti of Jerusalem, who had followed every word of the Palestine debate in New York, knew that the vote was no guarantee that the Jewish state would actually come into being. Between the vote on that late November afternoon and the expiration of the British mandate in Palestine, scheduled for May of the following year, lay a span of time that might well be decisive. Both men immediately set about to strengthen their forces for the battle that loomed ahead. Violent Arab-Jewish clashes occurred in Jerusalem and other parts of the country the day after the United Nations vote. The Jews were fearful lest Arab resistance would deprive them of the fruits of the partition vote. The Arabs were enraged at a decision that, in their view, deprived them of their patrimony. On both sides, there seemed to be no time to lose.

The search for arms now dominated the minds of Arab and Jewish leaders alike. In this vital quest, the Zionists were at a disadvantage. The right to buy arms openly on the international arms market was the prerogative of sovereign states. Lebanon and Syria, which had won their independence in 1943 and 1946 respectively, were legally free to purchase arms for the Arab cause. Syria's defense minister, for example, was able to place an order for 10,000 rifles with a leading arms manufacturer in Czechoslovakia. The Jews, on the other hand, had to resort to clandestine means. The Haganah, the underground Zionist army, bought up American surplus arms and machine tools that were destined to be converted into scrap metal. To bypass the British arms embargo, most of the equipment was broken down into its component parts, classified by code, and then shipped to Palestine in random bits and pieces under official import permits for such items as textile machinery. Another device used by Ben-Gurion's men was to place an order on the stationery of a sovereign state. One such order, from "Ethiopia," reached the same Czechoslovak arms manufacturer who had served the Syrians. That order, too, was filled. Thus by late 1947, a jostling for territory between Arabs and Jews was threatening to erupt into organized warfare between two desperate peoples.

In December 1947, the seven members of the Arab League met in Cairo to discuss the threat of a Jewish state in their midst. The states that were represented at this historic meeting were Egypt, Iraq, Saudi Arabia, Syria, Yemen, Lebanon, and Transjordan. Together, their leaders ruled some 45 million people and had at their command 5 regular armies. Azzam Pasha, the secretary-general of the Arab League, had labored patiently to reach a consensus among the seven Arab leaders, whose only common bond was their hostility to Zionism but who were otherwise deeply divided by historic rivalries and future ambitions. After protracted debate, the leaders resolved to "prevent the creation of a Jewish state in Palestine and to conserve Palestine as a united independent state."[9] Toward that end, they pledged to furnish the league with 10,000 rifles, 3,000 volunteers, and £1 million sterling to provide an immediate beginning for guerrilla operations against the Zionists in Palestine.

At the same time, David Ben-Gurion summoned his Haganah leaders to an emergency meeting in Jerusalem. "It is time," he told the men before him, "to start planning for a war against five Arab armies." [10] Ben-Gurion perceived the threat of war with the Arabs as a terrible menace that could strangle the Jewish state before it was born. On the other hand, he felt that if the Arabs insisted on going to war, the frontiers of the Jewish state would not be the boundaries assigned to it by the United Nations but those that the Jews could seize and hold by force of arms. If the Arabs rejected the United Nations decision and went to war, Ben-Gurion thought, that would give his people "the right to get what we could." [11] Thus, paradoxically, the Jewish leader turned the Arab cause into a handmaiden of Zionist aspirations.

As the two hostile armies engaged in strikes and counterstrikes that mounted in frequency and ferocity during the final months of the British mandate, events were taking place in Washington that once again placed the birth of the Jewish state in serious doubt. Shaken by the violence of Arab resistance and skeptical of Jewish military strength, President Truman was extremely reluctant to enforce the United Nations partition resolution with American troops even if such troops were part of a United Nations force. Moreover, the State Department continued to be deeply critical of partition and considered it to be legally unenforceable. In December 1947, the department prevailed upon the President to declare an arms embargo to the Middle East. Since under various agreements Britain was still free to ship arms to the Arabs, this embargo amounted to a ban on arms to the Jews. Perhaps most damaging to the Zionist cause was the fact that President Truman had become resentful of certain Zionist leaders, particularly Rabbi Abba Hillel Silver, who, in the President's opinion, had exerted indecent pressure to support the Jewish cause. Thus, the United States abandoned its support of the partition plan and now proposed an international trusteeship over Palestine. In desperation, the Zionists appealed to the

aging, almost blind, Chaim Weizmann who had enjoyed a
close relationship with the American President over many
years. On February 10, 1948, Weizmann wrote Truman a
letter asking "for a few minutes of [his] precious time."[12]
The request was refused.

Sitting at Weizmann's bedside, Frank Goldman, president
of B'nai B'rith, came up with a last-ditch plan to change
Truman's mind. He offered to telephone Eddie Jacobson, who
was once a partner with Harry Truman in a haberdashery
store and who, Goldman thought, might persuade the President to receive Dr. Weizmann. Jacobson responded favorably
and was granted an interview with the President on March
12. Truman at first was not receptive to the overtures of his
former business partner, but Jacobson persisted. His appeal
to the President made a crucial difference in Zionist fortunes:

> Chaim Weizmann is a very sick man, almost broken in health,
> but he travelled thousands and thousands of miles just to see
> you and plead the cause of my people. Now you refuse to see
> him because you were insulted by some of our American Jewish
> leaders, even though you know that Weizmann had absolutely
> nothing to do with these insults and would be the last man to
> be a party to them. It doesn't sound like you, Harry.[13]

According to the same account, President Truman, after a
long silence, looked Jacobson straight in the eye and said:
"You win, you baldheaded son-of-a-bitch! I will see him."[14]
One week later Truman met with Weizmann and promised
the Jewish leader that he would work for the establishment
and recognition of a Jewish state.

The battle was not yet won by the Zionists, however. On
March 19, United States Ambassador Warren Austin announced in the Security Council that the United States would
propose the suspension of the partition plan and the estab-

lishment of a temporary trusteeship in Palestine in its place. When a shocked and angry Truman wanted to know how such a thing could have happened, he discovered that Secretary of State George Marshall, who had not been privy to the President's personal pledge to Dr. Weizmann, had directed Austin on March 16 to make the trusteeship speech at the earliest appropriate moment. The Zionists were in despair, the Arabs were jubilant, Secretary-General Trygve Lie of the United Nations briefly considered resigning, and President Truman, according to his counsel, Clark Clifford, was "boiling mad." [15] He now had to go along with the trusteeship idea, at least for the time being, since yet another reversal would have deprived the United States of all credibility.

With the British mandate rapidly drawing to a close, the fighting in Palestine became increasingly desperate. In April 1948, Jewish extremists of the Irgun and Stern groups massacred the inhabitants of Deir Yassin, a small village near Jerusalem. Even though Ben-Gurion personally cabled his shock at the slaughter and the Chief Rabbi of Jerusalem excommunicated the Jews who had participated in it, Deir Yassin became a stain on the conscience of the Jewish state. Not only did it elicit demands for vengeance and retribution but, in the years ahead, it was to become a symbol of the homelessness of hundreds of thousands of Arab refugees. The mass exodus of terrified Arabs from Jewish-controlled areas began in earnest after this event. The Arab decision to encourage the refugees to leave and to broadcast the massacre in all its horror contributed to the growing panic. Thus, Deir Yassin marked the beginning of the Palestinian problem that was to haunt the Middle East for decades to come.

Several days after the carnage of Deir Yassin, Ben-Gurion sent Golda Meir on a final peace mission. Disguised as an Arab woman, Meir traveled to Amman for a secret meeting with King Abdullah of Transjordan to discuss the possibility of preventing a collision. The king proposed that the proclamation of the Jewish state be postponed and Palestine be kept united with the Jews autonomous in their areas. He also suggested a parliament composed equally of Arab and Jewish deputies. He desired peace, he told his visitor, but if his proposals were not accepted, he feared that war was inevitable. Meir replied that the postponement of the birth of a Jewish state was unacceptable and added that the Jews would fight as long as their strength lasted. Abdullah said that he realized that the Jews would have to repel any attack and that it was probably no longer in his power to act as mediator between his fellow Arabs and the Zionists. "Deir Yassin has inflamed the Arab masses," he said. "Before then I was alone. Now I am one of five and have discovered that I cannot make any decisions alone."[16] Thus, this last effort to stave off the catastrophe ended in failure.

In May, with the days of the British mandate numbered, the Jews faced a crucial dilemma. Should they proclaim the Jewish state immediately, or in the light of the erosion of American support and the massing of Arab armies, should they wait? On May 12, Ben-Gurion called a secret meeting of the provisional National Council to make such a decision. Opinion was sharply divided. Some council members felt that it would be wise to wait since the United States would probably not come to the aid of a self-proclaimed state but might do so if the Arabs acted first and invaded a United Nations-declared state. Others felt that the Jewish state would have to stand alone under any conditions and, hence, statehood should be proclaimed without delay. Ben-Gurion was for immediate statehood even though he gave the Jews only a 50-50 chance for survival. When the vote was taken, six of the eleven council members voted to go ahead. By a margin of one vote, the council decided to proclaim the new state on May 14, a few hours before the British mandate was to expire.

At 4 P.M. on May 14, 1948, two hours before the termination of the British mandate, David Ben-Gurion announced
the birth of Israel. The news triggered a frantic debate in the
United Nations General Assembly in New York, but the
world body was unable to reach a decision. A short time after
Ben-Gurion's proclamation, Warren Austin, on the personal
instruction of President Truman, announced that the United
States had recognized the new state of Israel. Shortly thereafter, the Soviet delegate followed suit. "We have been
duped," said Charles Malik of Lebanon in an assault of fury
upon the American and Soviet delegations. It was now 6:15
P.M. and the mandate had ended. Ben-Gurion broadcast a
personal message of thanks from Tel Aviv to the American
people. As he spoke, the building shook from the impact of
an Arab bomb. "The explosions you can hear," he told his
audience across the Atlantic, "are Arab planes bombing Tel
Aviv." [17] The war for Palestine had broken out.

At dawn on May 15, Israel was simultaneously invaded
by the Egyptian army from the south, the Transjordanian
Arab Legion from the east, and the forces of Syria and
Lebanon from the north. The total strength of the invading
Arab armies was approximately 23,500 men, equipped with
tanks, airplanes, heavy artillery, spare parts, and ammunition.
The Israelis had approximately 3,000 regulars under arms
plus 14,000 recruits. They also had 10,000 rifles, 3,600 sub-
machine guns, four ancient cannons smuggled in from Mex-
ico; they had no tanks. The United States and the Soviet
Union both disapproved of the invasion. Andrei Gromyko,
speaking for the Soviet Union in the Security Council on May
29, 1948, stated: "This is not the first time that the Arab
states, which organized the invasion of Palestine, have ignored
a decision of the Security Council or of the General Assembly."

At the end of several months' fierce fighting, interspersed by periods of truce, Israel was left in possession of the whole of Galilee, a section of central Palestine connecting the coastal area with Jerusalem, and the whole of the Negev. Jerusalem became a divided city. The entire area controlled by Israel in 1949 was somewhat larger than the area that had been allotted to the Zionists in the partition resolution of 1947. Thus, the Arab invasion had played into the hands of the Jews. Almost 1 million Arabs were rendered homeless by the conflict and entered Syria, Transjordan, and the Egyptian-controlled Gaza Strip as refugees. From their midst would rise the fedayeen and the Palestinian resistance fighters who would hold Israel responsible for the deprivation of their homeland. Thus, the bloody birth of Israel set the stage for a mortal conflict between two nationalisms—one Arab, the other Jewish—both equally desperate and equally determined to secure what to each was holy ground.

The Sinai Campaign and the Suez Crisis of 1956

Time did not appease feelings after the conclusion of the armistice agreements of 1949. On the Arab side, the plight of almost 1 million refugees constituted, by their very existence, a constant reminder of the alien Zionist presence. No matter how defensive or conciliatory Israel's policy would be, this massive displacement would make the Jewish state into a standing provocation in the eyes of the entire Arab world. The Jews, of course, were fearful of allowing the refugees to return to their former homes. How could 700,000 Jews risk the return of nearly 1 million Arabs to their land without also risking the destruction of the Jewish state? And yet, how could they refuse it without inflicting on innocent people the very injustice that they had themselves suffered in the Diaspora? Thus, the Jews took back a few, compensated some, but most continued to linger in refugee camps in Jordan, Lebanon, Syria, and Egyptian-controlled Gaza. At the same time, large numbers of Jews were driven out of Iraq, Yemen, Egypt, and Morocco.

During the early 1950s, Palestinian Arab fedayeen from the refugee population mounted raids on Israeli territory which steadily increased in ferocity and frequency. The Israelis, in turn, engaged in massive and powerful reprisals. Thus, despite the military armistice, a state of belligerency continued to exist.

In 1952, Gamal Abdel Nasser, who had distinguished himself in the Palestine war, became president of Egypt and was soon the unrivalled champion of Arab nationalism. He instituted a blockade on Israeli shipping through the Suez Canal and, in 1953, extended this blockade to include all goods being shipped to Israel. This left the Israelis with only one port, at Elath, at the head of the Gulf of Aqaba in the Straits of Tiran. In late 1953, Nasser began to restrict Israeli commerce through the straits by making its ships subject to inspection by Egyptian coastguards. In 1955, he broadened the blockade and included a ban on overflights by Israeli aircraft. In Israel, Prime Minister Ben-Gurion, who considered the port of Elath vital to Israel's survival, wanted to strike at Egypt immediately but was restrained by his colleagues. By 1956, relations between Egypt and Israel had reached the boiling point.

At this juncture, the Arab-Israeli conflict blended into a broader confrontation between Arab nationalism and the remnants of the Anglo-French, postcolonial presence in the Arab world. Two huge engineering structures, one long in existence and the other about to be constructed, brought this confrontation to a head: the Suez Canal and the High Dam at Aswan. President Nasser viewed the former as a leftover from colonial times and the latter as a modern pyramid, to be built as a symbol of a resurgent Arab nationalism.

The United States had initially agreed to help finance the Aswan High Dam through the World Bank, but Secretary of State John Foster Dulles was irked by President Nasser's decision to purchase arms from Czechoslovakia in 1955 and his recognition, a year later, of Communist China. As a result, the United States reneged on its pledge to finance the dam, ostensibly because the Egyptian economy was deemed to be unsound, and Nasser became incensed. In his rage, he declared that the United States "should drop dead of fury, but [it would] never be able to dictate to Egypt." [18] Two days later, in an emotional "declaration of independence from imperialism," he announced the nationalization of the Suez Canal which was partially owned by British and French financial interests. Thus, Britain and France were made to pay for Dulles' policy reversal and, fatefully, the two Western European powers now perceived a common interest with Israel: the removal of Gamal Abdel Nasser from power.

The perceptions of the British and French leaders now began to play a crucial role in the gathering crisis. In Britain, Anthony Eden was prime minister. Eden's memories of Hitler at Munich were still fresh and he now compared Nasser's actions to those of the German dictator in the 1930s. In the words of one thoughtful student of British policy at the time, the prime minister "saw Egypt through a forest of Flanders poppies and gleaming jackboots." [19] Guy Mollet, the premier of France, shared this perception. He had been an anti-Nazi resistance chief at Arras during World War II and now "saw Nasser as Hitler more plainly than anyone." [20] The two men became so obsessed with Nasser's action that "Lady Eden is believed to have complained that the Suez Canal was running through her drawing room." [21]

There was, of course, good reason for consternation in Britain and France. The International Convention of Constantinople of 1888 had provided that "The Suez Maritime Canal shall always be free and open, in time of war and in time of peace, to every vessel of commerce or of war without distinction of flag." Thus, the two Western powers considered Nasser's action as a violation of their legal rights. Moreover, to Britain, control of the canal symbolized her status as an empire and as a world power. To the French, who blamed Egypt for supporting the Algerian rebellion against France, seizure of the canal served as a kind of last straw. For both, the issue at stake was not merely safeguarding the economic rights of their shareholders in the Suez Canal Company; far more important was their emotional reaction to the seemingly insolent and Hitler-like nationalism represented by the Egyptian leader.

To Nasser, on the other hand, the Suez Canal had become the symbol of a shameful colonial past. Its architect, Ferdinand de Lesseps, had become an Egyptian folk ogre. Under his brutal direction, as Nasser saw it, more than 100,000 Egyptian workers had died to build a canal that was to belong not to them or their country but to a foreign company that profited for its own enrichment and never for Egypt's benefit. "Instead of the Canal being dug for Egypt," Nasser declaimed, "Egypt became the property of the Canal and the Canal Company became a state within a state. But now the days of alien exploitation [were] over; the Canal and its revenues [would] belong entirely to Egypt. We shall build the High Dam and we shall gain our usurped rights." [22]

These sharply divergent perceptions set the stage for a violent encounter. During the weeks that followed Nasser's action, the conflict broadened. Eden and Mollet privately sounded out American reactions to the situation. They were partially reassured by the fact that Secretary of State Dulles also appeared outraged by Egypt's action. In their conversations with Dulles, the British and French leaders again compared Nasser's action to Hitler's behavior at Munich and stated in the strongest terms that this type of Western appeasement must not be allowed to occur again. Secretary Dulles replied that "force was the last method to be tried, but the United States did not exclude the use of force if all other methods failed." [23] From this statement, Eden and Mollet inferred that the United States would, at best, present a united front with Britain and France in a show of force against Nasser and, at worst, remain benevolently neutral.

Britain and France now prepared for military action. They hoped to mount a lightning attack against Egypt, occupy the canal, depose Nasser, and then negotiate with his successor from a position of strength. In the course of these preparations, highly secret meetings took place with Israeli leaders for the purpose of coordinating the attack. Prime Minister Ben-Gurion and his chief of staff, General Moshe Dayan, were intent on seizing Gaza, the main base of fedayeen activities, and Sharm-el-Sheik on the Tiran Straits, from where the Egyptians maintained their blockade of the Gulf of Aqaba against ships bound for the port of Elath. Mollet pledged that if the Israelis would thrust into Sinai, French forces would join them, and Israel could seize Sinai and end the Egyptian blockade. Ben-Gurion hesitated; he feared that Egyptian bombers might attack Tel Aviv while Israeli forces were advancing into Sinai.[24] But when Eden pledged to use British airpower to prevent Egyptian air attacks on Israel, Ben-Gurion agreed to move into Sinai.

The final plans worked out among the three prime ministers were the following: Israel was to launch her attack on October 29. As soon as Dayan's troops began their advance into Sinai, Britain and France were to issue an ultimatum to Israel and Egypt, requiring them to cease fire, to withdraw their forces 10 miles on either side of the canal, and to "accept the temporary occupation by Anglo-French forces of key positions at Port Said, Ismailia and Suez." [25] When Israel had agreed to these terms and Egypt had rejected them, British bombers were to destroy the Egyptian air force and disrupt Egypt's communications and military capabilities in preparation for an Anglo-French invasion by paratroops from Cyprus and sea-borne forces from Malta. Then, when these forces had occupied the canal from Port Said to Suez, a further attack was contemplated, aimed at the occupation of Cairo, if necessary, in order to depose Nasser. As these arrangements were being concluded, by a fateful coincidence in time, thousands of miles away, Russian tanks rolled into Budapest to crush the two-day-old Hungarian revolt against Soviet domination.

On the afternoon of October 29, Israel's army launched its four-pronged advance against Egypt. Two thrusts were aimed at the canal while the third and fourth were to seal off the Gaza Strip and to seize Sharm-el-Sheik. On the following day, while Israeli forces were advancing rapidly across the Sinai Peninsula, Britain and France issued their prearranged ultimatum, which, in effect, told the Egyptians to retreat and the Israelis to advance. Caught by complete surprise, Nasser rejected the ultimatum but was unable to put up much military resistance. He was convinced, however, that world opinion in the United Nations would come to his rescue.

On October 31, British and French bombers began air attacks against Egyptian targets, including Cairo. In retaliation, Nasser sank ships in order to block the canal. Within six days, Israel overran the greater part of the Sinai Peninsula and achieved its main military objective, the occupation of Sharm-el-Sheik.

The United Nations entered the picture on October 30. The American delegation called for a meeting of the Security Council and, to the consternation of Britain and France, introduced a resolution calling upon Israel to leave Egypt without delay and asking all member states to "refrain from the use of force or threat of force." [26] The resolution was immediately vetoed by Britain and France. As the Security Council stood

paralyzed and the Anglo-French-Israeli action continued, Soviet Premier Nikolai Bulganin, in a news conference in
Moscow, warned of the possibility of a third world war and
declared that Soviet "volunteers" were ready to aid the Egyptian forces. He proposed that the United States and the Soviet
Union restore the peace through a joint show of force. This
suggestion was rejected as "unthinkable" by President Eisenhower. The United States was eager to see the Anglo-French
action ended, but it was equally eager to prevent the establishment of a Soviet presence in the Middle East.

On November 2, in an emergency session of the General
Assembly, the United States took a leading role in calling for
a cessation of the fighting and the immediate withdrawal of
the Anglo-French-Israeli forces from Egypt. The United States
found support for this action from a not particularly welcome
source—the Soviet Union. Thus, the United States found
itself in the paradoxical position of being allied in the United
Nations with its great antagonist in the cold war, and of being
at odds with its closest friends and allies, Britain and France.
By November 6, Britain had to yield. Confronted by United
Nations resolutions charging her with aggression, dismayed
by the action of the United States, and troubled by an increasingly hostile opposition at home, Prime Minister Eden
terminated his abortive venture. As one critical British analyst
summed it up: "The spectacle of over one hundred thousand
men setting off for a war which lasted barely a day and then
returning has few parallels in the long gallery of military im-
becility." [27] France had no choice but to follow suit, but Israel
still held on tenaciously to what her army had conquered in
the six days of the war.

The role of the American leadership, of course, was crucial
in the evolution of the crisis. Here, personalities played an
important part. Both President Eisenhower and Secretary
Dulles felt a sense of outrage because Eden and Mollet had

not bothered to consult them on a matter as important as military action in the Middle East at a time when a national election was imminent in the United States. From a purely military standpoint, only the Israelis were attaining their objectives. The Anglo-French punitive expedition seemed to be foundering and thus could not be presented to the General Assembly as a *fait accompli*. The United States, by supporting the Anglo-French venture, or even by taking a neutral view of it, would have risked the ill will of a large majority of the United Nations membership and, in addition, might have had to look on helplessly while the military action failed or bogged down. Moreover, such an American response might have persuaded many neutralists that the United States, by countenancing aggression in the Middle East, differed little from the Soviet Union which was aggressively crushing a rebellion in Hungary with military force. Most important, the United States feared the possibility of Soviet intervention in the Middle East through "volunteers" and the risk of sparking a major war through direct superpower confrontation in the contested area.

From the Soviet point of view, the Suez crisis constituted a great windfall: the British and French appeared to be digging their own graves in the Middle East and the United States seemed to be doing its best to help them. Thus, by appealing to the cause of Arab nationalism, the Soviet Union saw its opportunity to eject all Western influence from the Middle East and gain a foothold of its own there. The fact that Israel was allied with the two colonial powers also played into Soviet hands.

Britain and France were clearly the main losers in the Suez affair. In humiliation, they had to watch Nasser snatch a political victory from a military defeat. Abandoned by their closest and oldest ally, they had to admit that they could no longer act like great powers and that, in the last analysis, their initiative in world politics depended upon the decisions of the United States. The very issue that they had set out to rectify by force of arms—the internationalization of the Suez Canal—now seemed beyond redemption. For all practical purposes, the Suez crisis terminated Anglo-French authority in the Middle East. Suez had become another Dienbienphu.

The greatest victory in the Suez crisis was won by Arab nationalism. Nasser was now clearly master of the Suez Canal. The two great superpowers had supported him. Not only did he triumph in the showdown with Britain and France, but his other great foe, Israel, now came under increasing pressure to withdraw. Dag Hammarskjöld, secretary-general of the United Nations, had been successful in dispatching to the Middle East a specially constituted peace force, the United Nations Emergency Force (UNEF). Under strong American pressure, Israel agreed to evacuate most of the territories it had conquered from Egypt and, beginning on November 15, the UNEF soldiers replaced the Israeli troops. Only an explicit American guarantee, however, that Israel's right to free and innocent passage in the Gulf of Aqaba would not be infringed upon, persuaded the Israelis to evacuate the last fruits of their Sinai campaign, the Gaza Strip and the east coast of the Sinai Peninsula down to the Straits of Tiran. By March 1957, Israel had given up all the territories it had conquered, on the understanding that UNEF would prevent fedayeen raids from Jordan and the Gaza Strip. Hence, Israel emerged from the Sinai campaign with a marginal gain.

President Nasser was now at the zenith of his power. Among the Egyptian people he enjoyed the title of *rais,* or captain of the ship of state. With deep satisfaction, he watched the resignations of Eden and Mollet from their posts. Thus encouraged, he now planned to turn upon his archenemy, the Zionist state. In March 1957, he appointed an Egyptian civil governor of Gaza, a move that was viewed with indignation and misgivings in Israel. At the same time, Radio Cairo declared that "the Gulf of Aqaba will be closed to Israeli ships and our commandos will continue to sow terror in Israel." [28] Thus the seeds of the next war, which was to erupt a decade later, were sown.

The Six-Day War of 1967

Once again, time did not heal but exacerbated the tensions between the Arab states and Israel. Within the Arab world, deep rifts had appeared on the overriding question of policy vis-à-vis Israel. By early 1967, three basic positions had crystallized. First, the Syrians, who were the most radical and whose country was a major base for border raids against Israel, had created an organization named *El Fatah* or "conquest." Its commando units carried out attacks against Israel in the tradition of the earlier fedayeen raids. In addition, Syria's President Al Atassi demanded a war of liberation against Israel similar to the one being fought against the United States in Vietnam. Second, and at the other end of the spectrum, was King Faisal of Saudi Arabia, who was relatively friendly toward the West and who regarded the violent temper of the Syrians with considerable distrust. While the huge oil deposits of Saudi Arabia provided the king with a formidable economic weapon, they also made him dependent to some extent upon the Western nations for his revenue. President Nasser of Egypt found himself between these two rival factions. Eager to maintain his role as the embodiment of Arab nationalism, his ear was more sensitive to the gravitational pull of the Arab radicals than to the more conservative and traditional Arab leaders, such as King Faisal of Saudi Arabia and King Hussein of Jordan. This made him vulnerable to Syrian efforts to involve him in a larger war with Israel.

In April 1967, a major clash took place on the Israeli-Syrian border. Six Syrian MIG fighters were shot down by Israel in the course of the battle. El Fatah raids continued to mount in ferocity, and, on May 14, the prime minister of Israel, Levi Eshkol, declared that a serious confrontation with Syria would be inevitable if the attacks continued. The Syrians responded by declaring that Israel was concentrating huge armed forces on her border in preparation for an attack against Syria. Eshkol denied this charge and invited the Soviet ambassador to visit the areas in question. The Soviet diplomat refused. The pressure on President Nasser to help the Syrians was mounting rapidly. On May 16, Nasser proclaimed a state of emergency for the Egyptian armed forces and took measures to work out a joint Syrian-Egyptian defense agreement. The Syrian leadership, however, continued to taunt the Egyptian president by accusing him of "hiding behind the sheltering skirts of the United Nations Emergency Force." [29] A wave of emotion now spread throughout the Arab world from Casablanca to Baghdad. Demonstrations against Zionism took place in virtually every single Arab country. On May 16, the Palestine Service of Radio Cairo declared:

> The menace and challenge of Israel have persisted far too long. The very existence of Israel in our usurped land has endured beyond all expectation. An end must be put to the challenge of Israel and to its very existence. Welcome to aggression by Israel which will send us into action to destroy it! Welcome to the battle for which we have long waited! The hour of battle is imminent. In fact, this is the hour of battle.[30]

President Nasser chose to ride the emotional tide of Arab nationalism rather than to resist it. This meant, however, that he had to take an active part in escalating the crisis. Thus, he decided to terminate the presence of the United Nations Emergency Force in Egypt and the Gaza Strip. On May 18,

Foreign Minister Mahmoud Riad asked U Thant, secretary-general of the United Nations, to withdraw UNEF "as soon as possible." He reminded the secretary-general that the force had been stationed on Egyptian soil at the invitation of the Egyptian government and that its continued presence depended on Egyptian approval.

The United Nations Emergency Force had patrolled the 100-mile-long Egyptian-Israeli frontier for ten years. It had been stationed on the Egyptian side of the border but not on the Israeli side. During the decade of its existence, border eruptions had been kept to a minimum. The demand for its withdrawal caused considerable dismay at the United Nations. While U Thant never questioned Egypt's legal right to demand the withdrawal of the force, he expressed "serious misgivings" about its termination. He immediately referred the matter to the UNEF Advisory Committee. The Indian and Yugoslav representatives made it clear that their contingents were likely to be withdrawn in any case. Since they made up almost one-half of the 3,300-man force, this created additional pressure for withdrawal. Furthermore, UN forces were already being jostled out of their positions by Egyptian troops. Thus, the secretary-general complied with the Egyptian demand, reasoning that UNEF could no longer remain in the area if the consent of the host government were withdrawn.

Few actions have been discussed more heatedly by governments, the world press, and public opinion than U Thant's withdrawal of the United Nations Emergency Force. Criticism was particularly sharp in the United States, the United Kingdom, Canada and, of course, in Israel. The Israeli ambassador to the United Nations, Abba Eban, stated caustically that "the umbrella was removed at the precise moment it began to rain." U Thant answered these charges by stating that he had no alternative by law but to accede to a request that was rooted in Egypt's sovereign rights. He also reasoned that if he did not comply with the request of a sovereign government, consent for the admission of a United Nations peace-keeping force in a future crisis might be infinitely more difficult to obtain. Given all these conflicting considerations, the secretary-general made his difficult and fateful choice.

The withdrawal of UNEF brought the crisis to a new and much graver stage. Israeli and Egyptian forces now confronted each other directly across the border. Israel ordered a limited mobilization of reserves to which Egypt, on May 21, replied in kind. Encouraged by the ease with which he had accomplished the removal of the United Nations buffer force, and spurred by the groundswell of emotions in the Arab world, President Nasser, on May 22, announced the decision that was to become the direct cause of the Six-Day War: he closed the Straits of Tiran at the entrance of the Gulf of Aqaba to Israeli shipping, thereby blockading once again the port of Elath. In an emotional speech at the Egyptian Air Force Headquarters in Sinai he declared:

> The armed forces yesterday occupied Sharm-el-Sheik. What does this mean? It is affirmation of our rights and our sovereignty over the Gulf of Aqaba which constitutes territorial waters. Under no circumstances will we allow the Israeli flag to pass through the Gulf of Aqaba. The Jews threaten war. We tell them you are welcome, we are ready for war, but under no circumstances will we abandon any of our rights. This water is ours.[31]

The imposition of the blockade catapulted the crisis into the international realm. Israel had withdrawn from the Straits of Tiran only after she had received explicit assurances that the Western powers would guarantee freedom of passage for her ships. On May 23, Prime Minister Eshkol reminded the

Western powers to live up to their obligations and Abba Eban, Israel's foreign minister, was dispatched to Paris, London, and Washington to secure the necessary assurances.

The responses of the Western powers to Israel's appeal for help were sympathetic but did not amount to guarantees. President Lyndon Johnson described the blockade as "illegal and potentially dangerous to peace." It was unlikely, however, that in the light of the American experience in Vietnam, the United States would be prepared to risk military intervention in the Middle East. President Johnson, in fact, emphatically urged Israel not to take unilateral action. Little support came from anyone else. The British, too, were sympathetic but did not offer a definite commitment to keep the waterway open, and President De Gaulle of France, observing a glacial neutrality, stated: "France is committed in no sense or on any subject to any of the states involved." [32]

These responses were not reassuring to Israel. Increasing pressure was placed on Prime Minister Eshkol to assume a more belligerent position. On May 24, the United Nations Security Council convened but was unable to take any action whatsoever to lift the blockade. The sense of foreboding in Israel increased. On May 26, President Nasser asserted that the Gulf of Aqaba was only part of the major problem that was caused by Israel's aggression in simply existing; the response in Israel was electric. Pressure now became intense to appoint to the Ministry of Defense the hero of the 1956 Sinai campaign General Moshe Dayan. On the same day that Nasser delivered his belligerent address, his friend, Mohammed Hasanein Haikal, the editor of the leading Egyptian newspaper *Al-Ahram,* wrote a remarkably frank and perceptive article:

The closure of the Gulf of Aqaba means, first and last, that the Arab nation, represented by the UAR, has succeeded for the first time vis-a-vis Israel in changing by force a fait accompli imposed on it by force. To Israel this is the most dangerous aspect of the current situation, not who can impose the accomplished fact and who possesses the power to safeguard it. Therefore, it is not a matter of the Gulf of Aqaba but of something bigger. It is the whole philosophy of Israeli security. Hence, I say that Israel must attack.[33]

This was a fair assessment of Israel's predicament. On June 1, it was announced that General Dayan was appointed minister of defense. This was widely interpreted as a sign that Israel had decided that she could not depend on outside help and would therefore have to resort to a preemptive attack to break out of her hostile encirclement. On June 2, Ahmed Shukairy, leader of the Palestine Liberation Organization, called for a holy war for the liberation of Palestine. Addressing a large congregation in the Old City of Jerusalem, he declared that the Arabs wanted "fighters, not Beatles" and called upon Arab women to don battle dress, adding that "this is no time for lipstick and mini-skirts." Meanwhile, on June 3, General Dayan stated at a press conference that, while Israel welcomed all the help she could get on the diplomatic front, she wished to fight her own battles with her own troops. He added that he did "not want British or American boys to get killed" in the defense of Israel. Asked whether Israel had lost the military initiative, General Dayan replied: "If you mean to say we stand no chance in battle, then I cannot agree with you."[34] The brink was reached.

At 7:45 A.M. Monday, June 5, the Six-Day War began. The Israeli air force attacked Egyptian airfields in a series of lightning strikes. By the end of the week, the armed forces of Israel occupied the Sinai Peninsula, the Gaza Strip, the whole West Bank of the Jordan, the entire city of Jerusalem, and the Golan Heights. The armies of Egypt, Jordan, and Syria had been completely routed. Israel had destroyed or captured 430 aircraft and 800 tanks and had inflicted 15,000 fatal casualties on Arab troops. It had taken 5,500 officers and men as prisoners. Its own losses were 40 aircraft and 676 dead.

A study made by the Institute for Strategic Studies in London by Michael Howard and Robert Hunter summarizes the campaign:

> The third Arab-Israeli war is likely to be studied in Staff Colleges for many years to come. Like the campaigns of the younger Napoleon, the performance of the Israeli Defence Force provided a textbook illustration for all the classical principles of war: speed, surprise, concentration, security, information, the offensive—above all, training and morale. Airmen will note with professional approval how the Israeli air-force was employed first to gain command of the air by destruction of the enemy air-force, then to take part in the ground battle by interdiction of enemy communications, direct support of ground attacks and, finally, pursuit. The flexibility of the administrative and staff system will be examined and the attention of young officers drawn to the part played by leadership at all levels. Military radicals will observe how the Israelis attained this peak of excellence without the aid of drill sergeants and the barrack square. Tacticians will stress the importance they attached in this, as in previous campaigns, to being able to move and fight by night as effectively as they did by day. Above all, it will be seen how Israel observed a principle which appears in few military textbooks, but which armed forces neglect at their peril: the Clausewitzian principle of political context which the British ignored so disastrously in 1956. The Israeli High Command knew that it was not operating in a political vacuum. It worked on the assumption that it would have three days to complete its task before outside pressures compelled a cease-fire.[35]

On the deepest level, the secret of Israel's military success probably lay in the realization of every one of her citizens that if she had lost, it would have been the end of the nation's history. In that light, the Soviet delegate's comparison at the United Nations Security Council of Israel's offensive with Hitler's attack on the Soviet Union was hardly persuasive. In a sense, Israel's military system was the very opposite of that of Prussia in the nineteenth century. Whereas the Prussian system had resulted in the militarization of society, the Israeli approach led to the civilianization of the army. Officers maintained their authority not by orthodox discipline but by personal example. Thus, the Israelis got the utmost out of their men and their machines.

President Nasser was so shocked by the swiftness and efficiency of Israel's offensive that he believed, or purported to believe, that the United States and the United Kingdom had given assistance to the Zionists by maintaining an "air umbrella" over Israel. The truth was that in the Arab countries political fanaticism simply was no substitute for military expertise, and fantasies of victory could no longer mask the totality of the disaster.

Israel's leaders knew that they had to achieve their victory quickly to make it stick. They worked on the assumption that they had three days to defeat the Arabs before outside pressures compelled a cease-fire. In fact, they had four and needed five. The chorus of disapproval that arose even in the West when Israel ignored a United Nations cease-fire call and, on the fifth day of the war, opened its offensive against Syria, showed how narrow was the time margin in which Israel had to work. Israel knew that there was a tacit agreement between the two superpowers not to permit the Arab-Israeli war to escalate into a larger conflict provided the war was quickly brought to an end. Once it had ended, the great powers were reluctant to risk a second conflict in order to undo the victory that had been achieved in the first. Thus, a premium was placed on preemption and lightning speed of Israeli arms.

An analysis of the changes in power constellations after the

Six-Day War reveals some interesting comparisons and contrasts with the crisis of 1956. First, the Soviet Union had backed a loser this time, whereas she had been on the winning side a decade earlier. Most of the military hardware that the USSR had shipped to the Arab states was destroyed or captured by the Israelis. The United States, on the other hand, was on the winning side, and, superficially, her policy seemed successful. But on a deeper level, it was clear that the swiftness of Israel's victory had saved the United States from having to make some difficult decisions. Had the war gone badly for Israel or remained inconclusive, the United States might have been forced to intervene and risk a confrontation with the Soviet Union.

Israel, which had to withdraw in 1956, was determined this time not to yield its military gains except in exchange for an end to belligerency. Within six days, Israel had exchanged its vulnerability for a position of unprecedented military domination in the Middle East. Within two brief decades, a fledgling Jewish state in Palestine had become a formidable power.

The October War of 1973

Israel's swift and decisive victory in 1967 had left a legacy of shame and bitterness on the Arab side. Diplomacy had not been able to dislodge the Israelis from the five territories that they had captured from three Arab countries in June 1967: Sinai and the Gaza Strip from Egypt; Old Jerusalem and the West Bank from Jordan; and the Golan Heights from Syria. The UN Security Council had been able to adopt only a single resolution on the Middle East over a period of six years. That resolution, which was passed on November 22, 1967, linked a promise of secure and recognized boundaries to Israel with a promise of withdrawal from occupied territories to the Arabs. But neither side was willing to take the first step, and, therefore, the entire situation remained frozen. No face-to-face negotiations between Arabs and Israelis ever took place. The Arabs gazed across the cease-fire line with increasing fury and frustration as Israel made plans to populate the territories with Jewish settlers. Israel seemed bent on de facto annexation, and the Arabs seemed equally determined to prevent it.

Anwar Sadat, who became Egypt's new president after the death of Nasser in 1970, gradually and without much fanfare prepared the ground for an Arab counterattack. Unlike Nasser, the less flamboyant Sadat did not divide the Arab world but doggedly worked toward a consensus. The Soviet Union, while not prepared to give the Arabs offensive weapons against Israel, did replace the military hardware that had been captured or destroyed by Israel in 1967. The Soviets also trained Egyptian and Syrian commanders in Soviet military strategy and tactics in order to prevent a repetition of the debacle of the Six-Day War. By 1973, the Arabs were encouraged to believe that at least some of the lost territories could be regained by force of arms. Thus, the stage was set for yet another violent encounter.

On Yom Kippur, the Jewish Day of Atonement, Syria and Egypt launched a well-coordinated surprise attack. In the north, Syria attacked the vital Golan Heights, in an effort to regain the vantage point over Israeli settlements in the valley below. In the Sinai, Egypt threw a major military force across the Suez Canal, capturing Israeli positions on the eastern bank and sending Israel's defenders backward into the desert.

The Arab attack had not come as a complete surprise to the Israeli leadership. Defense Minister Moshe Dayan claimed several days later that he had had advance information that some sort of attack was imminent but had decided against a preemptive strike. The reason for this decision, according to

Mr. Dayan, was to "have the political advantage of not having attacked first, even at the expense of the military advantage." [36] Israel's image abroad would thus be improved with
resultant long-term political benefits.

The price that Israel paid for this apparent self-restraint
was heavy. On the Suez front, the Egyptians swarmed across
the canal in large numbers, laid down bridges, and landed
hundreds of tanks and other war materiel. They managed to
overrun the famous Israeli defense installation, the Bar-Lev
line, with heavy air and artillery assaults. The lightly defended Israeli positions had to be abandoned. On the Golan
Heights, an enormous Syrian force equipped with 800 tanks
plunged across the cease-fire line at four points. Commando
units landed by helicopter on Mount Hermon and seized a
major Israeli position. Overwhelmed by the force of the attack, Israeli defenders had to evacuate several outposts.

One explanation of these early Arab successes may be found
in Israel's perception of its own military superiority and of the
Arabs as notoriously poor, bumbling soldiers. The Israeli
leadership had convinced itself of its own superiority to such
an extent that it believed that any Arab attack would be suicidal. Israel, in short, was suffering from a case of military
hubris.

By the end of the first week of war, Israel had stemmed the
Arab onslaught, but the myth of its invincibility had nevertheless been shattered. Egypt had managed to insert almost
100,000 men on the East Bank of the Suez Canal and the
fiercest tank battles since World War II were raging in the
Sinai desert and the Golan Heights. Casualties were heavy on
both sides, and new Soviet ground-to-air missiles presented a
grave threat to the Israeli air force. Buoyed up by the successes
of Syria and Egypt, other Arab countries joined in the battle.
Iraq and Jordan supplied troops for the Syrian front, and
Saudi Arabia and other oil-rich Arab sheikdoms placed in-

creasing pressure on the United States to abandon its support of Israel.

As casualties mounted and both sides suffered staggering losses in war materiel, the superpowers entered the arena. The Soviet Union began to resupply the Arab states with ammunition and light weapons. When the United States decided to do the same for Israel, the Soviet Union escalated its supply operations to tanks and planes. This, too, was matched by the United States. Thus, by the end of the first week, the war had reached a new and dangerous plateau. Not only was the armor of both sides locked in a death struggle, but the fragile détente between the Soviet Union and the United States hung in the balance.

During the second week of war, Israel gradually gained the upper hand on both the Syrian and Egyptian fronts. After fierce tank battles in the Golan Heights, the Israelis not only threw back the Syrians but embarked on the road to Damascus. In the words of General Dayan: "We have to show them [the Syrians] that the road leads not only from Damascus to Tel Aviv, but from Tel Aviv to Damascus."[37] The Israeli advance into Syria came to a standstill at the village of Sasa, 20 miles from the Syrian capital.

On the Egyptian front, the Israelis, in a daring tactical maneuver, inserted troops on the West Bank of the Suez Canal on Egyptian territory. Their aim was to encircle the Egyptian troops on the East Bank in Sinai and to cut off their retreat across the canal back to Egypt. After massive air and tank battles, the Israeli objectives were attained. The Egyptian troops were trapped in two large pockets in Sinai and the Third Army was at Israel's mercy for its supply of food and water. At this juncture, with the balance shifting rapidly in Israel's favor, the superpowers once more intervened.

On October 21, acting with great urgency to protect its Egyptian ally, the Soviet leadership agreed on a formula for a cease-fire resolution with Secretary of State Henry Kissinger. This resolution, which was rushed through the UN Security Council on the following morning under joint Soviet-American sponsorship, provided for a cease-fire in place and called on all parties to start immediate negotiations toward implementing the 1967 Security Council plan for peace in the Middle East. The cease-fire began shakily, with the Egyptian forces trapped behind Israeli lines trying to break out and Israel seeking to destroy the Egyptian forces once and for all. A second cease-fire call still did not end the fighting. As a result, the Soviet Union proposed that a joint Soviet-American peace force be dispatched to the Middle East. This proposal was rejected by the United States which feared the possibility of a military confrontation in the area. The Soviet Union then declared that it would introduce its own troops into the area unilaterally. To this Soviet threat, President Nixon responded by placing the armed forces of the United States on military alert.

During the "alert" crisis, a compromise was worked out. The UN Security Council approved a third resolution sponsored by the nonaligned countries that authorized the secretary-general to send a UN buffer force to the area. This 7,000-man emergency force would be patterned after the old UN Emergency Force that had been created by Dag Hammarskjöld in 1956. It was to exclude the permanent members of the Security Council from active participation. To save face, however, the two superpowers insisted on sending a small number of observers into the cease-fire area. The first UN troops began to arrive from Cyprus on October 27. By then, all fronts were quiet. The precarious Soviet-American détente had held after all.

As the "October war" drew to a close after seventeen days of violent fighting, Israel had won another victory, but a costly one in blood and treasure. While it had managed to roll back the initial Arab advance and had assumed a commanding military position on both fronts, the price paid in human lives for this achievement was far higher than the toll that had been exacted in the war of 1967. The heavy losses made the victory a somewhat joyless one. Moreover, the immediate postwar Israeli attitude on the question of the occupied territories hardened. If an Arab surprise attack had been launched along the pre-1967 armistice lines, then Tel Aviv and Jerusalem—not the Golan Heights and the Bar-Lev line—would have had to absorb the initial shock. Thus, in the Israeli view, tens of thousands of their people could be killed if such a surprise attack were only slightly more successful than the one launched in October 1973. In Abba Eban's words:

> If we had been mad enough to abandon the Golan Heights and Sharm el Sheikh and all the Sinai and the whole West Bank, would not the massive attack launched on October 6 have murdered thousands of our civilians, devastated our population centers and brought us to catastrophe? I tell you, a massacre more hideous than Auschwitz would have been a real prospect and Israel's survival would be in doubt. To suggest a restoration of the pre-1967 lines is sheer irresponsibility in the light of what has been revealed.[38]

Just as the setbacks of the first few days of war were deeply etched on Israeli minds, so the Arabs cherished and glorified their short-lived victory. Despite his ultimate defeat, President Sadat proclaimed that "Egyptian forces had performed a miracle by any military standard" and had thus "restored the honor of the nation." Egypt and Syria had been able to break out of the frustration and futility of unending diplomatic stalemate. They had placed Israel on notice that it could not hold on indefinitely to occupied territory unless it was prepared to accept the risk of yet another war with the odds against it. As Egypt's foreign minister, Mohamed El Zayyat, put it:

> The Israeli attitude had been to assume that they were invincible and that we were meek and weak. They pictured Egyptians as people who would never fight. The argument that this occupied territory serves as a protective buffer for Israel—that was the argument of Hitler. What we are asking for is very simple: that our territorial integrity and the rights of the Palestinians be respected. These two elements are the *sine qua non* conditions for peace in the Middle East.[39]

Thus, the fourth round ended with positions hardened on both sides and with passions unallayed. The Israelis were embittered by the Yom Kippur surprise attack and, in their bitterness, tended to forget that the attack was launched in order to regain lost territories. The Arabs were so intent upon restoring their dignity and regaining lost ground that they believed that they had won even though actually they had lost. Neither side was able any longer to understand the fears of the other. All empathy was lost. The superpowers, for two weeks, had made the desert a proving ground for new destructive weapons. Kings played chess while pawns bled on the battlefield. Only when the kings were fearful that the battle might engulf them, too, did they stop the bloodshed. Once again, the United Nations was used as a rescue operation at the edge of the abyss. Frantic cease-fire resolutions had to take the place of preventive diplomacy. And only a fragile superpower détente prevented yet another fateful escalation with dire consequences for mankind. One positive result came out of the October War of 1973. Under superpower pressure, Israelis and Arabs did agree to meet in a peace conference in Geneva in December 1973. This was their first face-to-face diplomatic encounter in a quarter of a century. As Abba Eban put it: "For something to be born, the parents have to meet at least once." Chastened by four wars, Arabs and Jews alike began to feel that unless wisdom and reason ultimately prevailed, the only alternative seemed mutual exhaustion.

The role of the United States during and after the October War was primarily defined by Secretary of State Henry Kissinger. For the next three years, the Middle Eastern scene was dominated by the tireless peace-making efforts of this extraordinary statesman.

Kissinger's role in the October War can be described as neither pro-Israeli nor pro-Arab. In essence, it was pro-equilibrium. Before the war erupted, Kissinger perceived Israel as the stronger side and thus warned the Jewish leaders "not to pre-empt." But when he turned out to have been mistaken and Syria and Egypt launched their coordinated surprise attack, Kissinger switched sides and provided American military aid to Israel in order to restore the military balance. And when the Israelis, with this American assistance, gained the upper hand, Kissinger switched sides again and insisted on the rescue of 100,000 trapped Egyptian soldiers. When a cease-fire was finally proclaimed by the United Nations, both sides were exhausted and roughly even—exactly what Kissinger had wanted. It had always been his firm belief that only a war without victory or defeat could contain the seeds of peace.

As Kissinger surveyed the ravages of the October War, he conceived his plan for peace in the Middle East. He decided to subdivide the problem into manageable segments instead of addressing it in its totality. He would approach it step by step, beginning with the least forbidding obstacle, and then, after having built a basis of trust between the rivals, he would try to negotiate the more formidable hurdles. A first tentative step had already been taken. Egypt had agreed to talk to Israel. If Kissinger could achieve a military disengagement between Israel and Egypt, a momentum toward peace might then be set in motion. It would perhaps then be possible to leap over yet another hurdle and to effect a military disengagement between Syria and Israel. If such military interim agreements were possible, perhaps one might be able to move the rivals toward political accommodation. Once Egypt and Syria had entered into negotiations with Israel, Saudi Arabia might be persuaded to lift her oil embargo, and, if luck held, it might even be conceivable to think about a compromise between Israel and the Palestinians and a Jerusalem settlement. Such was Kissinger's train of thought. The peace-making process would be like a steeplechase, with each successive hurdle higher and more treacherous. But at least, Kissinger believed, the step-by-step approach would yield some limited successes and should not be a total failure.

The objective that Kissinger had in mind, of course, was equilibrium. Israel would have to withdraw from some of the conquered territories, but within the context of her national security. The diplomatic reemergence of the Arabs would be encouraged, but within a context of realism and responsibility. An effort would be made to woo the Arabs away from the Soviet Union. They would come to the United States be-because, in Kissinger's judgment, "they could get weapons from the Russians, but territory only from the United States." Thus, by delivering some real estate to the Arabs, Soviet power in the Middle East would be diminished and American influence strengthened. To achieve this objective, however, pressure would have to be applied on Israel. She would have to be encouraged to trade territory for security. And if Kissinger's reasoning was wrong, he would have to protect Israel by always being generous with arms.

Kissinger's step-by-step approach to peace was not greeted with general acclaim. The Soviet Union was highly critical and pushed for a general peace conference to be held in Geneva. There was also criticism in the United States. Numerous Middle East experts asserted that Kissinger's approach was that of a doctor who planned to stitch up only part of a wound while permitting a raging infection to continue unattended.

By concentrating on Egypt, these critics stated, Kissinger intended to woo the moderate Sadat away from the Arab camp. This would not only remove the most conciliatory voice from Arab councils, but it would postpone and ultimately make more difficult the moment of truth. The heart of the matter, Kissinger's critics declared, was neither Egypt nor Syria, but the problem of the Palestinians, which Kissinger had chosen to postpone indefinitely, not to mention Jerusalem, which he had chosen to ignore completely. Thus, as George Ball, one of Kissinger's most trenchant critics, put it, "the step-by-step approach was the work of a tactician when the times called for a strategist."

Kissinger was undaunted by these attacks. He believed that the aftermath of an inconclusive war was the best time for a concentrated peace effort. Shortly after the last shot had been fired, he decided to commit his skill, energy, and reputation to a highly personal diplomatic peace offensive in the Middle East. During the next few months, he would visit virtually every Arab capital, shuttle between Aswan and Jerusalem, and later between Damascus and Jerusalem. Sadat would call him "brother"; Faisal would welcome him even though he was a Jew; Hussein would pilot him in the royal helicopter; even Assad would learn to like him; and Golda Meir would have endless conversations with him in her kitchen. The end result of this extraordinary diplomatic *tour de force* was the successful negotiation of the first two hurdles. In January 1974, Kissinger was able to produce a military disengagement accord between Israel and Egypt, and four months later, after immense effort, he was able to achieve a similar accord between Israel and Syria.

The high point of Kissinger's "shuttle diplomacy" was the Sinai agreement between Israel and Egypt, signed in Geneva in September 1975.

The Sinai agreement bore the typical imprimatur of a Kissinger settlement. Neither side was happy with it but neither side was able to produce a better alternative that was acceptable to both. The Israelis promised to return two mountain passes and an oil field. In exchange, they received pledges from President Sadat to the effect that Egypt would refrain from the threat or use of force against the Jewish state. Sadat also agreed to continue negotiations toward a final peace agreement and to extend the mandate of the UN buffer force annually for at least three years.

What finally made it possible, however, for Israel to conclude the agreement was a specific American commitment that Kissinger had not made before. Kissinger offered to provide 200 American civilian technicians, who would be stationed in the Sinai *between* the contending parties. They would serve as a kind of early warning system in case either side planned an attack upon the other, and they would report to both Israel and Egypt. In addition, Kissinger pledged that he would recommend an American aid commitment of $2.3 billion to Israel. Israel, which did not trust the UN buffer force, found the pledge of a small symbolic American presence reassuring. The aid package, too, was attractive, and furthermore, Prime Minister Rabin could tell the opposition that Israel still retained over 85 percent of the Sinai and the entire Gaza Strip. Sadat received his coveted mountain passes and oil fields plus an American commitment of $700 million needed for the impoverished Egyptian economy. The 200 Americans were welcome too, since their presence only underlined Sadat's growing independence from the Soviet Union. Thus, Egypt gained some territorial allowances and Israel received political concessions. What could not be bridged between the parties directly was bridged by American commitments. Some senators grumbled that the 200 Americans in the Sinai reminded them of the beginning of Vietnam, but Kissinger was quick to point out that the Americans in the Sinai were civilians who were to aid both sides in keeping the peace, not soldiers who were to help one side to win a war.

On the whole, Kissinger was pleased with the second Sinai interim agreement. It was, after all, the first accord between Israel and an Arab nation that was not the immediate consequence of war. He knew that it was far from a genuine peace treaty, but he was convinced that his step-by-step approach was still the best way to proceed. In his judgment, most Americans were still willing to take great risks to preserve the state of Israel, but were *not* willing to take such risks to preserve Israel's conquests.

During most of 1976, a *deus ex machina* postponed the moment of truth for Israel. Syria and the Palestine Liberation Organization, Israel's two bitterest adversaries, turned on each other in a murderous war in Lebanon. While it lasted, Israel was in no mood to make concessions. By 1977, however, as Jimmy Carter assumed the presidency of the United States and Menachem Begin became prime minister of Israel, the Lebanese war had tapered off and a renewed Arab alliance confronted the Jewish state.

It had become clear by 1977 that the step-by-step approach had reached a dead end. The heart of the matter was now the problem of the Palestinians. Israel was confronted with a dreadful choice.

If she agreed to negotiate with the PLO and return some territories for the purpose of creating a Palestinian state, such a state would clearly be a dagger pointed at the heart of Israel. If, on the other hand, she refused to negotiate, she risked another war or another oil embargo, as well as slow economic strangulation and increasing isolation. Despite the risks involved, President Carter believed that, ultimately, Israel would have to face the Palestinians as a reality that would not go away, just as America, after more than two decades, had to adjust herself to the reality of a China that was Communist. There were now 3 million Israelis and 3 million Palestinians. Both were permanent realities and, sooner or later, a compromise solution would have to be discovered. The alternative was yet another war.

In November 1977 the world held its breath when, in a spectacular and unprecedented move, President Sadat visited the Jewish state and addressed the Israeli Knesset. While neither Sadat nor Prime Minister Begin made any substantive concessions during that first face-to-face encounter in Jerusalem, both leaders made a solemn pledge never again to go to war with one another. While peace, unlike war, does not break out, the Sadat mission was widely heralded as a major turning point in the thirty-year-old conflict between Arab and Jew. At last an Arab statesman had openly recognized the Jewish state. Two old enemies had suddenly become friends.

Conclusions

When people of good will despair of finding a solution, they tend to find solace in time as the great healer of wounds. This confidence in the power of time has not been warranted by the experience of the four wars between the Arab states and Israel. The shock inflicted on the Arab consciousness by the establishment of Israel and the resulting homelessness of a million native Palestinians grew more, rather than less, acute as Arab nationalism gathered momentum. This trauma was accentuated by the fact that Israel—four times its original size—was seen as an ever-growing menace by the Arab world. Many Arabs feared that if expansion continued at this rate, Israel would soon dominate the whole of Palestine.

On the Jewish side, time has turned Israel into virtually a garrison state. How strange it is to contemplate the fact that the Jews who lived homeless in the Diaspora for two millennia should, within the short span of two decades, create a state with such fearful military capability. Who would have guessed that the Jews, to whom military things were anathema, should now make them their first priority? Yet this is exactly what time has done.

Four times the Arabs made fatal mistakes that the Zionists used to their advantage: in 1948, five Arab armies invaded a Jewish state whose modest boundaries had been assigned to it by the United Nations. The Jews repelled the invaders and engaged in some annexation of their own, managing to enlarge their territory. The Sinai campaign of 1956 demonstrated vividly what Israeli arms could do even though the territorial gains had to be given up. In 1967, Nasser's blunder, the blockade of Aqaba, led directly to his humiliation and to Israel's spectacular victory. And in October 1973, the Israelis turned an initial setback into yet another costly victory. The question now remains what Israel will learn from the lesson of her triumphs and the Arabs from the bitterness of their defeats.

A victor's peace, history teaches us, is seldom lasting. Neither is total defeat. To be durable, a peace must be constructed on a measure of equality. The flush of victory sometimes makes the victor hard and brittle. He then no longer understands the pain and anguish of the vanquished. His realism then becomes another word for lack of empathy. This was the danger that Israel faced after 1973. The Arabs, on the other hand, unable to cope with a terrible reality, took refuge in their fantasies. Their dreams and their despair, rather than the facts, determined policy. They learned in 1967 what the Jews had always known: the utter desolation of defeat and homelessness. And in 1973, their honor had to be restored at all costs, even at the price of yet another setback.

There is one ultimate and final paradox that emerges from Israel's victories. The four wars with the Arabs created a situation in which 3 million Jews came to control territories that contained nearly 1.5 million Arabs. It is difficult to see how Israel can keep the fruits of victory and yet remain a Zionist state. It may be that within its boundaries it will be compelled to revert to the older concept of a Palestine that was once shared peacefully between Arab and Jew.

Perhaps this is the form that destiny assumes on earth. Zionism for the Jews was a response to the need to save their lives. In their own need and plight, they drove more than a million other human beings to despair. Of the two nationalisms that clashed in Palestine, the Jewish was militarily superior but not politically stronger. The vanquished are yearning for redress. Zionism, to endure, will have to find the courage not to inflict on others what had been inflicted on the Jews in history. This will take a generosity of spirit that had seldom been extended to the Jews in their Diaspora. According to their faith, they had been chosen to have a great capacity for suffering. Now, at long last, they are no longer chosen; they themselves must choose.

Notes

1. John Neary, "The Bloody Dawn of Israel," *Life* (May 1973), p. 28.
2. Dan Kurzman, *Genesis 1948* (New York: Signet, 1972), p. 26.
3. *Ibid.*, p. 27.
4. David Horowitz, *State in the Making* (New York: Knopf, 1953), p. 140.
5. *Ibid.*, p. 141.
6. Larry Collins and Dominique Lapierre, *O Jerusalem* (New York: Simon & Schuster, 1972), p. 27.
7. Kurzman, *op. cit.*, p. 38.
8. Collins and Lapierre, *op. cit.*, p. 30.
9. *Ibid.*, p. 78.
10. *Ibid.*, p. 80.
11. *Ibid.*, p. 81.
12. Kurzman, *op. cit.*, p. 120.
13. *Ibid.*, p. 123.
14. *Ibid.*, p. 124.
15. *Ibid.*, p. 126.
16. Collins and Lapierre, *op. cit.*, p. 345.
17. *Ibid.*, p. 300.
18. Anthony Nutting, *Nasser* (New York: Dutton, 1972), p. 143.
19. Hugh Thomas, *Suez* (New York: Harper & Row, 1966), p. 163.
20. *Ibid.*
21. *Ibid.*
22. Nutting, *op. cit.*, p. 145.
23. Anthony Eden, *Full Circle*, quoted by Herbert Feis in *Foreign Affairs*, (July 1960), p. 600.
24. Nutting, *op. cit.*, p. 163.
25. *Ibid.*
26. United Nations Document 5/3712, October 29, 1956.
27. Thomas, *op. cit.*, p. 164.
28. Keesing's Research Report, *The Arab-Israeli Conflict* (New York: Scribner, 1968), p. 8.
29. Michael Howard and Robert Hunter, *Israel and the Arab World: The Crisis of 1967* (London: Institute for Strategic Studies, 1967), p. 17.
30. *Ibid.*
31. *Ibid.*, p. 20.
32. *Ibid.*, p. 22.
33. Cited in *Ibid.*, p. 24.
34. Keesing's Research Report, *op. cit.*, p. 25.
35. Howard and Hunter, *op. cit.*, p. 39.

36. *The New York Times,* October 14, 1973.
37. *The New York Times,* October 21, 1973.
38. *Time* (October 29, 1973), p. 44.
39. *Ibid.,* p. 45.

Selected Bibliography

COLLINS, LARRY, and DOMINIQUE LAPIERRE. *O Jerusalem.* New York: Simon & Schuster, 1972.

HOWARD, MICHAEL, and ROBERT HUNTER. *Israel and the Arab World: The Crisis of 1967.* London: Institute for Strategic Studies, 1967.

KURZMAN, DAN. *Genesis 1948.* New York: Signet, 1972.

NUTTING, ANTHONY. *Nasser.* New York: Dutton, 1972.

STOESSINGER, JOHN G. *Henry Kissinger: The Anguish of Power.* New York: Norton, 1976.

THOMAS, HUGH. *Suez.* New York: Harper & Row, 1966.

7.

Why Nations Go to War

Even in our sleep
Pain that we cannot forget
Falls drop by drop upon the heart
Until in our own despair
Against our will
Comes wisdom
Through the awful grace of God.

Aeschylus

"If you look too deeply into the abyss," said Nietzsche, "the abyss will look into you." The face of war in our time is so awesome and so terrible that the first temptation is to recoil and turn away. Who of us has not despaired and concluded that the entire spectacle of war was a manifestation of organized insanity? Who of us has not had moments in which he has been tempted to dismiss the efforts of those working for peace as futile Sisyphean labor? Medusa-like, the face of war, with its relentless horror, threatens to destroy anyone who looks at it for long.

Yet we must find the courage to confront the abyss. I deeply believe that war is a sickness, though it may be mankind's "sickness unto death." No murderous epidemic has

221

ever been conquered without exposure, pain, and danger, or by ignoring the bacilli. But in the end, man's faculty of reason and his courage have prevailed and even the plague was overcome. The Black Death that ravaged our planet centuries ago today is but a distant memory.

I know that the analogy between sickness and war is open to attack. It has been fashionable to assert that war is not an illness but, like aggression, an ineradicable part of human nature. I challenge this assumption. While aggression may be inherent in us all, war is learned behavior and, as such, can be unlearned and, ultimately, selected out entirely. There have been other habits of mankind that seemed impossible to shed. In the Ice Age, when people lived in caves, incest was perfectly acceptable. No one except mother and sister was around. Today, incest is virtually gone. Cannibalism provides an even more dramatic case. Thousands of years ago, human beings ate each other and drank each other's blood. That, too, was part of "human nature." Even a brief century ago, millions of Americans believed that God had ordained white people to be free and black people to be slaves. Why else would He have created them in different colors? Yet, slavery, once a part of "human nature," was abolished because human beings showed a capacity for growth. The growth came slowly, after immense suffering, but it *did* come. "Human nature" had been changed. Like slavery and cannibalism, war too can be eliminated from mankind's arsenal of horrors.

It seems, however, that men abandon their bad habits only when catastrophe is close at hand. The intellect alone is not enough. Men must be shaken, almost shattered, before changing. A grave illness must pass its crisis before it is known whether the patient will live or die. Most appropriately, the ancient Chinese had two characters for crisis: one connoting danger and the other, opportunity. The danger of extinction is upon us, but so is the opportunity for a better life for all men on this planet.

We must therefore make an effort to look Medusa in the face and to diagnose the sickness. Diagnosis is no cure, of course, but it is the first and the most necessary step. I shall attempt this diagnosis by suggesting certain common themes from the six case studies.

When I first began work on the cases, I did not know what conclusions I would reach. I was afraid, in fact, that I might reach no general conclusions whatsoever. The landscape of war differed so much from case to case that I despaired of finding a reliable roadmap. As my work progressed, however, certain common themes emerged. Gradually, they took on shape and meaning and as I reached the end of my journey, they thrust themselves upon me with clarity and force. I hesitate to state these themes as definitive conclusions and prefer instead to set them forth in the hope that they might engage the reader in a dialogue. If he is challenged and pursues my quest to greater depths, I shall have been well served.

The first general theme that compels attention is that no nation that began a major war in this century emerged a winner. Austria-Hungary and Germany, which precipitated World War I, went down to ignominious defeat; Hitler's Germany was crushed into unconditional surrender; the North Korean attack was thwarted by collective action and ended in a draw; although the Vietnam war ended in a Communist victory, it would be far too simple to blame the Communists exclusively for its beginning; the Arabs who invaded the new Jewish state in 1948 lost territory to the Israelis in four successive wars; and Pakistan, which wished to punish India through preemptive war, found itself dismembered in the process. In all cases, those who began a war came out a cropper. The nature or the ideology of the government that started a war seems to have made little, if any, difference. Defeat came to aggressors whether they were capitalists or Communists, white or non-white, Western or non-Western, rich or poor.

In the nineteenth century, by contrast, most wars were won by the governments that started them. Only those who aspired to the big prize like Napoleon suffered ultimate defeat. War then was still a rational pursuit, fought for limited objectives. Twentieth-century aggressors, on the other hand, tended to be more demanding and more ruthless: they fought for total stakes and hence made war a question of survival. Those who were attacked had to fight for life itself. Courage born of desperation proved to be a formidable weapon. In the end, those who began the war were stemmed, turned back, and in some cases, crushed completely. In no case did any nation that began a war in our time achieve its ends.

In the atomic age, war between nuclear powers is suicidal; wars between small countries with big friends are likely to be inconclusive and interminable; hence, decisive war in our time has become the privilege of the impotent. It has become almost banal to say that the atomic age has fundamentally altered the nature of war. No nuclear power can tell another: "Do as I say or I shall kill you," but is reduced to saying: "Do as I say or I shall kill us both," which is an entirely different matter. Thus, when everybody is somebody, nobody is anybody. But it is not only nuclear countries that cannot win wars against each other. A small country with a good tie to a big ally also can no longer be defeated. The wars in Korea, Vietnam, and the Middle East all illustrate this point. The North Koreans were unable to defeat South Korea so long as the United States was willing to support the South and to neutralize the North's successes. And the South Koreans could not defeat the North so long as China and the Soviet Union were willing to render assistance. Thus, in the

end, the Korean War ended with the frontiers virtually un-
changed. The main difference was the large number of dead
Koreans on *both* sides. In Vietnam, the Soviet Union and
China sent enough supplies to offset the results of American
bombings; and the deserts of the Middle East became veritable proving grounds for the testing of new superpower
weapons. Thus, wars between small nations with big friends
will be interminable so long as the ally of the weaker side
is willing to continue his support. Neither side can win;
only the casualties mount. In our time, decisive victories seem
possible only for nations without big friends or for the
impotent. Thus, Bangladesh was able to break away from
Pakistan because none of the great powers considered the
issue important enough to restore the status quo by force
of arms. Nor did the genocidal violence perpetrated by the
Tutsi tribe against the Hutu people in Central Africa stir
the great powers into action. Thus, the paradox of war in the
atomic age may be summarized as follows: the power of big
states vis-à-vis each other has been reduced if not altogether
cancelled out, while the power of small and friendless states
vis-à-vis each other has been proportionately enhanced.

*In our time, unless the vanquished is destroyed completely,
a victor's peace is seldom lasting. Those peace settlements
that are negotiated on a basis of equality are much more
permanent and durable.* In 1918, Germany was defeated
but not crushed. Versailles became the crucible for Hitler's
Germany, which was then brought down only through unconditional surrender. The Korean settlement was negotiated
between undefeated equals. Both sides were unhappy, but
neither side was so unhappy that it wished to overturn the
settlement and initiate yet another war. An uneasy armistice
or truce was gradually recognized as a possible basis for a peace
settlement. The relative insecurity of each side thus became
the guarantor of the relative security of both. Israel learned

this lesson in October 1973. The victor's peace of 1967 had left the Arabs in a state of such frustration that they were compelled to try their hand once more at war. With their dignity restored in 1973, they found it psychologically possible to meet with Israelis in a face-to-face diplomatic encounter for the first time in a quarter of a century.

Turning to the problem of the outbreak of war, the case studies indicate the crucial importance of the personalities of leaders. I am less impressed by the role of abstract forces such as nationalism, militarism, or alliance systems that traditionally have been regarded as the causes of war. Nor does a single one of the six cases indicate that economic factors played a vital part in precipitating war. The personalities of leaders, on the other hand, have often been decisive. The outbreak of World War I illustrates this point quite clearly. Conventional wisdom has blamed the alliance system for the spread of the war. Specifically, the argument runs, Kaiser Wilhelm's alliance with Austria dragged Germany into the war against the Allied Powers. This analysis, however, totally ignores the role of the Kaiser's personality during the gathering crisis. Supposing Wilhelm had had the fortitude to continue his role as mediator and to restrain Austria instead of engaging in paranoid delusions and accusing England of conspiring against Germany? The disaster might have been averted and then the conventional wisdom would have praised the alliance system for saving the peace instead of blaming it for causing the war. In truth, the emotional balance or lack of balance of the German Kaiser turned out to be absolutely crucial. Similarly, the relentless mediocrity of the leading personalities on all sides no doubt contributed to the disaster. Looking at the outbreak of World War II, there is no doubt that the victor's peace of Versailles and the galloping inflation of the 1920s brought about the rise of Nazi Germany. But once again, it was the personality of

Hitler that was decisive. A more rational leader would have consolidated his gains and certainly would not have attacked the Soviet Union. And if Russia had to be attacked, then a rational man would have made contingency plans to meet the Russian winter instead of counting blindly on an early victory. In the Korean War, the *hubris* of General Mac-Arthur probably prolonged the conflict by two years, and in Vietnam, the fragile egos of at least two American presidents who could not face the facts first escalated the war quite disproportionately and then postponed its ending quite unreasonably. In the Middle East, the volatile personality of Gamal Abdel Nasser was primarily responsible for the closing of the Gulf of Aqaba which precipitated the Six-Day War of 1967. And in 1971, Yahya Khan, the leader of West Pakistan, took his country into war with India because he would not be "cowed down" by a woman. In all these cases, a fatal flaw or ego weakness in a leader's personality turned out to be of crucial importance. It may, in fact, have spelled the difference between the outbreak of war and the maintenance of peace.

The case material reveals that perhaps the most important single precipitating factor in the outbreak of war is misperception. Such distortion may manifest itself in four different ways: in a leader's image of himself; a leader's view of his adversary's character; a leader's view of his adversary's intentions toward himself; and, finally, a leader's view of his adversary's capabilities and power. Each of these is of such importance that it merits separate and careful treatment.

There is a remarkable consistency in the self-images of most national leaders on the brink of war. Each confidently expects victory after a brief and triumphant campaign. Doubt about the outcome is the voice of the enemy and therefore incomprehensible. This recurring atmosphere of optimism is not to be dismissed lightly by the historian as an ironic example of human folly. It assumes a powerful emotional momentum of its own and thus itself becomes one of the causes of war. Anything that fuels such optimism about a quick and decisive victory makes war more likely and anything that dampens it becomes a cause of peace.

This common belief in a short, decisive war is usually the overflow from a reservoir of self-delusions held by the leadership about both itself and nation. The Kaiser's appearance in shining armor in August 1914 and his promise to the German nation that its sons would be back home "before the leaves had fallen from the trees" was matched by similar scenes of overconfidence and military splendor in Austria, in Russia, and in the other nations on the brink of war. Hitler's confidence in an early German victory in Russia was so unshakable that no winter uniforms were issued to the soldiers and no preparations whatsoever made for the onset of the Russian winter. In November 1941, when the mud of autumn turned to ice and snow, the cold became the German soldier's bitterest enemy. Tormented by the Arctic temperatures, men died, machines broke down, and the quest for warmth all but eclipsed the quest for victory. Hitler's hopes and delusions about the German superman were shattered in the frozen wastes of Russia. The fact that Hitler had fought in World War I and seen that optimism crumble in defeat did not prevent its reappearance. When North Korea invaded South Korea, her leadership expected victory within two months. The Anglo-French campaign at Suez in 1956 was spurred by the hope of a swift victory. In Pakistan, Yahya Khan hoped to teach Indira Gandhi a lesson modelled on the Six-Day War in Israel. And in Vietnam, every American escalation in the air or on the ground was an expression of the hope that a few more bombs, a few more troops, would bring decisive victory.

Thus, leaders on all sides typically engage in self-delusions on the eve of war. Only the war itself then provides the stinging ice of reality and ultimately helps restore a measure of perspective in the leadership. The price for this recapture of reality is high indeed. It is unlikely that there ever was a war that fulfilled the initial hopes and expectations of *both* sides.

Distorted views of the adversary's character also help to precipitate a conflict. As the pressure mounted in July 1914, the German Kaiser explosively admitted that he "hated the Slavs, even though one should not hate anyone." This hatred no doubt influenced his decision to end his role as mediator and to prepare for war. Similarly, his naive trust in the honesty of the Austrian leaders prompted him to extend to them the blank-check guarantee that dragged him into war. In reality, the Austrians were more deceitful than he thought and the Russians more honest. Worst of all, the British leadership which worked so desperately to avert a general war was seen by Wilhelm as the center of a monstrous plot to encircle and destroy the German nation. Hitler, too, had no conception of what Russia really was like. He knew nothing of the history and depth of the Russian land and believed that it was populated by subhuman barbarians who could be crushed with one decisive stroke and then be made to serve as slaves for German supermen. This relentless hatred and contempt for Russia became a crucial factor in Hitler's ill-fated assault of 1941. Perhaps the most important reason for the American military intervention in Vietnam was the misperception of the American leadership about the nature of Communism in Asia. President Lyndon Johnson committed more than half a million combat troops to an Asian land war because he believed that Communism was still a monolithic octopus with North Vietnam its tentacle. He did this more than a decade after the death of Stalin, at a time when Communism had splintered into numerous ideological and political fragments.

His total ignorance of Asia in general and of Vietnam in particular made him perceive the Vietnam war in terms of purely Western categories: a colossal shoot-out between the forces of Communism and those of anti-Communism. The fact that Ho Chi Minh saw the Americans as the successors of French imperialism whom he was determined to drive out was completely lost upon the President. Virtue, righteousness, and justice were fully on his side, he thought. America, the child of light, had to defeat the child of darkness in a twentieth-century crusade. Mutual contempt and hatred also hastened the coming of the wars between the Arab states and Israel and between India and Pakistan. In the former case, the Arab view of Israel as an alien and hostile presence was a precipitating cause of conflict. And, in the latter, the two religions of Hinduism and Islam led directly to the creation of two hostile states that clashed in bloody conflict three times in a single generation.

If a leader on the brink of war believes that his adversary will attack him, the chances of war are fairly high. If both leaders share this perception about each other's intent, war becomes a virtual certainty. The mechanism of the self-fulfilling prophecy is then set in motion. If leaders attribute evil designs to their adversaries, and if they nurture these beliefs for long enough, they will eventually be proven right. The mobilization measures that preceded the outbreak of World War I were essentially defensive measures triggered by the fear of the other side's intent. The Russian czar mobilized because he feared an Austrian attack; the German Kaiser mobilized because he feared the Russian "steamroller." The nightmare of each then became a terrible reality. Stalin was so imprisoned by the Marxist dogma that capitalists would always lie that he disbelieved Churchill's truthful warnings about Hitler's murderous intent to which he was so blind that Russia almost lost the war. Eisenhower and

Dulles were so convinced that the Chinese would move
against the French in Indochina in the way they had against
MacArthur's UN forces, that they committed the first American military advisers to Vietnam. The Chinese never intervened but the Americans had begun their march along the
road to self-entrapment in the Vietnam quagmire. Arabs
and Israelis and Indians and Pakistanis generally expected
nothing but the worst from one another, and these expectations often led to war. The conviction held by Syria and
Egypt after 1967 that Israel intended to hold on to the
occupied territories forever was the immediate precipitating
cause of the October War of 1973, in which the Arabs made
a desperate attempt to reconquer their lost lands. And
Yahya Khan's perception of India's intention to fight on
the side of the secessionist movement in Bengal led directly
to his abortive and suicidal air attack.

*A leader's misperception of his adversary's power is per-
haps the quintessential cause of war. It is vital to remember,
however, that it is not the actual distribution of power that
precipitates a war; it is the way in which a leader thinks
that power is distributed.* A war will start when nations dis-
agree over their perceived strength. The war itself then becomes a dispute over measurement. Reality is gradually restored as war itself cures war. And the war will end when
the fighting nations perceive each other's strength more
realistically.

Germany and Austria-Hungary in 1914 had nothing but
contempt for Russia's power. This disrespect was to cost them
dearly. Hitler repeated this mistake a generation later and
his misperception led straight to his destruction. One of the
clearest examples of another misperception of this kind took
place in the Korean War. MacArthur, during his advance
through North Korea toward the Chinese border, stubbornly
believed that the Chinese Communists did not have the

capability to intervene. When the Chinese did cross the Yalu River into North Korea, MacArthur clung to the belief that he was facing 40,000 men while in truth the figure was closer to 200,000. And when the Chinese forces temporarily withdrew to assess their impact on MacArthur's army, the American general assumed that the Chinese were badly in need of rest after their encounter with superior Western military might. And when the Chinese attacked again and drove MacArthur all the way back to South Korea, the leader of the UN forces perceived this action as a "piece of treachery worse even than Pearl Harbor." The most amazing aspect of this story is that the real facts were quite available to MacArthur from his own intelligence sources, if only the general had cared to look at them. But he knew better and thus prolonged the war by two more years. Only at war's end did the Americans gain respect for China's power and take care not to provoke her again beyond the point of no return. Yet in the Vietnam war, the American leadership committed precisely the same error vis-à-vis North Vietnam. Five successive presidents believed that Ho Chi Minh would collapse if only a little more military pressure would be brought to bear on him either from the air or on the ground. The North Vietnamese leader proved them all to be mistaken and only when America admitted that North Vietnam could not be beaten, did the war come to an end. In both Korea and Vietnam the price of reality came high indeed. As these wars resolved less and less, they tended to cost more and more in blood and treasure. The number of dead on all sides bore mute testimony to the fact that America had to fight two of the most terrible and divisive wars in her entire history before she gained respect for the realities of power on the other side. In 1948, the Arabs believed that an invasion by five Arab armies would quickly put an end to Israel. They were mistaken. But in 1973, Israel, encouraged to the point of *hubris* after three successful wars, thought of Arab power only with contempt and of its own as unassailable. That, too, was wrong as Israel had to learn in the bitter war of October 1973. And in Pakistan, Yahya Khan had to find out to his detriment that a woman for whom he had nothing but disdain was better schooled in the arts of war than he, did not permit her wishes to dominate her thoughts, and, finally, managed to dismember Pakistan.

Thus, on the eve of each war, at least one nation misperceives another's power. In that sense, the beginning of each war is a misperception or an accident. The war itself then slowly, and in agony, teaches men about reality. And peace is made when reality has won. The outbreak of war and the coming of peace are separated by a road that leads from misperception to reality. The most tragic aspect of this truth is that war has continued to remain the best teacher of reality and thus has been the most effective cure for war.

As we move toward the close of the twentieth century, we face an awesome paradox: never before in history have we prepared so feverishly for a war that no one wants. No analysis of war in our time would be complete without at least a glance at our simultaneous efforts to build—and then to destroy, or at least control—weapons that could incinerate the earth.

The following is an eyewitness description of Hiroshima shortly after the city was destroyed by an atomic bomb in August 1945:

People are still dying, mysteriously and horribly—people who were uninjured in the cataclysm—from an unknown something which I can only describe as the atomic plague.

Hiroshima does not look like a bombed city. . . . I write these facts as dispassionately as I can, in the hope that they will act as a warning to the world. In this first testing ground of the atomic bomb . . . it gives you an empty feeling in the stomach to see such man-made devastation. . . . I could see about three miles of reddish rubble. That is all the atomic bomb left. . . . The Police Chief of Hiroshima . . . took me to hospitals where the victims of the bombs are still being treated. In these hospitals I found people who, when the bomb fell, suffered absolutely no injuries, but now are dying from the uncanny after-effects. For no apparent reason their health began to fail. They lost appetite. Their hair fell out. Bluish spots appeared on their bodies. And then bleeding began from the ears, nose and mouth.

At first, the doctors told me, they thought these were the symptoms of general debility. They gave their patients Vitamin A injections. The results were horrible. The flesh started rotting away from the hole caused by the injection of the needle. And in every case the victim died.

A peculiar odour . . . given off by the poisonous gas still issues from the earth soaked with radioactivity; against this the inhabitants all wear gauze masks over their mouths and noses; many thousands of people have simply vanished—the atomic heat was so great that they burned instantly to ashes—except that there were no ashes—they were vaporised.[1]

The bomb here mentioned, it should be noted, is now considered obsolete. Its capacity for destruction has been dwarfed by an even more total weapon—the hydrogen bomb. That this development has engendered a more intensive quest for disarmament than ever before in history is by no means surprising. Indeed, the price of failure in this quest is not likely to be merely the kind of devastation that was loosed on Hiroshima and Nagasaki. It may well be the extinction of man as the dominant form of life on this planet.

Since 1945 the issue of disarmament has assumed paramount importance and has unceasingly occupied the thinking of statesmen and technical experts everywhere. The United Nations General Assembly has dealt with it during every session and it is safe to predict that this pattern will continue. The two major antagonists in the East-West struggle have agreed that disarmament is the most important problem facing the world today. Yet, despite a strategic arms limitation treaty agreed upon at the Moscow Summit of 1972, not a single weapon, atomic or conventional, has been scrapped. Instead, we are still witnessing the fiercest and most relentless arms race in history. Why? In order to answer this question, we must analyze the disarmament dilemma in all its complexity.

If the objective of the builders of political order is a world without major disputes, the hope of those who would build order through disarmament is a world without weapons. In the view of the latter, arms races cause wars. If, as they see it, arms are permitted to accumulate, they sooner or later will be used. An arms race, therefore, becomes a relentless and self-propelling march to war. Both sides strain furiously to maintain or reclaim the lead. Finally, the tension reaches such a pitch that war is almost welcomed as a liberating explosion. If, on the other hand, nations are deprived of the means to fight, the proponents of disarmament maintain, wars will either cease to exist or, at worst, become relatively harmless. In the telling phrase of the late Soviet foreign minister Maxim Litvinov: "the way to disarm is to disarm."

Here we encounter the first crucial problem. Is it true, as the advocates of disarmament hold, that arms races cause the political tensions that drive nations to war? Or are the builders of political order correct in asserting that though arms races may precipitate war, the real source of international conflict must be sought in the political tensions between nations that lead to arms races in the first place? The former tend to regard the arms race as a basic cause of war, the latter merely as a symptom of political pathology. Both groups are prepared to admit that the problem is really a circular one: that arms races breed political tensions; that these in turn lead to the development and acquisition of more destructive weapons; and that this situation raises temperatures even further—until the violent climax is reached. But the two groups differ as to the most effective point at which to intervene in the vicious circle. Those who see arms races as a basic cause of war assert the primacy of international order building through disarmament. They maintain that halting the arms race will lead to a reduction in political tensions, which will likely result in an even further scrapping of weapons. On the other hand, a growing number of observers are defending the view that disarmament efforts are bound to fail unless they are preceded by more fundamental political accommodation. The way to disarm, according to this latter view, is not to begin by disarming but to concentrate instead on the settlement of political differences.

In view of the sharp disagreement on the nature and significance of disarmament, it is necessary to subject the modern record of disarmament negotiations to careful scrutiny.

Since the end of World War II, disarmament negotiations have been a permanent phenomenon. Yet none of the many conferences that have been held—whether inside or outside of the United Nations—has accomplished the elimination of a single atomic or conventional weapon. Even the SALT agreements were no exceptions. SALT I in 1972 was in essence a Soviet-American agreement not to construct antiballistic missile systems, and SALT II intends to limit the number of missiles on each side. Thus the two agreements limit the building of additional arms; they do not reduce existing arms. The most intensive disarmament efforts in Western history have therefore been virtual failures. The only successes on record antedate World War II, and one of these was of too brief duration to be termed an unqualified success. We shall now look into the causes of this discouraging record.

One important reason for these many failures is the inherently *static* nature of all disarmament. It is a fact of international life that many nations are constantly engaged in attempts to manipulate the existing distribution of power in their favor. An increase in armaments is an obvious means to accomplish this end. The goal of disarmament, on the other hand, is in essence the freezing of a certain distribution of power which will be acceptable to some, but never to all the powers concerned. Most nations conceive of themselves as dynamic actors on the international scene, hoping to move from strength to strength. Such states will have little patience with policies that would deprive them of an important means whereby they can grow in power and stature. Indeed, one of the greatest obstacles to disarmament is the fact that nations are less concerned with what they are than with what they would like to be.

The technical counterpart of this political truth has been the enormous difficulty of *measurement*. Each disarmament conference has to grapple with this stubborn problem. Once the delegates get down to specifics, they constantly find themselves compelled to "compare apples with oranges." Which is more valuable to a military arsenal—a destroyer or a tank? How does the striking force of the American Strategic Air Command compare to the Soviet land army? How many Polaris missiles should be scrapped for each Soviet intercontinental ballistic missile? How do 4 million men in reserve compare to 1 million in active service? Precision is almost impossible to attain. Each side in the East-West struggle has advanced proposals that would leave its superiority intact or reduce that of the other side. Since both the United States and the Soviet Union conceive of themselves as dynamic contestants for supremacy, neither has been willing to accept an arms reduction that would freeze it at a level of inferiority. The Spanish philosopher Salvadore de Madariaga has illustrated the point admirably through the analogy of an imaginary conference of animals at which "the lion wanted to eliminate all weapons but claws and jaws, the eagle all but talons and beaks and the bear all but an all-embracing hug."

The crucial cause of the failure of most disarmament negotiations is, of course, the absence of mutual trust. In technical terms this has meant that each side has attempted to impose rigorous requirements of *inspection* and *control* on the other in order to ensure that an agreement, once reached, would not be violated. Control and inspection are to be the technical substitute for mutual trust. But this condition has invited a circular problem: each side requires control because it does not trust the other; yet, the acceptance of a control system itself demands a high degree of mutual trust. In short, whenever nations have taken the position that there can be no disarmament without security, they have had to realize that foolproof security is equally impossible. A degree of mutual confidence is necessary for both disarmament and security. The major powers have been unable to escape from this predicament.

The control problem proved to be an insurmountable obstable at the very beginning of the nuclear disarmament negotiations in the United Nations Atomic Energy Commission in 1946. At that time, when the United States still had an atomic monopoly, it proposed a far-reaching control plan known as the Acheson-Lilienthal Report, or Baruch Plan. The purpose of the plan was to ensure that atomic energy would be used exclusively for peaceful purposes. To accomplish this end, the United States proposed the internationalization of all facilities producing atomic power. All atomic plants would be owned and operated by an Atomic Development Authority that would have the powers of inspection, accounting, and licensing. The American hope was to place atomic energy firmly under international control before the Soviet Union would end the American monopoly and engage in an atomic arms race with the United States. The plan was widely heralded as a generous offer which would place the power of the atom under the authority of a limited world government. The Soviet Union's response, however, was negative. It insisted upon the continuance of national ownership and operation of atomic plants and advanced a plan of its own, which proposed the destruction of all existing stocks of nuclear weapons and a legal prohibition of their future manufacture. Only after existing stockpiles had been destroyed and a treaty outlawing nuclear weapons concluded would the Soviet Union be ready to proceed to international inspection. Most immediately, then, the impasse revolved around the problem of priorities. The United States insisted on the priority of international inspection before it was willing to undertake the destruction of its nuclear stockpiles. Control would have to come first and disarmament would follow. The Soviet Union, on the other hand, insisted on the prior destruction of American stockpiles before it was willing to allow international inspection. It reversed the sequence: disarmament must come first and control would follow.

It would seem from the above that the United States' offer was a generous one, whereas the Soviet Union's rejection was an unreasonable act of caprice. After all, the United States made its offer at a time when it had an atomic monopoly. It would, therefore, appear that the Soviet Union, which had not yet developed its own atomic bomb, could only gain from the internationalization of atomic power. Actually, however, the picture is considerably more complex. It is true that the American offer was an enlightened act of statesmanship. But it is equally true that, given the state of mistrust between the two superpowers, there were valid reasons from the Soviet point of view for rejecting the Baruch Plan. First and most important, the plan would have perpetuated the American monopoly of atomic weapons. And beyond that, the Soviet Union feared that the proposed Atomic Development Authority would be dominated by the Western powers with the Eastern bloc in a permanent minority without the right of veto. In the words of Andrei Gromyko, the Soviet delegate:

> The Soviet Union is aware that there will be a majority in the control organ which may take one-sided decisions, a majority on whose benevolent attitude toward the Soviet Union the

Soviet people cannot count. Therefore, the Soviet Union, and probably not only the Soviet Union, cannot allow that the fate of its national economy be handed over to this organ.[2]

Most basically, Soviet suspicions grew out of the realization that only the United States would be in a position to cheat, that is, to withhold weapons from the authority, while the Soviet Union would be compelled to accept a permanent position of inferiority. All this is not to say that the United States' offer was not farsighted. What does seem clear, however, is that its chances of acceptance would have been considerably greater if it had permitted the continuation of national atomic research in the Soviet Union.

The struggle over priorities that began in 1946 continued without letup until the Moscow Summit of 1972. The United States and the Soviet Union both agreed that a viable disarmament treaty would have to include provisions for the prohibition of nuclear weapons as well as acceptable arrangements for control. The Soviet Union consistently defended the priority of prohibition in numerous "ban the bomb" proposals. These proposals were unacceptable to the United States, which feared that the Soviet Union would not accede to control once prohibition was accepted. The United States' insistence on the priority of control, on the other hand, was unacceptable to the Soviet Union because the latter consistently tended to regard all international inspection as a form of espionage. Hence the paradoxical situation that though both powers accepted the principle of simultaneous disarmament and control, they were unable to translate it into practice. Each side continued to postpone what for it would be the greater sacrifice and, instead, encouraged the opponent to take the first step. To try to expedite matters the French in 1958 introduced the ingenious formula: "Neither control without disarmament, nor disarmament without control but, progressively, all the disarmament that can at present be controlled." Though this proposal met the problem in principle, it, too, could not be applied in practice.

Fundamentally, the impasse stemmed from the fact that American proposals assumed a good deal of Soviet confidence in the United States, while the Soviet counterproposals assumed an equal amount of American faith in Soviet intentions. When the two rivals realized that this premise of mutual trust did not exist, they sought substitutes in various technical requirements for inspection and control. Yet they soon concluded that even such technical devices could never be completely foolproof; cheating would continue to be possible regardless of how intricate the safeguards. Indeed, there clearly seemed no other alternative: good faith was a necessary premise for *all* disarmament negotiations and arrangements.

The discouraging record of disarmament in the modern world supports the proposition that order is fundamentally not a military problem. Disarmament negotiations per se will not reduce the tensions between the major powers unless such efforts are preceded by at least a minimum of success in the settlement of outstanding political differences. This is really another way of saying that the problem of disarmament is not disarmament at all, but is in essence the problem of forging the bonds of political community among nations.

The frustrations over disarmament have led some thinkers to approach the problem in a somewhat different way: arms control rather than disarmament. Whereas the disarmer is primarily concerned with the actual scrapping of existing weapons, the arms controller is more interested in stabilizing the climate in which these weapons exist and in the prevention of additional arms buildups. The emphasis here is less on hardware and more on psychology. The hope is that progress can be made on issues related to disarmament, which might act as confidence builders and ultimately lead to actual disarmament agreements. In December 1959, for example, a treaty was signed among twelve nations with claims in Antarctica demilitarizing that continent. The signatories pledged themselves neither to establish military fortifications nor to carry out military maneuvers in the Antarctic. In 1963, in the wake of the Cuban missile crisis, the Soviet Union and the United States agreed on a partial nuclear test ban and established direct communications—a "hot line" between the White House and the Kremlin. In 1964 the United States offered one of its large nuclear reactors to international inspection by a United Nations agency, and in the same year the two superpowers agreed on cutbacks in their stockpiles of fissionable materials—the raw materials for atomic weapons—thus retarding the growth of "overkill" capacity on both sides.

In 1967, the two superpowers, after lengthy negotiations, agreed to work in earnest on a formula for a treaty banning the proliferation of nuclear weapons. In January 1968, they presented a joint draft treaty on nonproliferation to the seventeen-member disarmament conference in Geneva. The draft treaty was designed to freeze the "nuclear club" at its membership of five: the United States, the Soviet Union, the United Kingdom, France, and Communist China. Several hurdles confronted the negotiators. First, neither France nor China was expected to sign. Second, certain "threshold" countries such as India and Israel were reluctant to sign, the former for fear of China and Pakistan and the latter because of Egypt. Finally, the matter of inspection posed formidable obstacles. Would the treaty be policed through self-inspection, or a United Nations organ, such as the International Atomic Energy Agency? These and other knotty problems defied easy solution and made progress on the treaty slow and arduous. Nevertheless, the very fact of superpower cooperation on such a sensitive issue as nonproliferation provided grounds for optimism. In June 1968, another forward step was taken when the UN General Assembly gave its blessing to the draft treaty. Three nuclear and forty nonnuclear ratifications were now needed to make the document into a binding treaty. In March

1970, the nuclear nonproliferation treaty officially entered into force without the adherence of China and France. It has worked relatively well since then, although in 1974 India became the sixth member of the world's exclusive nuclear club.

Several other arms control treaties are deserving of mention. In 1967, the two superpowers agreed on a treaty in which each pledged itself not to militarize outer space. The treaty was approved by the UN General Assembly in 1967 and entered into force that same year. In 1971 a similar treaty was signed in relation to the seabed and the ocean floors. And in 1976 treaties were signed to ban chemical, biological, and environmental warfare. It is significant to note that none of these efforts achieved an actual reduction of existing weapons, but each went a long way in preventing their further dissemination and in preventing the construction of new weapons.

Despite these recent breakthroughs in arms control, the arms race remains a very real and very expensive fact of life. The money devoted each year to military expenditures is more than the total income of all the peoples of Africa and South and Southeast Asia. It is nearly three times what all the world's governments spend on health, nearly twice what they spend on education, and nearly thirty times what industrialized countries give in aid to developing countries. These massive military expenditures have continued to rise over the years despite the arms control agreements. Arms control has managed to slow down the mad momentum toward nuclear death, but not to arrest it.

While the anarchic nature of the nation-state system and its leaders has been chiefly responsible for wars in the past, the future may bring new challenges to our survival that emanate from nonstate entities. Self-styled patriots, liberation groups, criminal elements, and even individual terrorists may soon have access to nuclear technology and subject national leaders to atomic blackmail. When one considers the fact that, in 1976, an undergraduate physics student at Princeton University was able to write a paper on how to build an atom bomb, using publicly available materials, that possibility does not seem at all far-fetched. If the world's poor and hungry will not be able to persuade the world's rich to share their wealth on a more equitable basis, violence becomes an increasingly more probable scenario. Hence, as the twentieth century draws to a close, wars may erupt in the cracks of the state system as easily as among sovereign states themselves.

Despite the persistence of so much human tragedy and folly, it is nevertheless possible to conclude this study on a note of hope. *There has been a slow dawning of compassion and of global consciousness over humanity's bleak skies in our generation.* This has manifested itself both in a new awareness of and even resistance to the havoc that war wreaks upon the human spirit. It is no longer quite acceptable to our sense of logic that throwing a human being into a fire is an atrocity, while throwing fire on many human beings may be designated as a military operation. We can no longer quite understand how one man who kills another is punished as a murderer while another man who murders thousands anonymously from the sky may be acclaimed as a patriot or hero. This new dawning has come through dreadful suffering, but it *has* come. It took a world war to build the League of Nations and yet another world war to create the United Nations. And now, for the first time in human history, we are witnessing a new phenomenon: soldiers *without* enemies. Soldiers, since time immemorial, have always had enemies, but in our generation, more than 300,000 men have seen service in United Nations peace-keeping forces in many different parts of the world. These men were often shot at by *both* sides in a war, but their very existence has come to symbolize this new dawning of a global consciousness.

There have been even more concrete achievements that have begun to turn mankind away from war. For example, 1976 was the first year since 1939 in which the world was without a major war. Outer space, the seabed, and the ocean floor have been demilitarized, and the mad momentum of the arms race has at least been slowed. *At the very moment when mankind has the power to destroy the earth, men also have begun to perceive the planet as a whole.* If the most fundamental challenge of this generation was to help prevent another world war, the great challenge of the coming generation may be the preservation of the possibility of a decent life on spaceship earth. The atom bomb, through its own inexorable logic, has left no alternative to a negotiated world order. Similarly, problems of resources and scarcity will be surmounted on a global basis or not at all. Thus, in both cases, the brute logic of the insensate machine has dictated a modicum of world order: the terror of atomic fire in the former, and the prospect of people struggling for survival in the latter. *And out of this terror has sprung the recognition of the need for flexibility and change. The bomb must not become the earth, nor must the earth become the bomb.*

It is this new, slow dawning of compassion and of global consciousness that is our greatest hope. From this new spirit that is stirring deep within us we shall forge the weapons against war. Man has built *both* cathedrals and concentration camps. While he has descended to unprecedented depths in our time, he has also soared to greater heights than ever before. Man is not burdened with original sin alone; he also has the gift of original innocence.

Notes

1. Peter Burchett, the London *Daily Express*, September 5, 1945.
2. United Nations Security Council Official Records, March 5, 1947, p. 453.

Selected Bibliography

BLAINEY, GEOFFREY. *The Causes of War*. New York: Free Press, 1973.

CLAUSEWITZ, KARL VON. *On War*. New York: Modern Library, 1943.

JERVIS, ROBERT. *The Logic of Images in International Relations*. Princeton, N.J.: Princeton University Press, 1970.

————. *Perception and Misperception in International Politics*. Princeton, N.J.: Princeton University Press, 1976.

KAHN, HERMAN. *On Thermonuclear War*. Princeton, N. J.: Princeton University Press, 1960.

KISSINGER, HENRY A. *Nuclear Weapons and Foreign Policy*. New York: Harper & Row, 1957.

SCHELLING, THOMAS C. *Arms and Influence*. New Haven, Conn.: Yale University Press, 1966.

WALZER, MICHAEL. *Just and Unjust Wars*. New York: Basic Books, 1977.

WRIGHT, QUINCEY. *A Study of War*. Chicago: University of Chicago Press, 1942.

About the Author

On the eve of World War II, John G. Stoessinger fled from Nazi-occupied Austria to Czechoslovakia. Three years later he fled again via Siberia to China, where he lived for seven years. In Shanghai he served with the International Refugee Organization.

Dr. Stoessinger came to the United States in 1947, received his B.A. from Grinnell College in 1950, and then went to Harvard University, where he earned his Ph.D. in 1954. He has taught at Harvard, M.I.T., Columbia, and Princeton. In 1969 he led the International Seminar on International Relations at Harvard University, and in 1970 he received an honorary degree of Doctor of Laws from Grinnell College. From 1967 to 1974 Dr. Stoessinger served as acting director of the Political Affairs Division at the United Nations. He is now professor of political science at the City University of New York.

Dr. Stoessinger is the author of numerous books on international relations. *The Might of Nations: World Politics in Our Time,* now in its fifth edition, was awarded the Bancroft Prize by Columbia University in 1963 as the best book on international relations published in 1962. He has also written *The Refugee and the World Community, Financing the United Nations System, Power and Order, The United Nations and the Superpowers, Nations in Darkness: China, Russia, America,* and *Henry Kissinger: The Anguish of Power.* Dr. Stoessinger also served as chief book review editor of *Foreign Affairs* for five years and is a member of the Council on Foreign Relations.